In this book Rob Walker offers an original analysis of the relationship between twentieth-century theories of international relations and the political theory of civil society since the early modern period. He views theories of international relations both as an ideological expression of the modern state and as a clear indication of the difficulties of thinking about a world politics characterized by profound spatiotemporal transformations. International relations theories should be seen, the author argues, more as aspects of contemporary world politics than as explanations of contemporary world politics. These theories are examined in the light of recent debates about modernity and post modernity, sovereignty and political identity, and the limits of modern social and political theory.

This book is a major contribution to the field of critical international relations, and will be of interest to social and political theorists and political scientists, as well as students and scholars of international relations.

INSIDE/OUTSIDE: INTERNATIONAL RELATIONS AS POLITICAL THEORY

Cambridge Studies in International Relations is a joint initiative of Cambridge University Press and the British International Studies Association (BISA). The series will include a wide range of material, from undergraduate textbooks and surveys to research-based monographs and collaborative columns. The aim of the series is to publish the best new scholarship in International Studies from Europe, North America and the rest of the world.

Cambridge Studies in International Relations (cont. p. 235)

INSIDE/OUTSIDE: INTERNATIONAL RELATIONS AS POLITICAL THEORY

R. B. J. WALKER

Department of Political Science
University of Victoria

 CAMBRIDGE
UNIVERSITY PRESS

Published by the Press Syndicate of the University of Cambridge
The Pitt Building, Trumpington Street, Cambridge CB2 1RP
40 West 20th Street, New York, NY 10011-4211 USA
10 Stamford Road, Oakleigh, Melbourne 3166, Australia

First published 1993
Reprinted 1994, 1995

A catalogue record for this book is available from the British Library

Library of Congress cataloguing in publication data

Walker, R. B. J.
    Inside/outside: international relations as political theory / R. B. J. Walker.
        p.   cm.   (Cambridge studies in international relations; 24)
    Includes bibliographical references (p.   ) and index.
    ISBN 0 521 36423 X hbk 0 521 42119 5
    1. International relations. 2. Political science. I. Title. II. Series.
JX1395.W33   1992
327.1'01–dc20   91–42632 CIP

ISBN 0 521 36423 X hardback
ISBN 0 521 42119 5 paperback

Transferred to digital printing 2001

CONTENTS

PREFACE

In an old joke, lately invoking the perverse wisdom of some archetypal pre-modern Celt, a request for directions to get 'there' inspires advice about the inadvisability of starting from 'here'. In this book, I offer similar advice on the basis of a series of meditations on the constitutive distinction between political theory and international relations: between discourses that invoke an eternally present political community within and those that project an eternally absent community between modern sovereign states. I do so in two related senses.

Affirming the significance – though not the truth – of some of the most entrenched assumptions about the 'realities' of modern political life, I develop a sceptical stance about the possibility of understanding 'world politics' through the categories of modern theories of 'international relations'. This stance permits me to explore some of the boundaries of a modern political imagination confronted with demands that we move 'beyond' a geopolitics of static fragmentation. Challenging these same assumptions, however, I offer a reading of modern theories of international relations as a discourse that systematically reifies an historically specific spatial ontology, a sharp delineation of here and there, a discourse that both expresses and constantly affirms the presence and absence of political life inside and outside the modern state as the only ground on which structural necessities can be understood and new realms of freedom and history can be revealed. The inadvisability of attempting to get 'there' from 'here' derives from a specific construction of what it means to affirm a here here and there there, not from the impossibility of being other than we are now. Indeed, although my analysis is concerned with the spatial and temporal horizons prescribed by the constitutive distinction between life within and between sovereign states, it should not be taken as an argument that other possibilities are out of the question. My concern with the limits of the modern political imagination is informed both by a sense of the need for alternative forms of political practice under contemporary conditions and a sense that fairly profound transformations are currently in progress. But it is also informed by a sense that our understanding of these transformations, and of the contours of alternative political practices, remains caught within discursive horizons that express the spatiotemporal configurations of another era.

What is at stake in contemporary debates about the possibility of moving on, I argue, is less the perverse humour of some imaginary premodernity than claims about the character and location of political life prescribed by distinctly modern accounts of the sovereignty of states. Reading theories of international relations as a characteristic expression of a modern politics bounded in sovereign space, a politics nevertheless obsessed by the dangers of time and contingency, of a dissolution or an absence threatening the secure frontiers of an unproblematic identity within, I want to show how it has become so difficult to trace a route from here to there, from the apparently inevitable violence so often celebrated as 'political realism', to those other -- peaceful, just, global, human – aspirations whose presumed impossibility certainly cannot be regarded as a joking matter.

Though theories of international relations seem to me to offer a very weak purchase on the structures and processes that might plausibly be regarded as a world politics, they do offer a crucial expression of the presumed limits of a politics caught within the contradictions of the modern state. They tell us what it means to affirm a here here while insisting that the there there is either dangerous or unattainable depending on whether it is framed in space or in time. As expressions of the limits of modern politics, they reveal some of the crucial conditions under which modern political life is possible at all, as well as the conditions under which alternatives to the present have been rendered implausible or even unthinkable.

Though my concern with such broad themes as international relations, world politics, (post)modernity, and space/time might suggest otherwise, this book has a relatively restricted focus on a specific literature and academic discipline. I am acutely aware that the analysis is in constant danger of spilling over into vast areas of contemporary political debate, especially about class, race, gender, capitalism, the politics of representation and the aspirations and practices that might be affirmed now that the specifically modern articulation of identity/ difference, self/other and space/time has become so transparent and so fluid. I have tried to indicate some general directions in which such spillages might flow. I also hope to pursue some of them in a subsequent volume devoted to contemporary claims about world politics and political identity.

Similarly, although my stance in this book is primarily critical, it also seeks to express a positive sense of the possibility and the practical importance of treating international relations/world politics as a subject of critical and theoretical reflection. If the pages that follow retain more than a hint of frustration at the practical difficulties of engaging with international relations as political theory, they also grow out of rich conversations with many individuals working in and around the discipline of international relations who have resisted disciplinary expectations, encouraged and supported my obsessions, and forced me to rethink problems I would have preferred to leave well alone.

I have been engaging with most of the basic ideas developed in this book since the early 1970s, but would not have known how to put them together without the constant challenges and affirmations provided by my experiences in three contexts, for which I would like to express my appreciation. One has involved my participation, from about 1980, with the World Models Project and the very different perspectives brought to it by Saul Mendlovitz, Richard Falk, Rajni Kothari, Lester Ruiz, Radmila Nakarada, Vandana Shiva, Dhirubhai Sheth, Ashis Nandy, Yoshikazu Sakamoto and many others. One has involved my extensive collaboration with Warren Magnusson while teaching political theory over the past decade at the University of Victoria, as well as the support of many students, colleagues and friends in this place on the edge of many worlds. One can be traced to the moment in the mid-1980s when I discovered, to my considerable relief, that Richard Ashley, Michael Shapiro and James Der Derian had also been making their way over much the same terrain through an engagement with various currents of contemporary philosophical critique. Others who bear some responsibility for shaping my own understanding of this terrain include Ruth Abbey, David Campbell, William Connolly, Michael Dillon, Jim George, Stephen Gill, David Held, Bradley Klein, Friedrich Kratochwil, Richard Leaver, Andrew Linklater, Tim Luke, Michael McKinley, Andrew Mack, Ralph Pettman, Harry Post, Steve Smith, Roger Tooze, the late John Vincent and Cindy Weber: the list could go on and on, but enough is enough.

My most profound debts, however, both as source of reflection on the politics of self and other and as condition of the possibility of my writing about politics at all, are to my parents, and to Susan, Johanna and Caitlin, who know all to well that I have often not been there because I have spent too much time here writing about here and there.

Research support for this book has been provided by grants from the Social Sciences and Humanities Research Council of Canada and the

University of Victoria. I am especially grateful for the opportunity to spend time at the Center of International Studies at Princeton University in 1988–89 and at both the Department of International Relations and the Peace Research Center at the Australian National University in 1989, as well as the opportunity to teach at the International Institute for Semiotic and Structural Studies at the University of Hawai'i in 1991.

Parts of this book have appeared in earlier incarnations and I would like to acknowledge the opportunities I have been given to try out work in progress. Chapter 2 appeared in *International/Intertextual Relations*, edited by James Der Derian and Michael Shapiro and published by Lexington Books. Chapter 3 was first given at a conference organised by the Department of International Relations at the Australian National University and the original version appears in a volume of papers from the conference edited by Richard Higgott and Jim Richardson and published by that Department. Chapters 4 and 5 are derived from a long-abandoned project on epistemological dualism in the philosophy of social science; versions of the first have appeared in *Millennium: Journal of International Studies* and in a volume on *World Politics* edited by David Haglund and Michael Hawes and published by Harcourt Brace Jovanovich Canada, and a version of the latter has appeared in *International Studies Quarterly*. Chapter 6 is derived from a version published in the *International Journal*. Chapter 7 has appeared in *Alternatives*. Chapter 8 is derived from a long set of notes which appeared as a World Order Studies Program Working Paper from the Center of International Studies, Princeton University, and parts have also appeared in *Millennium*.

In revising arguments that usually began with an engagement with relatively arcane literatures in contemporary philosophy and social theory, I have tried to write in a manner that is accessible to those without much background in such literatures, and especially to those working within the discipline of international relations. Nevertheless, I hope the argument is also of interest to a broader audience, not least because its critical edge is ultimately directed less at the problems of international relations theory than at assumptions about modern social and political theory that have encouraged theories of international relations to be as they have become.

1 INTERNATIONAL RELATIONS AS POLITICAL THEORY

Outside and inside form a dialectic of division, the obvious geometry of which blinds us as soon as we bring it into play in metaphorical domains. It has the sharpness of the dialectics of *yes* and *no*, which decides everything. Unless one is careful, it is made into a basis of images that govern all thoughts of positive and negative. Logicians draw circles that overlap or exclude each other, and all their rules immediately become clear. Philosophers, when confronted with outside and inside, think in terms of being and non-being. Thus profound metaphysics is rooted in an implicit geometry which – whether we will or no – confers spatiality upon thought; if a metaphysician could not draw, what would he think? ... The dialectics of *here* and *there* has been promoted to the rank of an absolutism according to which these unfortunate adverbs of place are endowed with unsupervised powers of ontological determination.

Gaston Bachelard, *The Poetics of Space*

if it will kindly be considered that while it is in our interest as tormentors to remain where we are as victims our urge is to move on

Samuel Beckett, *How It Is*

Historical moments

Attempts to come to terms with the complexities, contradictions and opportunities of contemporary political life participate in a widespread sense of accelerations, disjunctions and uncertainties. The swift succession of events is already enough to induce vertigo, even among journalists, policy-advisors and other mediators of the moment. Moreover, passing events draw much of their significance from broader readings of the twentieth century – and of modernity more generally – as an age of unprecedented innovations and transformations. 'All that is solid melts into air', observed Marx in his paradigmatic account of the increasing dynamism of the modern world.[1] Paradoxically, perhaps, this remark has become more prescient than ever, despite, or perhaps even in part because of evaporating

1

hopes for an alternative to the capitalism that has so completely transformed human life over the past half-millennium.

The most trenchant reminder that ours is an age of speed and temporal accelerations has been the simultaneous dissolution of Cold War geopolitics and rapid entrenchment of a globally organised capitalism across the territorial divisions of Europe. The year 1989 is now firmly enshrined as a symbol of historical ruptures that have been felt everywhere. Structural rigidities and ideological certainties have given way to social revolutions and territorial fluidities. Ritualised attitudes and postures have atrophied, scholarly literatures have been declared redundant and policy-making elites have been forced to regroup. Even the most up-to-date cartographies have acquired the antique aura of mid-century maps of a world carved into formal colonies and empires.

No doubt there are still suspicions that beneath the surprises and contingencies lies a fundamental continuity of human behaviour, some hidden hand of utilitarian efficiency or tragic necessity that must soon reappear. The eternal return of power politics or the decisive confirmation of established teleologies: these, it might be argued, offer a more appropriate interpretation of contemporary trajectories than wild claims about innovation and transformation. The latest news of geopolitical aggression or the arrogance of great powers readily inspires old memories. Claims about the vindication of favoured philosophies of history – about the slightly delayed end-of-ideology and the final supremacy of capitalism and/or modernity and/or liberalism – have become a central motif of contemporary political debate. Established orthodoxies still retain the courage – and self-righteousness – of their convictions.

Focusing upon dramatic events, it is undoubtedly tempting to exaggerate the novelty of novelty. Dissolutions of Cold War and the re-writing of Europe seem misleadingly momentous when interpreted only in relation to the entrenched expectations of a world carved up at Yalta and Bretton Woods. An old order may be giving way to the new but, it might be said, we are likely to see the emergence of a new order that looks suspiciously like the old. The players or the polarities may change but the rules of the game are likely to stay more or less the same. This, after all, is the lesson that continues to be taught in so many appeals to a canonical tradition of political realism and to be reenforced through claims about the core principles of an international balance of power.

Even so, neither the drama of apparently familiar geopolitical conflict nor the celebration of ideological victories have been able to erase

2

a pervasive sense that the search for a lasting and stable order – for a resilient architecture that might withstand the assaults and erosions of temporal change, unexpected dangers and volatile fortunes – is increasingly tenuous. The demolition of the Berlin Wall may have signalled an opening across territorial space, but it equally signalled an awareness of temporal velocities and incongruities. Ancient memories and burnished resentments have meshed simultaneously with expanded credit and a sharp eye for the main chance. Nineteenth-century nationalisms thaw while geopolitical inertia gives way to an all-consuming global economy. Yalta may have established a settled order at the architectonic centre of world politics for almost half a century, but the speed of dissolution is more in keeping with the accelerative tendencies that have been charted by almost every account of modern economies, technologies and cultures as the most distinctive characteristic of the century itself. Dissolutions in Europe may have been followed by the concerted reassertion of great power dominance in the Persian Gulf, but even the imposition of a global military order by the greatest of great powers has seemed unlikely to restrain the unpredictable volatilities of regional antagonisms or the aspirations of oppressed peoples.

As a grand cliché about modernity, the claim that we live in an era of rapid transformations has even become a form of continuity among diverse currents of contemporary social and political thought. Ever since the possibility of a progressive history was elaborated during the European Enlightenment, modern thinkers have struggled to grasp the succession of events as an unfolding of a more or less reasonable, even rational process.

For early-modern writers like Hobbes, reason and order – both cosmological and socio-political – could be envisaged in relation to the discovery of permanent principles, the secular guarantees of a geometry that seemed to offer at least as good a bet as the increasingly dubious guarantees of Heaven. From the late eighteenth century, the guarantees of Reason were converted into the promises of History. For some, like Rousseau, these promises were distinctly ambiguous. For others, like Hegel, they were magnificent. Whether as Comtean positivism, Benthamite utilitarianism, Marxian revolution or Weberian disenchantment, subsequent social and political thought and practice has been articulated around powerful claims about change, novelty and transformation that have been common intellectual currency for at least two hundred years. Contemporary sociological research, for example, remains deeply indebted to the concern – shared by all the classical sociologists like Durkheim, and echoing Hobbes in a more historically minded age – with how a stable modern society can exist at all given the transformative quality of modern life.

In this context, contemporary vertigo has already acquired its own trusted antidote. The sense of acceleration that impressed so many thinkers in the late nineteenth and early twentieth centuries is easily turned from a problematic into a celebration. History, it can be said, is simply working out as it should. Development is evolutionary and progressive. The end of ideology is undeniably at hand. Modernity shall indeed be our salvation. If full-blooded Hegelianism or a crude theory of Progress seem to have too many side-effects, too much of the chauvinistic arrogance of nineteenth-century empires, a more benign treatment of rational choice theory, utilitarian ethics and the freedom of the market will suffice. And for those not wanting to seem too naive or trusting, the antidote may be swallowed with an appropriate coating of Rousseauean or Weberian scepticism. Modernity brings both emancipation and loss: not heaven on earth but the struggles of Sisyphus, the boring of hard boards, the demands of responsibility and community in a world in which secular principles have lost their heavenly glow.

Claims to novelty, in short, already have an appropriate location within the established conventions of contemporary intellectual life. Even the startling dissolutions and reconstitutions of 1989 can seem like business as usual once one is sedated by contemporary philosophies of history, by scholarly procedures that, no less than established political interests, are ready and willing to put novelties and uncertainties in their proper place.

Nevertheless, philosophies of history that depend on an affirmation – even a highly qualified affirmation – of the European Enlightenment or nineteenth-century theories of progress have themselves come to appear as artifacts of a world that has transformed beyond the imagination of eighteenth- and nineteenth-century prophets. Those philosophies of history are still captivated by a pervasive sense of space and territoriality. They promise to take us from here to there, from tradition to modernity, from modernity to postmodernity, from primitive to developed, from darkness into light. In this sense, they reproduce the fixing of temporality within spatial categories that has been so crucial in the construction of the most influential traditions of Western philosophy and socio-political thought. Whether moving from the dangers of sophistry to the eternal forms, from the sins of earth to the redemptions of eternity or from the vagaries of individual subjectivity to the objective certainties of nature, modern accounts of history and temporality have been guided by attempts to capture the passing

4

moment within a spatial order: within, say, the invariant laws of Euclid, the segmented precision of the clock or the sovereign claims of territorial states.[2]

Interpretations of momentous events have again begun to sediment into manageable routines. Speculations about grand civilisational transformations have become more familiar as the blinkers of Cold War fade and a new millennium beckons. But the experience of temporality, of speed, velocity and acceleration, is more and more bewildering.

Despite the bewilderment, this experience is now richly inscribed in the contemporary imagination.[3] Discourses of military strategy express worries about contracting response times and instantaneous decisions rather than about the logistics of extended territorial spaces. Discourses of political economy speak about the enhanced mobility of capital compared with territorial constraints experienced by governments and labour. The language of probabilities and accelerations now familiar from astrophysics contrasts sharply with the restrained dynamics expressed in the great Newtonian synthesis of cosmic order. A popular culture of freeze-frames, instant replays and video simulations is widely interpreted as an expression of a rapidly changing world of speed and contingency that increasingly eludes the comprehension even of all those theories, those one dimensional echoes of Durkheim, Weber and Marx, that once captured the unprecedented dynamics of modernity with such conviction.

Whether in the context of traumatic events, of accounts of modernity as variations on the themes of spatial extension and historical progress, or of more recent readings of what has been characterised variously as a posthistorical or postmodern condition, contemporary claims about novelty pose a range of fundamental problems for contemporary political thought and practice. In this book, I am concerned to explore some of these problems by examining how they have come to be expressed by contemporary theories of international relations.[4]

Theories of international relations, I will argue, are interesting less for the substantive explanations they offer about political conditions in the modern world than as expressions of the limits of the contemporary political imagination when confronted with persistent claims about and evidence of fundamental historical and structural transformation. They can be read, as I will read them here, as expressions of an historically specific understanding of the character and location of political life in general. They can also be read, as I will also read them here, as a crucial site in which attempts to think otherwise about political possibilities are constrained by categories and assumptions that contemporary political analysis is encouraged to take for granted.

Theories of international relations are more interesting as aspects of contemporary world politics that need to be explained than as explanations of contemporary world politics. As such, they may be read as a characteristic discourse of the modern state and as a constitutive practice whose effects can be traced in the remotest interstices of everyday life. To ask how theories of international relations demarcate and discipline the horizons beyond which it is dangerous to pursue any political action that aspires to the rational, the realistic, the sensible, the responsible or even the emancipatory, is to become acutely aware of the discursive framing of spatiotemporal options that has left its mark in the quiet schism between theories of political possibility within and theories of mere relations beyond the secure confines of the modern territorial state. To ask how theories of international relations manage to constrain all intimations of a chronopolitics within the ontological determinations of a geopolitics, within the bounded geometric spaces of here and there, is to become increasingly clear about the rules under which it has been deemed possible to speak about politics at all. As discourses about limits and dangers, about the presumed boundaries of political possibility in the space and time of the modern state, theories of international relations express and affirm the necessary horizons of the modern political imagination. Fortunately, the necessary horizons of the modern political imagination are both spatially and temporally contingent.

Historicity and spatiality

The problematic character of modern theories of international relations has been widely discussed, especially in relation to the presumed bankruptcy of established intellectual traditions, the untidy proliferation of research strategies, an unseemly dependence on the interests of specific states and cultures, and the hubris of empirical social science. In the readings to be developed here, however, I want to show how this general sense of dissatisfaction must become especially acute when the historically specific understandings of space and time that inform the primary categories and traditions of international relations theory are challenged by speculations about the accelerative tendencies of contemporary political life.

The most important expression of these understandings, indeed the crucial modern political articulation of all spatiotemporal relations, is the principle of state sovereignty. They are also apparent in persistent debates about the validity of claims about political realism in relation to equally persistent claims about historical and structural trans-

6

formation. Consequently, much of my analysis is explicitly concerned with the specific spatiotemporal valorisations that may be traced in claims about state sovereignty and political realism. I will argue that, as they have been articulated as theories of international relations, claims about political realism are an historically specific consequence of contradictory ontological possibilities expressed by the principle of state sovereignty, and not, as is so often asserted, an expression of ahistorical essences and structural necessities.

At the very least, I am concerned to show that much more is going on in the construction of claims about state sovereignty and political realism than is usually apparent from even the most theoretically and methodologically sophisticated literature in the field. If it is true, as so many have concluded on the basis of diverse research strategies, that claims about state sovereignty and political realism simply fail to grasp the dynamics of contemporary world politics, then it is necessary to be clear about the conditions under which it has been assumed to be possible to engage with contemporary rearticulations of spatio-temporal relations. Familiar controversies about whether states are obstinate or obsolete, or whether so-called non-state actors play a significant role in contemporary world politics, or even whether states are becoming caught within networks of interdependence or func-tional regimes, do not take us very far in this respect. On the contrary, a large proportion of research in the field of international relations remains content to draw attention to contemporary innovations while simply taking a modernist framing of all spatiotemporal options as an unquestionable given. While it is not surprising that a discipline largely constituted through categories of spatial extension should experience difficulties coming to terms with problems of historical transformation and temporal acceleration, the implications of these difficulties have remained rather elusive.

Part of my aim in reading persistent claims about state sovereignty and political realism as attempts to resolve, or more usually to forget about, the spatiotemporal conditions of contemporary political prac-tice, is to explore some of the implications of recent attempts to canvass the possibility of an explicitly critical attitude within the theory of international relations. Few would argue that such an attitude is now flourishing. Many even seem to feel that such an attitude would be undesirable. Certainly, the absence of a moment of critique in this context has provided one of the conventional measures by which to distinguish international relations theory from most other areas of contemporary social and political analysis. In fact, I will argue, the absence of a critical edge to most theories of international relations is a rather special case. The distinction between theories of international relations and other forms of social and political analysis is itself an expression of the limits of a political practice that seeks to be other than what it has already become within the spatial horizons of the territorial state.

While my analysis draws upon ideas and strategies of investigation that have become familiar from broad and still controversial literatures about postmodernity and poststructuralism, I am primarily concerned to show how moments of critique that are already present in modern theories of international relations have been lost or forgotten through textual strategies that conflate, polarise and reify specifically modern accounts of spatiotemporal relations. In this context, for example, I am interested not only in the pervasive discourses in which political realists constantly confront idealists and utopians, but also the manner in which the possibility of a critical theory of international relations has been erased by a privileging of epistemological and methodological prescriptions that simply take historically specific–modern–ontological options as a given. The spatial framing of the relation between an autonomous subject set apart from the objective world is especially crucial, for it resonates with the same modernist dichotomies that have been reified so smoothly within claims about state sovereignty and political realism. Epistemologies that simply affirm these dichotomies are not obviously the most appropriate place from which to investigate a world in which boundaries are so evidently shifting and uncertain.

As a theory, or complex of theories, constituted through claims about sovereign identity in space and time, international relations simply takes for granted that which seems to me to have become most problematic. I prefer to assume that any analysis of contemporary world politics that takes the principle of sovereign identity in space and time as an unquestioned assumption about the way the world is – as opposed to an often very tenuous claim made as part of the practices of modern subjects, including the legitimation practices of modern states – can only play with analogies and metaphors taken from discourses in which this assumption is also taken for granted: hence much of the contemporary appeal of utilitarian micro-economic theory as a way of explaining patterns of conflict and cooperation between states. For all that they have been advanced under the banner of an epistemologically rigorous social science, utilitarian stories about rational action remain explicitly literary devices and carry enormous ontological and ideological baggage. Shifting allusions from that which is assumed to be known – the rational action of sovereign individuals in a market – to that which has to be explained – the

8

rational/irrational action of sovereign states in an anarchical system/ society – they especially have encouraged the uncritical affirmation of claims to sovereign identity in space and time that might be better placed under rather more critical suspicion.

While my explicit focus is on modern Anglo-American theories of international relations, and on attempts to develop a critical posture towards them, I am also concerned with broader theoretical analyses of the rearticulation of spatiotemporal relations in late or postmodernity, and with what the specific experiences of international relations theory might tell us about the limits of our ability to comprehend and respond to contemporary spatiotemporal transformations more generally. Reading theories of international relations as a constitutive horizon of modern politics in the territorial state, I want to clarify some of the difficulties besetting attempts to envisage any other kind of politics, whether designated as a world politics encompassing the planet, as a local politics arising from particular places, or as somehow both at once – the possibility that seems to me to be both the most interesting but also the one that is explicitly denied by modernist assumptions about sovereign identity in space and time.

In this broader context, especially, it is difficult to avoid two sources of controversy that have become apparent in the contrasting meanings now assigned to modernity and to the designation of the present as either post or late. Both the character and contemporary fate of modernity are difficult to pin down in this respect. On the one hand, modernity has been characterised as either a privileging of space over time or as a culture of historical and temporal self-consciousness. On the other, contemporary accelerations have been understood as a reassertion of either temporality or spatiality.

As they have descended from claims about the ancients and the moderns, claims about modernity usually refer to a form of life associated with the emergence of those autonomous subjectivities and unbridgeable chasms charted by Descartes, Galileo and Hobbes, celebrated by Kant, and reified in popular characterisations of Enlightenment reason. As they have descended from various cultural movements over the past century or so, they refer more to a sensitivity to the fragility of those autonomous subjectivities and the impossibility of those chasms between subject and object, language and world or knower and known. The theme of modernity as an era not only of rapid socio-political, economic and technological transformations but also of a new consciousness of temporality and the contingency of specifically modern experiences, has been especially familiar since the late nineteenth century. In fact, much of the recent literatures on the dynamics of late or postmodernity, as on late capitalism, may be read as a recovery and extension of ideas once associated with, say, Baudelaire, Bergson and Nietzsche as well as Marx.[5] Many of these ideas have long been explored in relation to literature and aesthetics under the rubric of modernism, although they have been largely erased from the dominant currents of social and political thought in favour of the progressivist teleologies of modernisation theory. Where many of the characteristic themes of postmodern and poststructuralist thought seem strange and even dangerous in the context of ideologies of modernisation, they are more likely to seem quite familiar to those who understand modern cultural forms precisely as responses to the renewed appreciation of temporality and contingency that was so characteristic of late nineteenth- and early twentieth-century intellectual life in Europe.

While much of the contemporary concern with speed and acceleration may be found in intellectual currents that are modern in this latter sense, as well as in currents that are more convinced that modernity is an evaporating condition, theories of international relations remain deeply informed by the ontological horizons of early modernity, although many elements of the late-nineteenth-century crisis of historicism are readily visible in some versions of the claim to political realism. In fact, I will argue, reiterated appeals to political realism simply obscure contradictions that have long been troublesome to theorists of modernity. This is especially the case with recently influential attempts to articulate a so-called structural or neorealist theory of international relations, attempts which I read as yet another attempt to avoid serious ontological difficulties through a gratuitous appeal to epistemological necessities.

The double diagnosis of modernity as a field of spatial separations or of historical consciousness encourages a double diagnosis of contemporary trajectories. Some writers identify modernity in relation to characteristic claims about evolutionary teleology and progressive history. Impressed by the speed and accelerations of the contemporary era, they speak of a new spatial awareness, characterising postmodernity as a transition from time to space, from temporal continuities to spatial dislocations. Others, focusing more on the constitutive moments of early-modern thought, analyse modernity primarily in spatial terms, notably in relation to the spatial separation of the self-conscious ego from the objective world of nature, the aesthetics of three dimensional perspective, and the demarcations of the territorial state. Contemporary conditions are then understood as a revalorisation of temporality.

The historical and theoretical problems posed by these contrasting conceptions of the spatio-temporal character of modernity are obviously very complex, and pose serious difficulties for the analysis of contemporary political life. They are implicated, for example, in an important tension within the literature on modern political economy. Much of this literature has inherited Marx's insight that the dynamic character of capitalism implied the inevitable destruction of space by time: all that is solid melts into air. Analyses of the capitalist state, however, have had to explain the ability of political structures to preserve a sense of spatial integrity, whether in the name of territoriality or national identity. This tension is felt in the continuing rift between international relations and international political economy as forms of enquiry, a rift that is often, and not very helpfully, characterised as one between base and superstructure or between high and low politics.[6] They are also implicated in analytical procedures and disciplinary boundaries that simply reproduce obsolete distinctions between space and time in a world that seems more appropriately characterised by patterns of intricate connections. Nevertheless, especially because my explicit focus is on a discipline that has been constituted as an analysis of relations between states conceived primarily as spatial entities, I treat the primacy of space in the cultural and intellectual experience of the early modern era as crucial, as setting the conditions under which later accounts of temporality – including those given by Marx – could be articulated as a linear and thus measurable progression.

For my purposes here, contemporary claims about novelty and transformation in political life give rise to three groups of problems in particular.

One group concerns the interpretation of those structures and processes through which modern political identities have been constituted historically. Such interpretation is sometimes marked by a concern with culture, especially in relation to the emergence of nationalism as the most powerful expression of collective solidarities. Sometimes it is informed by various kinds of political economy, especially in relation to the state as an expression of particular interests. Sometimes it is informed by a multiplicity of perspectives on the development of individual subjectivities, especially in relation to the social construction of class, race and gender, to ideologies of possessive individualism and to the micro-politics of childhood. As I emphasise in the final chapter, however, analyses of culture, state, class, gender, race or individual subjectivity as expressions of modern political identity have been systematically marginalised in this context, primarily because the character and location of modern political identity is already taken for granted in the claims of state sovereignty. Consequently, I am primarily concerned with the constitution of modern political identities in relation to the claims of state sovereignty, and thus to the early-modern resolution of competing claims to a universally conceived humanity, on the one hand, and to the particularistic claims of citizens on the other.

A second group of problems concerns the categories within which accounts of historical change have been framed in modern social and political theory. In this context, I am especially interested in the continuing impact of familiar tensions between philosophies/ideologies of Enlightenment and Despair:[7] between universalising accounts of progress and the end of history and the countercurrent of Romantic or disenchanted pluralism that has come to both challenge and affirm our most influential accounts of where we have come from, where we might be going to and, consequently, who in fact 'we' are. For my present purposes, the still elusive figure of Max Weber is especially important in this respect. It is through Weber, I will contend, that it is possible to see how these tensions have been insinuated into modern theories of international relations, and insinuated in such a manner that both the philosophical issues at stake in, and the political consequences of, these twin readings of historical possibilities have been more or less forgotten.

A third group of problems concerns those contemporary forms of theoretical critique – especially those that have been fixed under the eminently unsatisfactory labels of postmodernism, poststructuralism and so on – which seek to engage with the discursive horizons that still sustain and legitimise both the prevailing accounts of political identity and our most influential philosophies of history.[8] Here I want to insist that many of the themes that have been introduced into contemporary social and political theory under these labels have already been at play for most of this century. They have even been at play in theories of international relations, despite the reluctance with which the modern discipline of international relations has explicitly engaged with theoretical or philosophical questions of any kind.

It is in this context, especially, that I want to explore the successful marginalisation of almost all forms of critical scholarship in international relations through a rhetorical appeal to accounts of novelty and continuity that are rooted in specifically modern claims about sovereign identity. On the one hand, I will argue that this discipline has been marked by a systematic forgetting of the conditions under which it has been able to sustain both its knowledge claims and its

12

ideological reach. On the other, I will suggest that perspectives now emerging under the rubrics of postmodern and particularly poststructuralist critique do permit some clarification of what these conditions are. They do so primarily by engaging with claims about modern political identities and philosophies of history that are deeply inscribed in the central categories, debates and discursive rituals of the discipline.[9] As so many political analysts have said so often, power is often most pervasive and effective amidst the silences of received wisdom.

With each of these three groups of problems and questions, all of which may be understood as aspects of our contemporary puzzlement about the historicity of human existence, I am concerned with the degree to which an increasing preoccupation with speed, temporality and contingency undermines established categories of analysis in what has conventionally been one of the most spatially oriented sites of modern social and political thought. Most specifically, I am concerned with the degree to which contemporary transformations can be understood as challenges to the spatial resolution of claims about the possibility of meaningful political community within states and the impossibility of anything more than transient modes of accommodation between them. This resolution, expressed in the claim to state sovereignty, is the crucial condition that both permits and encourages the constitutive distinction between two traditions of thought about, and analysis of, modern political life: a tradition of properly political thought on the one side and a tradition of international relations theory on the other. This distinction between inside and outside, whether made explicitly, as it usually is in the theory of international relations, or tacitly, as it usually is in texts about political theory, continues to inform our understanding of how and where effective and progressive political practice can be advanced.

The sovereignty of states is, of course, often taken to be the most important fact of life in a world of more or less autonomous authorities. Indeed it is so important that it is usually taken for granted, left as an abstraction or a technical venue for legal squabbles. But claims to sovereignty involve very concrete political practices, practices that are all the more consequential to the extent that they are treated as mere abstractions and legal technicalities. Moreover, these practices are exercised quite as much within disciplinary discourses about international relations as they are in the routines of state-craft.[10]

To pursue speculations about the transformative quality of contemporary trajectories with any theoretical rigour, I will argue, is

13

necessarily to put in doubt the spatial resolution of all philosophical options that is expressed by the principle of state sovereignty – a resolution which is in any case always in doubt and subject to constant deferral, as well as subject to constant attempts to affirm its natural necessity. To put the point as succinctly as possible: if it is true that contemporary political life is increasingly characterised by processes of temporal acceleration, then we should expect to experience increasingly disconcerting incongruities between new articulations of power and accounts of political life predicated on the early-modern fiction that temporality can be fixed and tamed within the spatial coordinates of territorial jurisdictions.

This point is often lost in endless controversies about whether states are here forever or are about to disappear into some global cosmopolis. Indeed, the discursive form of these controversies is often much more interesting than the constructions of empirical evidence deployed to decide whether the head or the tail of this particular red herring should be swallowed first. What is at stake in the interpretation of contemporary transformations is not the eternal presence or imminent absence of states. It is the degree to which the modernist resolution of space–time relations expressed by the principle of state sovereignty offers a plausible account of contemporary political practices, including the practices of states.

Furthermore, to the extent that contemporary accounts of temporal accelerations evade the familiar clichés of modern philosophies of history, they also put in doubt the manner in which challenges to the principle of state sovereignty are conventionally advanced; that is, on the ground of universalising claims about peace, justice, reason and humanity in general. This ground is precisely the condition under which claims about state sovereignty were advanced in the first place. It cannot offer the possibility of effective critique.

This is one of the key insights that have been sustained by at least some contributors to the postmodern turn in twentieth-century social and political theory.[11] It is an insight that I want to pursue here in a series of meditations on the discursive rituals through which modern theories of international relations have been constructed as a clearly defined but only intermittently problematised horizon of modern political thought and practice. Approaching questions about political identity and historical change by reflecting on the implications of the postmodern turn for theories of international relations, I want to explore how we are now able, or unable, to conceive of other possibilities, other forms of political identity and community, other histories, other futures.

International relations and the horizons of modern political theory

The sense that modern political life and thought is severely constrained within inherited intellectual horizons is fairly widespread. This sense of constraint is felt in popular scepticism towards established political ideologies. It characterises influential currents of contemporary social and political theory.[12] It finds a particularly interesting and important articulation in modern theories of international relations.

In this context, theories of international relations appear less as a set of variations on the theme of power politics – undoubtedly their most popular guise – than as a celebration of an historically specific account of the nature, location and possibilities of political identity and community. As a celebration, however, they are also a warning. They specify the limits within which the celebration may be conducted. They express authoritative reservations about how far and under what conditions this particular account of political identity and community can be sustained in either space or time. As a discipline concerned with the delineation of borders, the inscription of dangers and the mobilisation of defences, the analysis of international relations offers a particularly clear account of what it means to suggest that modern political thought is somehow endangered, in crisis, in need of repudiation, reaffirmation or reconstruction.

For the most part, accounts of the limits of modern political thought echo familiar rhetorical and critical strategies. Prevalent theoretical perspectives, it is often said, are out of touch with contemporary trajectories. Calls to dispense with the old and bring in the new become a chorus of reassurances that progress is indeed possible. Alternatively, dominant modes of thought are said to express the special interests of particular groups, classes or societies: so away with the parochial and ideological in favour of greater openness and universality. One of the most striking aspects of contemporary political analysis, however, has been an increasing concern with the limits of these familiar analyses of limits. The preoccupation, even obsession, with transcending inherited horizons has itself come to be seen as a characteristic aspect of the traditions that must now be regarded with suspicion.

This particular suspicion is in part what has made the postmodern turn and the scholarly strategies of post-structuralism so disconcerting to established forms of critical analysis. They involve not only a certain scepticism about inherited intellectual, ideological or ethical claims but

15

also about the possibility of moving to lusher pastures on the other side of the hill. The claim that the grass is in fact greener elsewhere, whether mapped as some realm of transcendant universals or inscribed in the essential qualities or rational capacities of humanity as such, has long been the explicit or tacit ground on which critique of inherited traditions has been deemed possible and legitimate. Without this possibility, this way out that is so often expressed in simple spatial metaphors of a journey to somewhere else, it is frequently assumed that we are left only with a conservative idealisation of the present as the best of all possible worlds or a merely nihilistic or relativistic deconstruction of any ground on which to engage in a progressive politics at all. This assumption is profoundly misleading.[13]

There is no doubt that theories of international relations express the limits of modern political thought in ways that are open to conventional forms of critique. These theories can be understood as the product of specific historical conditions that have now passed.[14] They can also be understood as ideological expressions of the parochial interests of particular societies.[15] They can even be understood in relation to the institutionalisation of specific academic disciplines and especially to the characteristic controversies of political science, the discipline that has had the greatest influence on the development of international relations as a mode of enquiry.[16] Yet while there is undoubtedly room for further critique of this kind, it remains exceptionally difficult to specify either the political grounds on which such a critique can be made or what its practical implications might be.

If theories of international relations express, say, spatial and temporal assumptions about political community that crystallised in early-modern Europe, as I believe they do, then it is not at all clear what it might now mean to ground critique in some other kind of political community, unless, for example, we invoke some purely abstract conception of humanity as such. Fortunately or unfortunately, and despite influential claims advanced by certain philosophical, ethical and religious traditions, humanity as such is not a meaningful political category. This is, after all, precisely the dilemma that was recognised by all those early-modern theorists who had to come to terms with the collapse of universalistic accounts of political, religious and metaphysical hierarchies.[17] It is for this reason that texts by Machiavelli and Hobbes remain significant for contemporary thinking about world politics, and not because these texts capture eternal verities about *realpolitik* or international anarchy.

Similarly, if theories of international relations can be understood as expressions of the *Pax Britannica* and *Pax Americana* in which they have largely been constructed, it is again not clear how it might be possible to specify some less parochial and hegemonic way of speaking about an alternative or more inclusive community. Even if early-modern conceptions of political identity and community are beginning to lose much of their plausibility, as again I believe they are, convincing accounts of alternative possibilities are notoriously difficult to find. They are difficult to find because the spatiotemporal resolutions through which early-modern accounts of political community were constituted, and then formalised by the principle of state sovereignty, have become so firmly rooted in modern thought and practice. They are often just as firmly rooted in aspirations for radical critique as they are in the most self-satisfied forms of conservative apologetics.

It is this presumed impossibility of even conceiving an alternative to the account of political community that emerged in early-modern Europe that is expressed by the most influential forms of international relations theory under the hyper-elastic label of political realism. Conversely, the pressing need for some alternative to realist tales of doom and gloom has become the common ground – usually designated as idealism or utopianism – of most of those who seek to criticise theories of international relations as obsolete and parochial ideology. In both cases, the historical specificity of this rendering of historical options is systematically obscured by philosophically trivial but discursively effective claims about, for example, inherited intellectual traditions, the relation between truth and power, and essentialistic theories about the state on the one hand and human nature on the other.

It is for this reason that suspicions about modernist philosophies of history and the imperatives of universal reason are so important for contemporary attempts to understand the horizons of the modern political imagination. They are especially important, for my purposes in this book, because they put into critical relief the assumptions about identity/difference, self/other, inside/outside, History/contingency and imminence/transcendence that have permitted theories of international relations to be constructed as a discourse about the permanent tragedies of a world fated to remain fragmented while longing for reconciliation and integration.

When placed in relief in this way, the characteristic debates of the discipline of international relations can be seen to confirm the established horizons of modern political discourse in general. Against those who are fearful of the postmodern turn because it undermines the possibility of escaping from the dangers of a fragmented world, therefore, I want to draw on poststructuralist suspicions of the conditions under which such an escape has been deemed desirable in

17

order to show how this very hope of escape has itself made effective critique more or less impossible.

Theories of international relations are a particularly interesting context in which to pursue the implications of poststructuralist suspicions of attempts to transcend inherited intellectual and political horizons because, at least as much as any other modern intellectual discipline, they are explicitly concerned with the politics of boundaries. They seek to explain and offer advice about the security and transgression of borders between established forms of order and community inside and the realm of either danger (insecurity, war) or a more universalistically conceived humanity (peace, world politics) outside. To be concerned with the implications of the postmodern turn for theories of international relations, therefore, cannot be simply a matter of importing the latest intellectual fad from elsewhere, in the way that certain forms of micro-economics or systems theory have been imported to provide models, metaphors and professional legitimacy for specific theoretical orientations and methodological strategies. It must, rather, involve trying to understand how theories of international relations – theories of relations across borders – have been constituted on the basis of historically specific and increasingly contentious claims about what it means to establish, defend or transgress borders, whether territorial or intellectual.

In focusing on the horizons of modern political theory, however, I do not wish to deny that for many or even most students of political life, established principles and assumptions remain more or less adequate to contemporary conditions. Still less do I want to deny a certain continuity between some forms of a critical affirmation of modernity and perspectives opened up by the postmodern turn. What is at stake here is not another grand schism between modernity and postmodernity, despite the recent prevalence of this seductive but profoundly misleading rendition of the alternatives before us. To construct an account of contemporary debates in this way would be to remain well within the established conventions of modernist discourse and their distinctive construal of what is normal or pathological, conventional or radical, legitimately identical or subversively different. While admitting continuity, however, I do want to challenge those affirmations of modernity that have degenerated into dogmatisms of one kind or another.

Claims to political realism, I will argue, have especially assumed this role, though in a distinctively ambivalent and therefore interesting fashion. Much less ambivalently, and much less interestingly, claims about modern social science have often taken on a similar quality.

18

Whether drawing on a positivistic distaste for metaphysics or simply starting from assumptions about rationality, objectivity and individual autonomy that have become hegemonic within modern liberal societies, modern social science has been prone to reduce all awkward questions to difficulties of method and technique. I am especially concerned here with the extent to which distinctions between fact and value, about the logic of empirical explanation and, above all, about the presumed priority of epistemology over ontology and axiology, have systematically obscured the highly contentious character of claims about sovereignty and political realism.[18]

Nonetheless, the unself-critical character of so much social science, especially in the analysis of international relations, should not detract from the significance of attempts to understand modern political life as a positive historical achievement or to extend established principles in a more emancipatory direction. In the specific context of international relations theory, for example, emerging literatures express a growing interest in a more ethically inspired form of liberalism, one that aspires to some kind of Kantian republicanism or even a perpetual peace between autonomous political communities.[19] More significantly, perhaps, several attempts have been made to elaborate critical theories of international relations which seek to fulfil the promises of modernity rather than to call them into question.[20]

These attempts clearly resonate with a broader tendency within recent social and political thought. Perhaps the best-known project here has been Jürgen Habermas' ambition to rewrite Enlightenment aspirations for a universal reason while acknowledging at least some of the contradictions inherent in those aspirations that had so depressed Weber and Habermas' predecessors in the so-called Frankfurt School of Critical Theory.[21] Comparable projects are to be found in Hans Blumenberg's celebration of the capacity for self-assertion that he sees as modernity's great achievement[22] or in Charles Taylor's attempt to clarify contemporary moral dilemmas through an historical grasp of the achievement of self-identity.[23]

What makes much of this literature interesting, however, is not the simple affirmation of modernity, of the kind that is all too common in modern social science, but a careful even if sometimes reluctant acknowledgment of the highly problematic status of modernity. It is a sensitivity to this problematic character, in fact, that sustains the attempt to recapture or elaborate achievements -- autonomy, freedom, rationality – that are known to be very fragile. Much of the same might be said, of course, about many of those who have been turned into rather simple-minded advocates of progress and universal reason.

Indeed, in my view, it is often just as helpful to engage with, say, Hobbes, Spinoza, Rousseau, Hume, Kant, Hegel and Marx in order to appreciate the problematic character of modernity as to those who have absorbed the lessons of Nietzsche, Foucault and Derrida. Those who would confidently lay claim to modernist epistemologies in order to discipline contemporary eruptions of scepticism might usefully remember, say, Hobbes' reflections on language or the difficulty such early-modern thinkers had in responding to the demands of a purely secular political order.

This is one reason why many of the recent debates that try to force a rigid division between modernity and postmodernity are so misleading, no matter what important insights such a distinction can sometimes convey. Much of the postmodern turn can be understood as a series of attempts to reclaim or reconstruct or even to finally create some practical space for, say, a Kantian concern with the conditions of the possibility of knowledge or the meaning of autonomy in a world in which the secular guarantees of Reason and History can no longer console us for the death of God. It can also be understood as a multifaceted struggle to come to terms with the possibility of a critical or emancipatory political practice given the extent to which the great secular substitutes for God in modern political thought – Reason, History, the sovereign state, the sovereign individual and the universal class – have themselves come to seem so problematic.[24]

Most specifically, I want to suggest that many of the intellectual perspectives opened up by the postmodern turn can be understood as a way of trying to make some sense of what it might now mean to speak of world politics rather than just inter-state or international relations.

Despite the extent to which the terms international relations and world politics have come to be treated as synonyms, they also suggest a radical incompatibility. The early-modern resolution of all spatio-temporal relations expressed by the principle of state sovereignty implies a fundamental distinction between a locus of authentic politics within and a mere space of relations between states. While it is easy enough to ignore this distinction by reducing all social action to some crude common denominator – the struggle for power, instrumental rationality, universal ethics – most serious political analysis has been forced to respond to the difficulty of simply translating assumptions established in relation to statist forms of political community into that realm in which such community is assumed to be absent. Hence the constant warnings about the dangers of the 'domestic analogy' or the special antipathy reserved for utopianism that have been so much a part of modern theories of international relations.[25] But hence also the distinctive silence of prevailing political traditions when confronted with claims about the need for some more cosmopolitan response to the collective experiences of a global economy, a planetary ecology or a technology specially designed for species suicide.[26]

The conditions under which we are now able – or unable – to conceive of what it might mean to speak of world politics, and thus of the spatiotemporal rearticulation of political community, are largely defined in terms of assumptions enshrined in the principle of state sovereignty. It is precisely these assumptions that are put into question, though not for the first time, by the convergence of philosophical critiques that have informed the postmodern turn. Again it should be clear that to engage in a postmodern exploration of what it might now mean to speak of world politics cannot involve a simple dismissal of all that has gone before. It does, however, require a re-engagement with the historically constituted limits of prevailing discourses about international relations/world politics without simply assuming that the historically specific resolutions of all spatiotemporal options expressed by the principle of state sovereignty are the only ground from which critical thought and emancipatory practice can be generated.

Meditations on the disciplinary practices of a discipline

As a sequence of meditations on a discourse about the horizons of modern politics, this book has no straightforward thesis or conclusion. It is motivated more by a sense of the difficulty of speaking coherently about politics at this historical juncture than by any confidence that anyone or any one theoretical orientation offers a clear way forward. It most certainly rejects the notion that the postmodern turn offers some new research paradigm as these have come to be conceived within modern social science. But it does have a loosely articulated guiding theme, one that remains exceptionally difficult to specify except at a very general level.

If the early-modern principle of state sovereignty that still guides contemporary political thought is so problematic, as these meditations suggest, it is necessary to attend to the questions to which that principle was merely an historically specific response. While there is undoubtedly some difficulty in claims about the continuity of questions over time, it does seem to me that questions about political identity, and thus about the legitimation of various forms of inclusion

21

and exclusion, are no longer adequately answered in the territorial terms we have inherited from early-modern Europe and reproduced so readily in the name of state and nation. This has always been a contested answer, although the terms of contestation may have now become more complex and insistent. Questions about political identity, however, do seem to be increasingly central to attempts to specify some content to a term like world politics. They also seem increasingly resistant to the entrenched research strategies deployed both in the name of the discipline of international relations and of forms of political theory that are content to treat the sharp distinction between political theory and international relations as an implicit premis.

Consequently, it also seems necessary to attend to the most fundamental assumptions about the relation between unity and diversity and between space and time through which the early-modern answer was fixed and permitted to enter into the most pervasive practices of modern political life. Against those who would continue to preserve international relations as a discipline of dogmatisms and reifications, I want to suggest that claims about contemporary world politics necessarily engage with the most fundamental questions about contemporary political life. Rather than continue to be a site at which the characteristic interrogations of political theory are marginalised and deferred, it ought to be a site at which such interrogations are conducted most persistently. And against those who would insist that fundamental questions can still be resolved within modernist assumptions about the relationship of unity and diversity in space and time, I want to suggest that it is precisely these assumptions that make it so difficult to envisage any kind of meaningful political identity in a world of profound temporal accelerations and spatial dislocations.

These meditations have both a more and a less explicit focus. Of most immediate concern are specific moments of controversy within the discipline of international relations since 1945. The most important of these have occurred under the guise of the grand antinomy between political realism and political idealism or utopianism. I read the former as a plurality of discourses about difference in both space and time, and the latter as the discourse that makes claims to political realism possible in the first place. Contrary to almost all the conventional wisdom, I will suggest that the dominant tradition of thinking in this discipline is not political realism, which is in any case best understood as a highly mobile and diversified strategy of theoretical evasions. It is, rather, that constitutive claim to universality that has come to be both known and ridiculed as idealism and utopianism. Those other controversies that are usually placed at the centre of accounts of the development of the discipline – about state-centricism and globalism or about socio-scientific methodologies – I also read as variations on this central antinomy. I read this antinomy, in turn, as a specific articulation of philosophical options expressed by the principle of state sovereignty. Concurring with supposedly realist claims about the significance of the principle of state sovereignty, I argue that theories of international relations tell us less about the character and consequences of state sovereignty than the principle of state sovereignty tells us about the categorical structures of international relations theory. Beginning with typical or influential statements about research options that have been made by contemporary scholars, I try to destablise the assumptions these statements take for granted and then to show how other ways of thinking might be opened up.

Less explicitly, I am concerned to set in motion a range of ideas which respond to the dilemmas of political identity, historical change and the possibility of critique given an awareness of contemporary accelerations and uncertainties. One line of analysis begins with those early-modern theorists who managed to articulate a new – modern – account of autonomous subjectivities in the wake of the dissolution of medieval hierarchies. In this context, I am especially concerned to know how it is still possible to treat Machiavelli and Hobbes as critical thinkers despite the ferocity with which they have been reduced to mere cyphers in a supposed canon about the necessities of power politics.

A second line of analysis is indebted to a range of thinkers who sought to respond to the critique of Enlightenment rationalism at the turn of this century. Because of his direct influence on some of the best-known theorists of international relations like Hans J. Morgenthau and Raymond Aron, I focus especially on the legacy of Max Weber.

The third set of ideas is associated with the heterogeneous entanglement of postmodernists, poststructuralists and interpretive theorists who have developed searching critiques of the claims to autonomous subjectivity that were worked out in the early-modern era and tenuously reaffirmed by Weber. Here my main inspiration comes from Michel Foucault, but only because I have found him to be a particularly challenging and sensitive entry into ways of thinking about language, identity and power that seem to me to be indispensable for thinking about politics in the late twentieth century. While I do not wish to overemphasise the connections that might be drawn between Weber and Foucault,[27] I have found it useful to think of these two extraordinarily complex thinkers as fertile sites for engaging with the relationship between claims about modernity, on the one hand, and about sovereign identity on the other. As broad sites of philosophical and political controversy, they have provided me with a context in which to draw upon some elements of the specifically deconstructive critique of sovereign identities associated with Jacques Derrida as well as an even broader – but here rarely explicit – intellectual heritage marked especially by the names of Kant, Marx and Nietzsche.

Like many books on international relations, I begin with Machiavelli; or, rather, with what it has come to mean to claim that one should begin with Machiavelli. I then work my way through problems that have been posed by the three 'great debates' that are generally acknowledged to mark the development of the discipline – debates about realism and idealism, about appropriate method and about the obstinacy or obsolescence of the state. I engage with realism by puzzling about the continuing influence of claims about a tradition of international relations theory in which the name of Machiavelli has retained a prominent role. A parallel puzzlement informs my discussion of claims about the need to bring ethics more forthrightly into contemporary discussions of international relations.

Themes raised in these discussions of realism and idealism are then recast in relation to more recent controversies arising from attempts to privilege certain modes of empirical and rationalistic enquiry. I am especially concerned to highlight the extent to which ontological, axiological and ideological problems are pushed aside in favour of a more epistemologically conceived understanding of social inquiry, and the extent to which claims about political realism manage to elide fundamental contradictions between structuralist and historicist commitments.

In chapter 6, I address the spatial framing of the primary disciplinary categories more explicitly, focusing especially on the characteristic opposition between claims that the territorial state will be ever-present or is now imminently absent, and on the transformation of horizontal territorialities into apparent hierarchies in the so-called 'levels of analysis' schema, undoubtedly the key classification of explanatory options encouraged by this discipline. In chapter 7, I try to move across the boundary between inside and outside in order to develop a reading of modern theories of democracy in the context of international relations. The very attempt to make such a move, however, merely accentuates an awareness of the limits of modern political thought and practice inscribed by boundaries of the state, and especially of the limits of the particularistic communities within which it has become possible to articulate specifically modern accounts of universality.

In all of these readings of key debates, conceptual options and methodological injunctions, my concern is to destabilise seemingly opposed categories by showing how they are at once mutually consti-tutive and yet always in the process of dissolving into each other. The nice straight – spatial – lines of demarcation between inside and outside or realism and idealism turn out to be shifting and treacherous. Unsur-prisingly, I end up at that other conventional starting point, the principle of state sovereignty. Concurring with the judgment that it is indeed necessary to take this principle as the key feature of modern political life, I seek to show how this judgment tells us more about the constitutive imagination of *modern* political life than about the determinations and possibilities of the political worlds in which we now live.

2 *THE PRINCE* AND 'THE PAUPER'

The politics of origins

In canvassing the problems and achievements of contemporary theories of international relations, Kal Holsti has succinctly repeated a familiar refrain. 'International theory', he says, 'is in a state of disarray.'

> In the past decade, the three-centuries long intellectual consensus which organised philosophical speculation, guided empirical research, and provided at least hypothetical answers to the critical questions about international politics has broken down. New conceptions and images of the world, and how it works in the diplomatic, military, and commercial domains, have arisen. Scholars have offered trenchant criticisms of the 'realist' tradition, which goes back to Hobbes and Rousseau, severely challenging the assumptions and world views upon which it is based. Some have outlined alternatives, not so much because they promise better understanding through methodological innovation, but because they are supposedly more consistent with contemporary realities. The continued underdevelopment of many new states, combined with the startling pace of technological transformation, have raised new kinds of questions about international politics, questions which were not relevant to the kinds of problems contemplated by our intellectual ancestors and most of those working within the realist, or classical tradition.[1]

In this passage, Holsti stresses three themes that have been common to many attempts since at least the mid-1970s to take stock of how we ought to examine the 'realities' of international relations. There is the observation about 'paradigm proliferation', about the loss of a clear consensus as to what the study of international relations involves, both substantively and methodologically. There is the connection drawn between this tendency towards paradigm proliferation and a sense that the phenomena being studied are changing in ways inadequately grasped by established theoretical orientations. And, finally, there is the reference to 'the tradition', specifically the classical or realist tradition, in this case linked explicitly to the names of Thomas Hobbes and Jean-Jacques Rousseau.

Enormous literatures now exist both on the proliferation of research orientations and on the claim that the substantive character of international relations is being transformed. However, both literatures rest upon a stance towards the prior claim that there is in fact a tradition, 'a three-centuries long intellectual consensus' which may be understood as both a point of departure and a distillation of conventional wisdom. This claim has been subject to relatively little critical attention, especially in the United States where the analysis of international relations has absorbed the unfortunate habit, characteristic of so much social science, of treating 'the tradition' as both naturally given in the 'great texts' and largely irrelevant to the analysis of modern human affairs. Even where the history of political thought is taken seriously, and where the difficulties in the way of understanding any particular text are well known, it remains almost a truism to claim that there is an identifiable tradition of international theory against which current tendencies in both theory and practice can be situated, measured, and judged.

Reference to such a tradition may be justified as a simple practical convenience. The story to be told has to begin somewhere. But it is not always easy to begin at the beginning, if only because the identification of a point of origin depends on where we think we are now. Thus, a practical convenience is always liable to turn into a powerful myth of origin. Other points of departure are rendered trivial or even unthinkable. The highly problematic character of claims about origins, continuities, teleologies, progressions and ruptures is conveniently forgotten.[2]

The identification of a tradition of international relations theory has now become especially problematic. We live in a world in which there has been a proliferation not only of research paradigms in the academic analysis of international relations, but also of myths of origin more generally. The Hegelian trek to universality still echoes as 'progress', 'development' or 'modernisation', but living within 'modernity', we are just as likely to be bemused by histories as seduced by *Geist*. Even from the centres of fading empires, amid ample evidence of fundamentalist self-righteousness about past and future, origins shift and recede. Reified temporal horizons give meaning to where we think we may be going. They also provide a sense of who this 'we' is. All too often, 'we' turn out to be those who have 'progressed', 'developed' or 'modernised', to be distinguished from 'they' who have not. These horizons seem increasingly tenuous, certainly inadequate as a way of orienting either serious academic analysis or progressive political practice.

Contemporary claims about intellectual traditions are caught between an awareness that dominant myths of origin – all those stories about a move from backward to advanced, from passionate to rational, from barbarism to enlightenment – harbour an embarrassment of subtexts (ethnocentricism, racism, the arrogance of empires, the butchery of wars and extermination camps) and a realisation that these stories still inform the most basic categories through which we understand and act in the world. The term *development*, for example, now demands quotation marks, a distancing of accounts of what is going on in particular societies from the evolutionary teleology with which the term is indelibly associated. Caught in this way, contemporary social and political thought has become embroiled in far-reaching debates about the character, potential and sustainability of modernity. A questioning of received temporal horizons – of myths of origin, of accounts of continuity and discontinuity, of reified teleologies – has become a precondition for engaging with the literature on contemporary social and political thought at all.

The questioning often leads to familiar answers. Marx could resolve a critique of the achievements of capitalism through a Hegelian claim about the universal subject of History. Even the pessimistic Weber could resolve his deep ambivalence about rationalisation through an appeal to a new hero, the proto-existential individual. Drawing on both, while also displaying a deep nostalgia for Kant, Jürgen Habermas can still see ways of fulfilling the promises of Enlightenment through practices of communication.

Yet anyone now trying to come to terms with Marx, or Weber or Habermas, not to mention the ingrained habits of Anglo-American liberalism or 'commonsense', quickly finds that the promises of Enlightenment seem very elusive. The grand Hegelian trek – whether written as a Hebrew parable of fulfilment in time, or a Greek story about the journey from becoming to being, or an Enlightenment claim about universal reason – has been put into radical doubt by a broad range of contemporary philosophical currents, of which poststructuralism is only the most insistent. Meanwhile, and in a less rarified atmosphere, we are becoming increasingly aware of other stories, of people who have been written out of the Hegelian script. For those drawing on other chronologies, other cultures, and other traditions, dreams of a universal History appear more convincingly as the particular claims of a culturally specific history, as claims arising from historical practices in which universalist aspiration is closely entwined with the legitimation of domination.[3]

To move from a seemingly innocent reference to a tradition to these large questions about the philosophy of history is obviously to enter upon very murky and contestable terrain. Most scholars trying to make sense of the contemporary world are likely to turn back very quickly. This is especially the case among theorists of international relations, who have often shown a certain pride in their immunity to theoretical and philosophical diversions. Whether they defend their claim to hardheadedness and realism in an empiricist account of socio-scientific explanation or in the supposed pragmatism of public policy analysis, they are likely to suggest that loose references to a tradition are indeed just a convenient place to start, a polite way of locating their concerns within an established disciplinary matrix. If pushed, such scholars are likely to suggest an appropriate division of labour, just as there is between, for example, political science and political theory; except that the distinction between political theory and political science is itself grounded in what are widely judged to be dubious assumptions about the possibility of distinguishing between normative and empirical concerns. If we have learnt anything at all from the debates about science and values from the 1960s and 1970s, it is that empirical theory or policy analysis cannot be isolated arbitrarily from the meta-theoretical and philosophical assumptions that are so often drowned out by loud appeals to 'objectivity' or 'reality'.

References to a tradition of international relations theory are by no means innocent. This is not to say that they are entirely misleading. They offer us a number of important clues about the historically constituted nature of both the theory and practice of international politics. But – particularly as they are inserted into textbooks, into passing references and obligatory footnotes – accounts of a tradition serve to legitimise and circumscribe what counts as proper scholarship. Indeed, the silences and limits engendered by claims about a tradition of international relations theory ought to be of pressing concern to students of contemporary political life in general, and not only to the apparently discrete discipline of international relations. Two aspects of the prevailing rendition of this tradition are of particular interest here.

The first concerns the rather peculiar relationship between theories of international relations and other areas of contemporary social and political enquiry, a peculiarity that is brought into especially sharp focus by contrasting responses to the problems posed by claims to a tradition. Although the twentieth century has seen many attempts to lay Hegel's *Geist* to rest, most contemporary social and political analysts still work on the basis of assumptions about a tradition of social and political thought, whatever unfortunate anachronism or deification of great texts has occurred, simply because it is possible – even necessary – to interpret history as a long march to modernity. From the high ground of modernity, critical voices, especially those echoing Nietzsche or Heidegger, may be dismissed as dangerous relativists, as unwilling to recognise the obvious achievements of progress or at least to put up with the costs of disenchantment with sufficient Weberian fortitude.

In the case of theories of international relations, however, the high ground of modernity gives way to shifting sand much more easily. The 'tradition' of international relations theory, with all its claims about necessities of state and the priority of power over ethics, is often articulated explicitly in opposition to a modernist reading of historical progress. Certain Nietzschean cadences, selectively heard and crudely harmonised with many other sceptical voices, are not difficult to detect in some of the more influential formulations of what a tradition of international relations theory involves. Ironically perhaps, but significantly, both defenders of a claim to a tradition of international relations theory and those who share a post-Nietzschean scepticism towards any such claim share a deep distrust of the grand trek to modernist universalism. The irony of this convergence is especially apparent in the recent forms of critique to which claims about a longstanding tradition of international relations theory have been subjected. Contrary to all those portrayals of the great debates in international relations theory as a contest between a relativist realism and a universalist idealism, for example, the self-identified political realists have recently found themselves being challenged on the ground of historicism and difference – precisely the ground that has been identified as the preserve of those who are willing to face up to the tragic necessities of power politics in a system of sovereign states. And whether in terms of scientific method, or of the utilitarian categories of liberal political economy, many contemporary (structural or neo-) realists have been caught trying to defend a tradition that can be traced back to Thucydides while also laying claim to the universalistic categories of modernity.[4]

The second aspect of the presumed tradition that is of concern here is 'Machiavelli'. More than almost anyone else, certainly more than either Hobbes or Rousseau, it is the name of Machiavelli that has come to symbolise what the tradition of international relations theory is all about. It is indeed necessary to take Machiavelli very seriously. He suggests crucial insights to those seeking to develop a critical perspective on contemporary international relations in particular and political life in general. To take Machiavelli seriously, however, cannot involve a simple submission to the caricature of tradition. On the contrary, Machiavelli can be read in ways that problematise the most basic assumptions on which claims about the tradition are based. Contrary to both the so-called realists who treat Machiavelli as one of their own and the so-called idealists who castigate him for his supposed realism, Machiavelli poses questions about political community and practice that may still be pursued even though his answers expose his own limited historical and conceptual horizons.

This is emphatically not a matter of making a claim about 'what Machiavelli really said' that may be counterposed to the caricature of the tradition, nor to demonstrate once again that Machiavelli was not a Machiavellian. It is, rather, to indicate one way of identifying some of the discursive practices that have turned an historical problematic into an ahistorical apology for the violence of the present. It is also to suggest a connection between the attempt to develop a critical dimension to international relations theory and emerging forms of political practice. To meditate on the identification of Machiavelli with claims about a tradition of international relations theory is to begin to see how it might now be possible to think otherwise: to use references to a tradition not as a legitimation of reification and closure, but as a source of critical opportunity. Even – or perhaps especially – *The Prince*, that supposedly most 'realist' of texts, I will suggest, must be read as a refusal to take any claim to an origin as an innocent act.

The tradition of international relations theory: three variations

Although references to a tradition of international relations theory are common enough, they are far from monolithic.[5] Some start with the Greek city-states, others with the Italian Renaissance, and others with the mature states-system of eighteenth-century Europe. There are also minor variations in the selection of authors and texts claimed to represent the tradition. Beyond this, however, it is useful to distinguish three rather different ways in which the tradition is identified and described. Although they are all closely related, the first two have been particularly susceptible to reification into an ahistorical claim about the unchanging realities of international politics. In the third version, the central issue that is at stake in the manner in which claims to a tradition of international relations theory have been articulated becomes more readily apparent.

There has been, first, the account of a permanent debate, the persistent confrontation between the houses of realism and idealism. E. H. Carr's rendition remains paradigmatic; Ian Clark's identification of Rousseau with a 'tradition of despair' and Kant with a 'tradition of optimism' is a typical recent echo.[6] With varying degrees of qualification, it informs surveys of the discipline and textbook categorisations of the main theoretical traditions. This account may feign sympathy for both sides, or it may be openly partisan. In either case, we find something rather similar to all those textbook histories of philosophy in which the eternal debate between rationalists and empiricists bears an uncanny resemblance to categories popularised as a consequence of Kant's attempt to synthesise them. In this case, also, it is not unreasonable to suspect that claims about an eternal debate rest upon an historically specific framing of the available alternatives.

This account of the tradition as a two-way debate has often been challenged. From one direction we find the Martin Wight–Hedley Bull triad in which something identified with Hugo Grotius acts as a kind of sensible middle road.[7] However, as with all appeals to a middle road, the intended compromise reenforces the legitimacy of the two poles as the limits of permitted discourse. From another direction, similar problems beset Stanley Hoffmann or even Hans Morgenthau, who, while rejecting the house of idealism, feel uncomfortable with a pure power politics and thus seek refuge in a Weberian 'ethic of responsibility'.[8] But again, as with Weber himself, the 'ethic of absolute ends' remains the silent possibility against which necessities and responsibilities are articulated. While dismissed as impractical, universalist aspiration provides the horizon against which the Sisyphean efforts of statesmen are to be judged.

In a second formulation, the partisans of realism claim victory. The eternal dialogue becomes an essentialistic monologue, although a number of theatrical figures – Thucydides, Machiavelli, Hobbes, Rousseau, Hegel, Morgenthau, Carr – are invited to read the script. Here terms like *power, state* and *national interest* appear with great regularity, interspersed with claims about human nature or political necessity, structural determinism or the tragic condition of human existence in general. For the most part, the list is constantly repeated as an article of faith, although the odd complaint about anachronism or even gross misrepresentation can certainly be found. Occasionally, serious attempts are made to justify the linking of names in this way into a continuous tradition. R. N. Berki's synthetic attempt to treat political realism as a 'mature attitude' towards the inherent instability of political life or Friedrich Meinecke's classic account of the doctrine of *raison d'état* stand out in this respect.[9]

In the third formulation, the tradition is defined by negation, by what it is not. And what it is not, by most accounts, is political theory. Sometimes this is intended to suggest that it is concerned with human relationships that are not subject to a centralised authority, as if centralised authority were a precondition for political life in general rather than a characteristic of some forms of political life in particular. In its more important rendition, however, the account of a tradition by negation – perhaps best represented by Martin Wight's celebrated essay on why there is no international theory – suggests that theories of international relations theory are marginal to political theory, marginal, that is, to the specific form of political community celebrated in claims about a tradition of properly political thought.[10] Theories of international relations are said to be characterised precisely by a refusal of the Enlightenment vision of universal progress, by a willingness to face up to contingency, pluralism and violence. Moreover, instead of an appeal to a tradition of classic texts there are references to the 'relative scarcity', 'unsystematic nature' and 'intellectual and moral poverty' of the scattered writings of historians, statesmen and the occasional philosopher. Like the other two versions of the appeal to a tradition, Wight's account sets important constraints on what theories of international relations can or cannot be. But instead of a prohibition against idealism or utopianism in general, the limits are defined by a particular form of idealism – by the political theory of life within states. International relations theory must therefore avoid the 'domestic analogy'. It must not transpose the universals, the teleology, the Whiggish History characteristic of accounts of political life within states into accounts of relations between states.

Wight argues an explicit case for what is more usually rendered as a simple and ahistorical contrast between political community within and international anarchy without. Moreover Wight's simultaneous appeal to a middle ground, whether one reads this as a reclamation of Hugo Grotius or of David Hume, makes the contrast less sharp than usual. Most significantly, Wight situates his analysis in an account of the historical context in which this spatial differentiation became constitutive of modern political life in the transformations of the late medieval era.[11] The myth of an eternal tradition almost collapses in the face of a sustained historical analysis. Unfortunately, the myth of an eternal debate remains in the background. Wight's three categories seem as deeply reified as those of Carr. Historical analysis gives way once again to a tradition that provides us with both a myth of origin and a clear boundary beyond which theories of international relations should not trespass.

Even so, in Wight's rendition, the problem at least becomes a little clearer. The difficulty is not the dubious list of names or the endless great debate, but the manner in which theories of international relations become framed as a counterpoint to another great tradition – that other long list of names and texts that populate courses in the history of *political* thought. It seems that theories of international relations are always destined to be the poor relation of something somehow more 'authentic', more 'political', more 'critical'; or at least to be always struggling to catch up with all those concepts, techniques and aspirations that can be taken for granted by those concerned with human communities within states.

Machiavelli and political community

Machiavelli's entry into this problematic is at once straightforward and disconcertingly complex – much like Machiavelli's own writing. He has entered into popular discourse as the paradigmatic 'realist'. He has become the most privileged icon, the most resonant symbol, the name (almost) at the top of the list of names, the writer of the text that more than any other has become synonymous with 'the tradition'. Read as the paradigmatic realist, he is immediately reduced to instant formulas – about the priority of power over ethics, about the necessity of violence and intrigue in the affairs of state, about ends justifying means and *raison d'état*.

All of which is clearly not to read Machiavelli at all, but to endorse a caricature, a product of a long, complex and particularly suspicious interpretive history. For many scholars, in fact, this interpretive history is at least as interesting as anything Machiavelli himself ever wrote.[12] As part of a reified tradition, Machiavelli remains elusive, embedded in layer upon layer of translations, anachronisms, interpretations and reinterpretations. Perhaps more than any other figure who has been implicated in the tradition of international relations theory, Machiavelli's name is indicative of how claims to 'realism' are intricately bound up with textualisations, reifications, idealisations and mystifications. At the very least, there is an interesting contradiction between substantive claims about a hard material reality, about the uncompromising necessities of power and violence that are so easily invoked by an appeal to political realism, and the textual strategies through which these claims are lodged within contemporary scholarship.

34

It is true that *The Prince* is a seductive text, in more ways
Numberless students have been impressed by its seemingl
grasp of the way people act. Too many of these students,
say, have gone on to teach international relations. Yet the difficulties
with this typical initial impression are clear enough. Although there
may be continuing controversies about and conflicting interpretations
of the meaning and significance of Machiavelli's texts, the received
caricature cannot survive even a moderately attentive first reading.

The seemingly straight-forward insistence on the necessity for
deception and dirty deeds if a prince is to remain in power – the things
that usually lead to claims about the way Machiavelli distinguishes
power from ethics – is immediately rendered problematic by the
attempt, in chapter 8, to distinguish between violence in general and
the minimum recourse to violence in pursuit of *virtù*. The concept of
virtù itself explodes with meanings and resonances that render any
straight-forward translation into modern terms extremely precarious.
The historically specific resonance of the term *virtù* is paralleled by the
specialised focus of the entire text. The first few chapters of *The Prince*,
with their binary classifications of different types of states, make it
clear that this particular text is referring only to the special problems of
new states. The text that is so often treated as the unproblematic origin
of tradition is itself obsessed with the highly problematic nature of
origins, of beginnings, of foundations, of the establishment and subsequent politics of traditions. Moreover, *The Prince* turns out to be one
text among many. To read the *Discourses on Livy*, or the *History of
Florence* or *The Art of War* is to become even more aware that
Machiavelli writes in the context of some very particular circumstances, that he is someone who has to be understood within the
broader context of Renaissance life and culture.

Far from being someone in touch with some timeless essence of
political life, Machiavelli appears within this broader perspective as
someone trying to make sense of historically specific circumstances,
and trying to do so in the discursive categories then available to him.
As, say, Quentin Skinner and John Pocock have argued at considerable
length, Machiavelli had to struggle to speak about an emerging form of
political community – the city state – in categories dominated by the
sensibilities of Christian universalism. To read Machiavelli in the light
of even a superficial acquaintance with this kind of literature is to see
that while it may be possible to trace a 'tradition' that may be called
Machiavellian, it is one concerned less with 'realism' or 'power politics'
than with 'humanism' or 'republicanism' or 'civic virtue'. It may also be
possible to trace a number of important antecedents and precursors,

but such an exercise does not take us automatically along a mythical highway back to Thucydides. Instead we encounter Roman historians, Cicero, interpreters of Plato such as Polybius, and even Aristotle.[13]

Still, despite this more complex figure who emerges from the specialised literature of the 'new historians', it might be argued that the traditional caricature is not entirely without foundation. One might admit that while Machiavelli may be invoked too frequently in a crude and unscholarly way, it does make some sense to identify him as someone who managed to articulate the most pressing problems of international relations theory in a forceful and provocative manner. After all, whatever else he may have written, he did write specifically about the prince (read statesman) in a situation of extreme danger (read international relations). He did speak of the dangers of allowing a universalist ethic to over-ride the pluralist or historicist ethics (as opposed to a simple power politics) necessary for creating and sustaining a community of *virtù* (read civil society or state). Thus while the identification of Machiavelli with a crude distinction between idealism and realism, understood as a distinction between ethics and power, must be called into question, Machiavelli might still be saved as the theorist who most incisively articulates the fundamental distinction between two ontologically distinct forms of political life, whether this is understood as public and private ethics or as political life within states and international relations between states.

Furthermore, his distinction between necessary and unnecessary violence, his insights into what Sheldon Wolin has called an 'economy of violence',[14] may even be invoked as a link between the Machiavellian sense of *virtù* and Weber's ethic of responsibility. In this sense, Machiavelli might even be rescued from the more extreme renditions of 'the tradition' and adopted by all those who seek some middle ground between freedom and necessity, is and ought, reality and possibility – except that, as Machiavelli himself kept insisting, it is no easier to work towards the middle than to begin at the beginning.

None of these lines of argument permit us to classify Machiavelli as the arch-realist. They suggest, on the contrary, that his primary concern was not international relations at all. To the extent that he was concerned with international relations and military affairs – and they certainly preoccupied him extensively – it is as a consequence of his account of the possibilities of political life within states. If it is useful to identify him with a tradition at all, it is a tradition concerned with the possibility of establishing a life of *virtù* within autonomous political communities. The reference, quite obviously, is to a classical conception of the *polis*, to a specific understanding of the location and character of political life within a bounded territorial space. Because this bounded space is identified as the location of political community, as the container in which republican *virtù* can flourish, the outside comes to be understood as the place where political community – as opposed to hegemony – is impossible.

In this sense, Machiavelli can be read as confirming the account of a tradition suggested by Martin Wight. It is, moreover, a tradition framed as a problem, a question, an interrogation. Accounts of a tradition as either a permanent dialogue or eternal monologue serve to affirm answers: this is the way it is, or this is the way it must be. But Machiavelli is not someone who is usually understood as a source of convincing answers to questions about political life. He may offer maxims and advice to princes, or sketch the broad outlines of how a republican polity might be sustained, but his positive recommendations are always tentative. He is more usefully approached as an explorer, an interrogator, someone who poses questions about what politics can be under new historical and structural conditions. And these new conditions, of course, involve a shift from the hierarchical continuities of medieval life, feudal modes of production and the claims of empire to the radical autonomies and separations of early-modern Europe, capitalism and the states-system. The formulation of a tradition of international relations as the negation of a tradition about political community within an autonomous bounded space must be the crucial point of engagement with contemporary theories of international politics because it focuses explicitly on the novel and highly problematic character of the autonomies and separations to which Machiavelli, and early-modern Europe in general, had to respond.

If thinking about international relations is to be understood as a tradition by negation, then it makes little sense to speak of a tradition of international relations theory as such. It is, rather, necessary to come to terms with the conception of political community that is being negated. There can be no meaningful reference to a tradition of international relations theory without specifying what one means by a tradition of political theory.

In this context, however, Machiavelli can be read in sharply contrasting ways. Machiavelli both affirms a particular understanding of what a political community can be and, equally important, suggests how that conception of political community must be brought into question. While from one direction Machiavelli can usefully be understood as someone who articulates a conception of political life that depends on a capacity to distinguish between life inside and outside a spatially organised political community, between self and other, community and anarchy, from another direction the very terms that Machiavelli is led to deploy can also be read as calling this distinction into question.

Machiavelli and temporality

Although Machiavelli spends a considerable amount of energy writing about military affairs, his observations in this context are at least as much an expression of his conception of political community as of the character of international relations. Take, for example, his discussion of fortresses in the twentieth chapter of *The Prince*. Fortresses he says

> are sometimes useful, then, and sometimes not; it depends on the circumstances. Moreover, if they help you in some respects, they will be harmful in others. The subject may be clarified in the following way: if a ruler is more afraid of his own subjects than of foreigners, he should built fortresses; but a ruler who is more afraid of foreigners than of his own subjects should not build them ... The best fortress a ruler can have is not to be hated by the people: for if you possess fortresses and the people hate you, having fortresses will not save you, since if the people rise up there will never be any lack of foreign powers ready to help them.

Concluding his discussion, he writes:

> Bearing in mind all these things, then, I praise anyone who builds fortresses and anyone who does not, and I criticise anyone who relies upon fortresses, and does not worry about incurring the hatred of the people.[15]

Two themes are conspicuously absent from this analysis, although they do not entirely escape his attention elsewhere. There is little sense that Machiavelli is concerned with treating fortresses as elements of an inventory of forces, as part of some strategic balance of power. Nor is there any concern with how new technologies might render fortresses obsolete. Rather Machiavelli's primary emphasis is on two other themes, both of which illustrate his understanding of the possibilities of political community rather than his distillation of the enduring realities of international relations.

The first involves the direct connection he makes between military affairs and the idea of civic *virtù*, between the qualities of skill and courage, virility and virtuosity, and the requirements of citizenship within the political community.[16] While it is true that the virile warrior may be required to engage in conflict outside the community, the qualities represented by the warrior, the man of *virtù*, are presented first and foremost as the qualities necessary for effective participation and citizenship within the community.

The second theme is closely related to the first, but is usually framed in a more abstract form. It concerns Machiavelli's insistence that political affairs, whether these concern fortresses or princes, must be understood and judged 'according to circumstances'. His fundamental complaint about fortresses is that they are fixed, that it is too easy to rely upon them as a guarantee of permanence. They inhibit a capacity to respond to changing conditions. Similarly, the *virtù* of a prince is understood in terms of a capacity to respond to *fortuna*, to the capricious bitch goddess who is 'the arbiter of one half of our actions'. *Fortuna* is in turn compared to 'one of those ruinous rivers that, when they become enraged, flood the plains, tear down the trees and buildings, taking up earth from one spot and placing it upon another'.[17] Thus, the concept of *virtù* invokes not only the military qualities of the warrior and civic qualities necessary for citizenship but also the qualities through which the virile hero is able to seduce *fortuna*, to prepare the banks and dikes against the oncoming flood.

In short we have, in a specifically Renaissance humanist language, in the images and metaphors of Machiavelli the poet rather than of Machiavelli the prototypical political scientist or realist, an account of political life as occurring in time.[18] This is not the linear time of universalist history. Machiavelli's understanding of time involves cycles and returns, contingencies and unpredictabilities. It is distinctively premodern. Yet although it is possible to trace the roots of Machiavelli's own understanding of time, it is more useful in this context to understand what conception of time it is articulated against. Most obviously, Machiavelli repudiates the prevailing Christian doctrine that political life is subordinate to eternity. Where the Christian tradition, and especially St Augustine, had downgraded political life as merely temporal, as at best a preparation for the universal kingdom of God, Machiavelli reverses the polarity. For him, politics is in the end a greater passion than God. In the context of an all pervasive discourse of universals, Machiavelli thus draws upon a number of traditions in classical political thought that insist on the importance of the world of time and becoming, not least Aristotle's account of man as a political animal and Roman conceptions of the republic as permitting the highest form of political life.

Where the Christian tradition saw everything that occurs in time as tainted with original sin, and where the Platonist tradition saw everything that is not understood as participating in Being or unchanging form as merely occurring in the world of flux, *doxa* and illusion,

Machiavelli insists on the possibilities of greatness in time, a greatness that is not in need of completion by either philosophy or grace.[19] These possibilities do not depend on unchanging laws. Machiavelli's image of time as a river in flood contrasts sharply with Hobbes' deterministic image of liberty as a river necessarily descending a preordained channel.[20] Instead, Machiavelli offers maxims, mere tennis play as Hobbes would insist, advice about how to prepare for the coming of *fortuna*: establish institutions, create respect for laws and customs, secure the support of the people, create an armed citizenry; above all, expect change to occur. Once *fortuna* arrives, even such maxims are of little use. Political greatness depends on a capacity to judge whether it is better to lie low, to submit to *fortuna*, or to 'command her with audacity'. Once *fortuna* departs, Machiavelli cautions against giving in to either self-esteem or self-pity, for *fortuna* is sure to return again.

Committed to a politics that responds to the temporal contingency of life in this world, Machiavelli is prepared to face up to the consequences that, according to both classical and Christian inheritances, must be drawn once one abandons the possibility of transcending the contingencies of time through an appeal to Being or eternity. Political life, according to Machiavelli, requires a capacity to recognise and manipulate illusions, rather than erase them in favour of Goodness, Truth and Beauty. It also involves being prepared to resort to violence, to understand the positive benefits of class conflict, and to see an armed citizenry as a necessary component of a political community worthy of being remembered and imitated at some other time. Or, to put this less negatively, political life calls for the special skills appropriate for confronting *fortuna*: the skills of civic *virtù*, prudence and caution, the capacity to generate a lasting and stable order in the midst of temporal flux and contingency.

None of which has endeared Machiavelli to those for whom temporal contingency is intolerable, and for whom the story of modernity as the trek to universality is so comforting. For them, even time has a meaningful order, a promise of fulfilment, reason, justice and peace. It is within the discursive politics that are thereby established that Machiavelli is enshrined in the account of the tradition as a great debate. The historical problematic confronted by Machiavelli comes to be framed in terms of another historical problematic. Machiavelli's specifically Renaissance humanist attempt to articulate a politics of time occurs in the context of historically constituted discourses – both classical and Christian – in which time is understood as a problem to be overcome either through fulfilment in time or by fixing a home for man in space – the state.

Machiavelli and the politics of displacement

Machiavelli articulates an account of politics in time against the prevailing universalistic categories of the medieval world. Yet it is these very universalistic categories that provide the broad context in which Machiavelli, and the Renaissance humanists more generally, could work, could attempt to articulate an alternative account of the possibilities of political life. This is why the history of Machiavelli interpretation is so interesting. The most influential accounts of what he was doing have for the most part been grounded in precisely the kind of universalistic categories that Machiavelli sought to challenge. Once read without the prior disposition to insist that human conduct ought to be guided by some underlying universalist ethical norm, it is not difficult to see that Machiavelli goes to some trouble to distinguish between acceptable and unacceptable behaviour. Machiavelli's political ethics may not be persuasive, but it requires a fair degree of interpretive violence to treat him as simply unethical, as the evil genius of *realpolitik*. Where Machiavelli himself may be understood as struggling to articulate a politics of time against a dominant discourse of universalisms, it has been fairly easy for those drawing upon some variant of those universalisms to reconstitute this struggle as merely a capitulation to relativism, or evil or sophistry. This move is not exactly rare in the annals of rationalism, monotheism or, indeed, in contemporary debates about modernity.

It is especially interesting to see how this move has occurred in the context of international relations theory. Here, we can see a displacement of the 'problem of Machiavelli' onto the distinction between political community and international relations. Even though Machiavelli's positive political theory makes little sense unless read in the context of the classical account of life within a political community, Machiavelli has come to be associated primarily with theories of the relations between states – the realm in which it has become more or less legitimate, even if distasteful, to abandon universalist principles in favour of an amoral *realpolitik*. Not only has the conventional interpretation turned Machiavelli into a simple relativist, but he has been given a particular space in which to act – not the community in which peace and progress are possible but the supposed home of pure power, the so-called international anarchy.

This move is crucial, and it allows us to see what is at stake in the formulation of a tradition of international relations theory as, in Martin Wight's sense, a negation of a tradition of political theory. It also indicates what is being obscured by constantly repeated claims about a

41

tradition understood as either an eternal debate or an eternal mono-logue. Simply put, Machiavelli has come to symbolise both a negation and a displacement of a tradition of political thought, a tradition that explicitly links a meaningful political life to the pursuit of universals within a territorially bounded space. As a negation, Machiavelli has been forced to occupy the ground of pluralism, relativism and power politics that is defined against the possibility of an ethical universalism. As a displacement he has been pushed into the space of international anarchy, into that realm of 'relations' rather than of 'politics', of barbarians, of others who are understood to be beyond the limits of our political community, our political identity, our peace, justice and good government.

To put this more provocatively, if it is necessary to identify a tradition of international relations theory, then the most appropriate candidate is not 'realism' but 'idealism'. For what is systematically obscured by the reifying claims about political realism as a tradition is that realism has been constituted historically through the negation and displacement of a prior understanding of political life understood in the context of universalist aspirations. For all that self-styled realists may complain about the dangers of idealism, cosmopolitanism or the misplaced domestic analogy, the tradition of political realism as we have come to know it is unthinkable without the priority ascribed to universalist claims within political theory. Conversely, political theory, while generally silent about what goes on beyond the boundaries of the sovereign community, itself depends upon the silences of inter-national relations theory to make its own claims to universalism plaus-ible. Rather less provocatively, perhaps, if one is to speak meaningfully of a tradition of international relations theory at all, it must be an account that places the discursive practices of negation and dis-placement at the centre; that is, one that insists on the mutually constitutive nature of thinking about life within and between political communities.[21]

The significance of Machiavelli in this respect is rather ambiguous. Three themes are relevant here. First, Machiavelli himself is quite clear about the continuity between life within political communities and relations between them. Conflict with other communities is, for Machiavelli, an integral aspect of the armed citizenship necessary for civic *virtù*. Second, despite the extent to which Machiavelli has been interpreted as merely a theorist of relativism and contingency, of *doxa* and illusion, he did struggle to articulate a meaningful politics in time. In doing so, he drew upon conceptions of time that make little sense to us. Yet we also are in many ways caught in a predicament that would have been familiar to Machiavelli – not a predicament of international anarchy, but a crisis of political consciousness arising from a loss of faith in universalist history. Third, while Machiavelli may have reversed the polarity among the conventional categories available to him, his own rejection of the dominant pole did little to undermine the claim that a politics of time could be erased by a politics of space. It is no accident that the next icon in the tradition is Hobbes: not the theorist of an international state of nature, but the theorist of political community as architecture, as the embodiment of sovereign and geometrical reason.

Thinking with and against Machiavelli

That Machiavelli should have been the subject of such a highly contested, not to say passionate interpretive history, and yet have been placed so comfortably in the received tradition of international relations theory is of more than passing interest. Claims about such a tradition in general or about Machiavelli in particular identify the nature of the problem to be addressed, and situate it within a discursive space that both defines and limits the legitimate responses to the problem that has been identified. Even from these brief remarks here, it should be clear that Machiavelli especially can be read in ways that undermine any simple claim to a tradition. As a point of departure he ought to be profoundly unsettling. There is both less and more in Machiavelli's writings than is usually implied by the claim that international relations is essentially Machiavellian in nature.

There is less, in that Machiavelli does not present, say, a structuralist account of international anarchy, such as the one so often attributed – falsely – to Hobbes. Structuralist accounts of the international system draw upon ontological, and thus political commitments that are significantly different from those to be found in Machiavelli's writings. Contrary to some translations, there is no clear statement to the effect that the end justifies the means. There is no clear notion of national interest defined as power. It may well be possible to read these things into Machiavelli's writings, but this is to engage in a rather different enterprise, one that is difficult to reconcile with established scholarly procedures.

There is more, in that Machiavelli draws upon a range of themes, especially those associated with classical conceptions of the *polis*, that are concerned with the establishment of a political community, one that aspires to *virtù*, to the good, although obviously not to a conception of ethical life that would find favour with followers of, say,

43

Thomas Aquinas or Immanuel Kant. There is more also in that Machiavelli insists on the problematic of establishing human communities in time, rather than of the need to finally abolish time in favour of a kingdom of ends, a metaphysics of being, a transcendent universal to be labelled as Reason or Justice or Peace. The significance of this insistence is not restricted to thinking about international relations. It applies also to those who understand political life as the attempt to seize the centres of state power, who understand the state as the fixed point of identity, whether as the prince acting boldly against *fortuna*, the legal sovereign claiming legitimacy through reason, or as the Weberian hero standing resolutely 'able to do no other', before the intensifying clash of values within a rationalised modernity. For ironically, while Machiavelli contested the universalism of the static universals of his time, and contested it on the ground of the temporality of human existence, the Machiavellian community, the state, has itself come to be treated as the static universal, the fixed point from which the world may be commanded by the latter-day heroes who claim power and legitimacy in a world of evident flux.

It is in this context that the contrast between the typical practices through which Machiavelli is inserted into the tradition of international relations theory and the key moments of Machiavelli's analysis in *The Prince* is so striking. Even though there are scholars who resolutely insist on a more historically and textually sensitive reading of theories of international relations, it is the brief references, the short assertions, the accumulating textbooks, the obligatory footnotes, and the revealingly short-tempered responses to the idealists and critics that are more relevant in practice. Here we find the insistent assertion that there is a tradition, an origin, a code, a centre, a home from which one can set out to explore the contingencies and transformations of the world outside. It is exactly the politics of such a claim that is challenged by Machiavelli's observations about fortresses: one should not rely on a fixed point of reference. What has worked before may not work again. Even though one might imitate earlier expressions of *virtù*, there can be no reliance on a tradition that makes claims about how things have always been, still are, and always will be. 'The man who adapts his course of action to the nature of the times', says Machiavelli, 'will succeed, and likewise ... the man who sets his course of action out of tune with the times will come to grief.'[22] To establish a tradition, as with establishing a long-standing community of *virtù* is, for Machiavelli, a challenge, a matter of political practice, something to be achieved through action. Inheritor of at least some aspects of the classical theory of the *polis* that he is, he knows that once such a community, such a tradition, is established, it is bound to succumb to *fortuna*, probably sooner rather than later. Machiavelli is just as obsessed with endings as he is with beginnings.

Even recognising that Machiavelli is more usefully understood as a theorist of political practice, of the possibility of creating new forms of political community, rather than as the theorist of the unchanging realities of *realpolitik*, it is still evident that his own understanding of what political practice entails has distinct limits. To begin with, not only is his attempt to articulate a politics of time predicated on an archaic cosmology, but it also embodies a degree of male chauvinism that is in some ways even more embarrassing than is usual in the great texts of political theory.[23] Beyond this, for all his attempts to articulate a politics of time, his vision of political practice is constrained within two crucial horizons. These horizons also may be understood as historically contingent rather than eternally fixed. Consequently, Machiavelli's politics of time may be turned against his own commitments to a politics of space. On the one hand there is the horizon of scholastic universals against which Machiavelli articulates his conception of a political community in time. On the other hand there is the space of the state within which it is possible to aspire to *virtù*, even if only for a brief period. Both of these horizons have been subject to historical change.

Scholastic universalism gave way to a more secular universalism associated with the scientific revolution, the Enlightenment, and modernity in general. There are certainly connections between these universalisms, but histories of Western thought are rather full of stories about how particular accounts of what constitutes a universal have been challenged by others. There is little reason to expect such challenges to cease; there may even be some hope that any future rethinking of what it means to make a universalistic claim might not be so insistent on subsuming all differences into an all-embracing unity. The difficulty confronting those who try to understand contemporary patterns of integration and internationalisation on a global scale is not a lack of empirical evidence. It is, rather, the temptation to speak about global processes within historically and culturally specific, and by now seriously misleading accounts of what universality must entail. Those who invoke an empiricist legitimation of liberal utilitarianism under such rubrics as 'interdependence' or 'international regimes' are no less susceptible to this temptation than those who express a more normative aspiration for 'world order'.

Similarly, the horizon presented by the spatial form of the state has changed historically. It was only after Machiavelli that the principle of state sovereignty came to be framed within the context of the Euclidean–Galilean principle of absolute space rather than the complex overlapping jurisdictions of the medieval era. There is no reason to expect that understanding of political community to remain unchanged; with global flows of capital and the internationalisation of production, we live in a world in which the complexity of spatial relations is more obvious than the simple legalistic maps of state sovereignty. Moreover, it was only after Machiavelli that it became possible to pretend that the state is a fixed form, a pretence expressed initially in the legal codes of territorial sovereignty, and echoed more recently in the reifying categories of so many socio-scientific analyses of international balances of power and foreign-policy decision-making. The difficulty with realism in this sense is not the insistence on the importance of the state, but the lack of much serious analysis of what a state is. Bald assertions consistent with ahistorical claims to state-sovereignty have been accepted all too easily as a substitute for a properly theoretical account of the state as an historically constituted and constantly reconstituted form of political life.

None of this is to suggest that the state is withering away, that pluralism is necessarily giving way to universalism. It is to insist that our understanding of what it means to engage in particular communities, whether particular is understood in local, cultural or regional terms, is just as likely to change as is our understanding of what it means to claim universality. If, as for Machiavelli, the most important, and certainly the most interesting political question concerns how new forms of political community are to be established – the question for which Machiavelli saves his 'most illustrious examples' – it is clear that Machiavelli's own answer is historically contingent. If we are to treat Machiavelli seriously then we might bring his question to bear on our own era without becoming obsessed with the limits of his own answers, or with the supposed answers that have ossified into accounts of a tradition as a permanent dialogue/monologue. Neither the realist appeal to an eternity of states nor the idealist appeal to a universal community tell us very much about politics in this sense. The myth of a tradition of international relations theory, like a myth of a tradition of political theory, makes it very difficult to think about politics at all. Both affirm answers to questions that they no longer take seriously.

Neither the politics of contemporary debates about modernity nor the problems of political practice in an era of rapid and confusing transformations are to be taken lightly. But they do take the concerns of those engaged with international relations into the centre of contemporary thought and practice, rather than leave it at the margin, the pauper ever subservient to the glories of the prince and his substitutes. Not least, they point to yet another way in which Machiavelli might be reconstituted in a tradition, this time one in which he is coupled with, say, 'Plato' and 'Marx'.

In this rendition, Machiavelli would appear not as one of a group of realists or proto-totalitarians, but as an important theorist of language. Plato understood very clearly what was at stake in the declining credibility of Homeric myth, and articulated an alternative language of philosophy, of general concepts, of universals.[24] Marx understood very clearly the processes through which human labour came to be reified into commodities, into the abstract generalities of money to be exchanged in a market, abstract generalities that found their expression in the class-specific universalisms of political economy. Machiavelli struggled to articulate a language of particulars, a language in which to speak about *lo stato* against a discursive hegemony of scholastic universals. It is interesting that in a century when so much political thought has been obsessed with language, and when so much of international life occurs as 'strategy', 'games', and other discursive formations, theorists of international relations should have shown so little concern with Machiavelli's insights into the politics of language.[25]

But then, one should not feign innocence about this rendition of a tradition either. Those concerned with the politics of language encounter another debilitating account of the relation between language and world, between idealism and realism/materialism. We return to the dilemmas of modernity and to the last-ditch attempts by the defenders of modernity to hang on to the promised certainties towards which Machiavelli encourages us to be so sceptical. Perhaps the pragmatists, empiricists and policy analysts are right to turn away in order to deal with more manageable topics. But they cannot do so innocently.

From origins to disjunctions

Contemporary explorations of world politics commonly begin by invoking a tradition, a starting point from which historical trajectories, theoretical innovations and future aspirations may be charted and judged. Appeals to this tradition of political realism underwrite the rituals through which students are introduced to the theory of international relations, and thus disciplined both to think of the realities of relations between states as fundamentally different from life within states and to repudiate hopes for a future free from the tragic necessities of power politics.

Once claims to such a tradition are examined with any degree of care, however, uncertainties and instabilities set in very quickly. For some purposes, it is enough merely to remember the methodological injunctions absorbed by any student of the history of ideas in trying to interpret any text, especially one written by someone no longer around to tell us what he – always a he – was trying to say. In this manner, accounts of a tradition of international relations may be understood as a consequence of a familiar relapse into anachronism and mythologising, and the task at hand can then be understood as the provision of a more accurate and scholarly reading of what Thucydides, Machiavelli, Hobbes, Rousseau and the rest were up to.[26]

The discussion so far has partly subscribed to this line of thought, though without accepting the view that the meaning and significance of particular writers and texts eventually might be pinned down with some confidence. Rather, I have used the contrast between realist caricature and several lines of interpretation that have been pursued in the recent scholarly literature on Machiavelli to introduce two other themes that I want to explore from several different directions in the rest of this book.

First, I have suggested that if one tries to think both with and against Machiavelli – the supposed arch-realist in spite of the bewildering interpretive practices through which he has become known to us – it is possible to emphasise certain Machiavellian motifs so as to open up precisely the sort of alternative possibilities that invocations of Machiavelli are usually used to prohibit.

Second, I have argued that if one is to make any sense of a tradition in which Machiavelli might be usefully located it is necessary to be sensitive to the specific questions to which Machiavelli was seeking to respond rather than to reify the repertoires of answers – supposedly to be found in his texts – which tell us how things are and how they might be. To focus on Machiavelli is to be especially concerned with questions posed as a consequence of the shift from hierarchical continuities to the autonomies and separations of a specifically modern world. It is in this context that it is possible to see why the account of a tradition of international relations theory affirmed by Martin Wight remains so important. The consequence that must be drawn from this account, however, is that any account of a tradition of political realism as such must be a fundamentally misleading point from which to start an analysis of modern world politics. If Wight is correct, in his initial insight at least, then it is necessary to begin by examining the account of political life within autonomous communities which makes possible the claim to a realist tradition about relations between such communities.

In the following chapter, I examine the extent to which this account is not only the positive ground against which theories of international relations have been constituted by negation but is also present *within* accounts of a tradition of international relations. That is to say, I want to replay and recast themes so far introduced in relation to claims about political realism in relation to the supposedly opposing claims that are said to constitute a tradition of political idealism. The key debates here have been posed in terms of 'ethics' or 'normative' theory. And instead of claims about a point of origin, we find claims about an intersection, an absence or gap that must be – or cannot be – erased. Again, I suggest, these claims obscure much more than they reveal.

3 ETHICS, MODERNITY, COMMUNITY

At the intersection

What is often characterised as an intersection marked 'ethics and international relations' is once again a site of industriousness and vitality. Stanley Hoffmann has even gone so far as to suggest that the appearance of a renewed literature seeking to treat relations between states as a proper subject for ethical inquiry has been one of the two major developments in the analysis of world politics over the past decade.[1] For Hoffmann, it shares this honour with the 'scientific' (or liberal-utilitarian) analysis of conflictual co-operation and inter-state regime formation.

This chapter is motivated by a similar sense of the importance of work being conducted under the sign of 'ethics and international relations'. It is also interested in its relation to the recent popularity of liberal-utilitarian accounts of inter-state co-operation. But I am concerned primarily with the extent to which so much of the literature is informed by the highly problematic assumption that 'ethics and international relations' is indeed the name of an intersection, a junction between two separate areas of disciplinary inquiry. This image reflects a pervasive sense that the task before us is primarily one of application or extension. 'Ethics' comes to be understood as an achieved body of principles, norms and rules already codified in texts and traditions. And 'international relations' is understood as a realm of recalcitrant practical problems in dire need of greater moral scruple. Hence the possibility, for example, of applying principles from just-war doctrine to practices of nuclear deterrence, or of extending accounts of distributive justice initially framed in relation to autonomous individuals into accounts of the obligations of autonomous states.

This image is especially troubling because it is sustained by a series of additional dichotomies that are regularly denounced as implausible guides to the subtleties and complexities of human affairs. An opposition between utopianism and realist power politics, the Cartesian divide between matter and consciousness and the positivist injunction to separate the normative from the empirical have all served to reinforce the conviction that 'ethics' and 'international relations' are, at least under present conditions, fundamentally incongruous terms.

Here I want to develop a different account of what is at stake in references to 'ethics and international relations' than is suggested by the image of an intersection and to examine some of the conditions under which it is possible to speak of ethics and international relations in the late twentieth century. Specifically, where the previous chapter sought to problematise and destabilise certain constitutive claims about origins and historical trajectories enshrined in accounts of a tradition of international relations theory, here I want to further problematise the pattern of presence and absence which found one important expression in Machiavelli's explorations of the possibility of political community under novel historical conditions, a pattern which finds a particularly important expression in a very large proportion of the literature on ethics and international relations.

Ethics, I will suggest, is not a repository of principles awaiting application; it is an ongoing historical practice. And far from being devoid of ethical principles, the theory of international relations is already constituted through accounts of ethical possibility. Neither suggestion is in any way novel in principle, at least in the context of contemporary philosophy or political theory. But together they permit a critical stance towards much of the recent literature on international relations not on the familiar ground that it dares to take ethical questions seriously despite the prevailing wisdoms of realism, materialism and positivism but because it does not take the difficulty of speaking about ethics in the modern world seriously enough. Analysis of the conditions under which it is now possible to speak of ethics at all has become a familiar part of contemporary ethical enquiry.[2] Theories of international relations, I will suggest, are especially interesting in this respect as expressions of the limits within which claims about ethics are – or are not – reconcilable with claims about the spatio-temporal articulation of political identity and community. To query the intersection marked ethics and international relations in the light of postmodern and post-structural suspicions is not to engage in ethical nihilism, as is often charged, but to place the connection between ethical claims and conceptions of political community back on the agenda of serious enquiry and practical action.

My procedure will be to sketch three distinct readings of the theory of international relations both as the embodiment of accounts of ethical possibility and as a discourse in which specific spaces are

51

reserved for speaking about ethics. The first reading offers an account of how discussions of ethics and international relations have been shaped by claims and counter-claims about emancipation and enlightenment over time. The second reading focuses on the spatial resolution of philosophical options formalised in the principle of state sovereignty. The third reading is concerned with accounts of a society of states, that is, with attempts to mediate between claims about temporal community and spatial or geopolitical anarchy.

Each of these readings is intended to resonate with themes introduced in the discussion of Machiavelli in the previous chapter. The explicit linkage, however, is the perhaps even more obscure figure of Max Weber, in whom it is possible to find Machiavellian motifs recast in a distinctively modern guise. With Weber, who arguably has been the single most important voice in contemporary debates about international relations, autonomies and separations continue to be of central importance, but these are grasped in relation not to *fortuna* as a capricious temporal energy but to characteristically twentieth-century debates about history and modernity. I argue, first, that the significance of the relationship between theories of modernity and theories of international relations has been systematically obscured by claims about socio-scientific epistemology on the one hand and about traditions of idealism and realism on the other; and, second, that to engage in serious reflection about ethics and international relations now is necessarily to be suspicious of the modernist categories through which the interaction between two seemingly autonomous disciplines has been treated as the main highway to a better future.

Temporality, Weber and the dialectics of Enlightenment

It is not difficult to understand the urgency with which the need for greater attention to ethical questions is now pressed. We confront manifold dangers, and are constantly reminded of multiple outrages. The litany is familiar: threats of nuclear annihilation; new patterns of inclusion and exclusion fostered by the global reorganisation of economic life; quandaries posed by novel technologies of production, destruction and reproduction; an emerging awareness of ecological fragility; and a continuing recourse to torture, disappearances and even genocide. The primary ground for ethical reflection no doubt remains a capacity to identify the intolerable. And, at a certain level, it is not difficult to identify a range of intolerable features of modern life: the tremendous resources devoted to potential species extermination;

the legitimacy of forms of economic development that continue to bring extreme wealth to some while threatening the very survival of others; the rapacious destruction of the planetary habitat in the name of progress and profit; the flagrant abuse of established human rights. From the South Bronx to the West Bank, from the proliferation of refugee camps to emerging patterns of inclusion and exclusion almost everywhere, the intolerable is always visible to those who would nevertheless celebrate the achievements of the modern world.

Phasing the matter this way, the crucial dilemma is already apparent. Even to begin such a listing is to recognise that judgments about what is to be tolerated are sharply contested. Consequently, discussion invariably moves from consideration of particular cases to attempts to shape universal principles of conduct that might guide rules and laws, cultures and institutions – principles that can be treated as foundational, as permitting the delineation of some Archimedian point from which contention and scepticism may be tamed and controlled.

The problem of scepticism was sharpened in classical Greece, and it is in that context especially that the possibility of a properly ethical life became tied to the possibility of philosophy. Not everyone has been persuaded by this move, and many have echoed suspicions of the kind articulated by Sextus Empiricus. For the most part, however, hopes for a firm foundation for ethical principles have been shaped by philosophical claims about the way the world is. These claims have been shaped and reshaped through the interplay between philosophy, religion, science and the broad cultural and ideological dynamics generated by specific social formations. Ethical traditions have thus come down to us bearing the marks of complex intellectual contention and social struggle. Yet in whatever way one cuts into that daunting edifice known as the history of philosophy, and however one understands philosophy as a socially and historically constructed practice, it is clear that modern philosophy has been very strongly guided by a privileging of questions about how the world is to be known, and thus about how knowledge is to be justified. Epistemology has become the key entry into philosophical inquiry. The epistemological turn, associated especially with the scientific revolution of the seventeenth century, still provides the most powerful context in which ethical questions are posed and ethical claims are judged.[3]

Linked in this way to the ambitions of philosophy in general and, increasingly, to the attempt to overcome a specifically epistemological scepticism, ethical inquiry has become caught up in contemporary debate about the achievements of modernity. On the one hand, ethical claims have been articulated on the basis of a positive reading of modernity, whether this is understood as an achieved condition or an incomplete project. On the other, scepticism is turned against modernity itself, sometimes just in terms of the epistemological guarantees established by a Galileo or a Descartes, and sometimes in terms of the prior assumption that ethical conduct must be tied to the claims of philosophy at all.

Paradoxically, the celebration of modernity as the primary condition for ethical conduct often brings with it a devaluation of ethics as a serious topic at the same time that the very possibility of ethical discourse is affirmed. This devaluation can take two related forms. In one, seriousness is associated with empirical or positive knowledge of what is. Claims about how the world is, or rather how it is to be known, become separated from claims about how the world should be. In this rendering, facts are separated from values, empirical science is distinguished from normative theory, and objectivity is opposed to subjectivity. In another form, values tend to be equated with the way the world is already, or rather with the way the world has become under the progressive logic of modernisation and utilitarian calculation. In both cases, questions about ethics appear to be relatively trivial. Modernity has already brought the good life, or at least provides the general principles and social dynamics through which any remaining dilemmas may be resolved.

Conversely, to bring the achievements of modernity into question is to raise serious doubts about the very possibility of creating universal principles of conduct. Such doubts are not novel. In either its Pyrrhonian, Cartesian or Humean forms, scepticism has long played a crucial role in both stimulating and deflating claims to universal validity. But doubt has been an especially persistent theme among philosophers and socio-political analysts in this century. In putting into question the link between ethics and a modernist celebration of scientific and social progress, contemporary social and political thought has become obsessed once again with the threat of relativism: with the fear that this century might be known retrospectively not only as one of extreme barbarisms, but also one in which the grand ambitions of Enlightenment reason and universalist principles finally collapsed in traumatic ruin.

The effects of a deep rift between those who would celebrate or are sceptical towards the achievements and potential of modernity are readily apparent to any student of contemporary theories of international relations. The most straight-forward effect arises from the development, since 1945, of the Anglo-American discipline of international relations as a modernist social science. Here the two different meanings assigned to the term 'normative theory' are symptomatic. On one reading, the normative is distinguished from the empirical. The normative is then associated with the history of political thought, that is, with pre-modern forms of political analysis articulated without the benefits of modern accounts of scientific explanation and research methodology. The institutionalised opposition within US political science between the kind of political theory represented by Leo Strauss and the claims of a positivistic empiricism remains paradigmatic in this respect, despite widespread assurances that we have now entered a post-positivistic or post-behavioural era. On another reading, one bearing the unmistakable hallmarks of utilitarianism in general and liberal micro-economics in particular, the normative has become associated with what Max Weber identified as formal rationality, and thus with what amounts to the efficient pursuit of established ends by instrumental means.

Thus insofar as the analysis of international relations is situated within the broader ambitions of modernist social science, questions about ethics are either deferred as mere theory and philosophy or simply subsumed into an account of the way the world is presumed to be. This goes a long way towards explaining much of the character of the literatures on world order on the one hand and on conflictual co-operation and international regime formation on the other. In effect, ethical dilemmas are subjected to a one-sided version of Weber's account of modernity in terms of the 'specific and peculiar rationality' of Western civilisation. The difficulty, however, is that Weber's own account of modernity is distinctively two-sided. Although he offers a qualified, even resigned, accommodation to modernity, Weber also offers a paradigmatic indictment of modernity as a realm in which both meaning and ethical life are rendered increasingly problematic. This is the side of Weber that becomes visible once the discipline of international relations is situated not within the aspirations of modern social science but in relation to enigmatic claims about a tradition of political realism.[4] It is through this historicist side of Weber that it is possible to see the effect of a more negative reading of modernity on the theory of international relations.

References to Weber are always difficult. He has become institutionalised as a founding father of sociology through a particularly tortuous episode in the history of contemporary social and political thought. Yet despite his posthumous recruitment as an apologist for value-free social science, his ambivalence towards modernity, and thus his intense concern with the possibility of ethical conduct, has never been completely erased. It was certainly plain enough to Raymond Aron,

Hans J. Morgenthau and other figures associated with realist portrayals of the tragedies of international politics.[5]

It remains unclear how best to conceptualise Weber's concerns. Despite the reappearance of Weber as a serious political thinker, one no longer reconcilable with the polished sheen once given to an empiricist icon, scholarly analysis still remains uncertain even about how to formulate Weber's guiding question. A concern with the process of rationalisation as the guiding principle of modern forms of social organisation is clearly important, but considerable controversy has arisen out of attempts to interpret this concern in terms of Weber's politics, especially his allegiance to a specifically German form of nationalist liberalism, or in terms of his philosophical anthropology, especially his concern with the nature of personality in the modern world.[6] Still, Weber's analysis of the process of rationalisation is obviously at odds with the spirit of Hegel's reading of history. Weber did not share the optimistic view of a universalising history that Marx could still take more or less for granted. Instead, we hear the voices of Nietzsche. God is dead. We live in a disenchanted universe. Rational calculation remains possible, but rational calculation offers not one shred of advice about how one should live.

For Weber, modernity is characterised by an intensifying clash between instrumental rationality and the realm of substantive values. As instrumental rationality advances, so the spheres of life in which meaning and values are affirmed become both marginalised and given a heightened significance. This tension introduces the fundamental paradox of modernity: in a world characterised by increasing rationalisation of all aspects of human existence, there is no rational way of deciding among an irreducible plurality of value commitments. Where Kant had advanced an account of ethics in which autonomous moral choice resided in a capacity to act according to principles that can be universalised, Weber offered an account of ethical life in which autonomous choice must be made not according to the requirements of universal reason but through a value-creating act of will. In short, an account of modernity framed as a universalising history of (instrumental) rationalisation is simultaneously an account of modernity as a realm of non-rational or criterionless choices about ultimate values.

Weber participates in a complex and widespread scepticism about modernity that characterised much socio-political theory and philosophy at the turn of the century. Weber's own response to it is fairly idiosyncratic. But interpreted as a specific expression of broader tendencies, Weber's formulations have been of enormous significance for the mediation of the critique of modernity within the theory of international relations. Three themes are worth special emphasis.

There is, first, the opportunity that Weber's work offers for explaining the presence of value relativism, power politics and the recourse to violence despite the advance of reason and civilisation. This opportunity is made available as an analysis of modern life in general. It requires reference neither to an analysis of class struggle nor to the structural configuration of relations between states. Moreover, the more strictly secular aspects of Weber's account of modernity may be augmented by a more theological reading, notably by a pessimistic account of modern life after the fall from both divine grace and secular knowledge. It is through Weber, especially, that realist forms of international relations theory have incorporated themes not only from Nietzsche but also from Luther and Augustine.[7]

There is, second, the opportunity of responding to this tragic vision of modern life if not with hope then with a resigned fortitude. For while insisting that value-relativism is a necessary consequence of progressive rationalisation, Weber also attempted to articulate an appropriate response to the dilemmas this posed. He attempted to preserve a capacity to decide autonomously about ultimate values in the face of the inexorable spread of instrumental reason. This autonomy may be realised by the individual, in which case Weber may be interpreted as a proto-existentialist. It may also be realised by the state, in which case we arrive at an account of Weber the advocate of a nationalistic power politics. The ethical irrationality of the world is turned into the struggle between value spheres, of which the state, that claimed monopoly on the legitimate exercise of power in a given territory, is the most powerful expression. In either case, autonomy can imply relativism. Existentialism may be interpreted in this way, while Weber's statist power politics has been recognised as being all too close to Carl Schmitt's conception of the total(itarian) state or the practices of the Third Reich.[8]

On a more positive interpretation, however, Weber can be understood as a proto-existentialist precisely because he was attempting to sketch the characteristics of a new type of individual, one capable of facing up to the demands of the age, one capable of finding meaning amidst disenchantment and the iron cage. In a similar vein, he was concerned to delineate the requirements now demanded of those charged with political authority. Hence his account of an ethic of responsibility, one he counterposes to both an ethics of conviction and to a purely instrumental concern with means. Weber's account of an ethics of responsibility attempts to combine a passionate devotion to a cause with the ability to calculate the consequences of one's actions. *Wertrationalitat* meets *Zweckrationalitat*. The vision is austere, but it is a perfect foil to the tragic tensions with which he thinks it is now necessary to live. It is this vision that has tempered the account of power politics found in some realist accounts of international relations. Weber's own formulation of an ethics of responsibility held out little hope for any mitigation of international conflict. Indeed, for Weber, responsibility to one's own value sphere implies the necessary intensification of international conflict. But the possibility of devising a more co-operative account of responsible conduct in foreign policy has appealed to many who have echoed Weber's tragic account of political life in the modern world.

The difficulty with this position, however, is already apparent from Weber's own account of what an ethic of responsibility can be. There is, in Weber's view, no rational way of deciding on criteria for judging what is responsible conduct, or to what and to whom one's responsibility should be directed. In effect, the meaning of responsibility is left hanging between a Kantian imperative to autonomous action in conformity with a universal moral law and an imperative to decide on the basis of one's own autonomous will (or in terms of international relations, on the non-rational will of one's own autonomous nation). Consequently, the sorry legacy of so much realist analysis of international relations has been either a constant relapse into the empty category of national interest or the amplification of personal judgment into appropriate criteria for state policy.

The third implication of Weber's ambivalence towards modernity is that it is evidently dangerous. His struggles with the threat of nihilism, historicism and relativism, with the legacies of Nietzsche's prophecies, have been quietly excised from the conventional record. Aron's debt, at least, is made explicit, but Morgenthau and E. H. Carr are more reticent, to say the least. Michael Smith is perfectly correct to insist that 'Weber's delineation of the issues established the terms of realist discourse that endure to the present day.'[9] But it is seriously misleading to suggest that his neglect among scholars of international relations is surprising. His neglect in this context is merely one aspect of a broader pattern of interpretive history. Weber has been the subject of a powerful politics of forgetting, an erasure of the connection that was once drawn between modernity and nihilism, between modernity and the darkest scepticism about the fulfilment of ethical possibilities through the realisation of universal reason.

Against this background, Hoffmann's judgment that a burgeoning literature on ethics and international relations and the 'scientific'

analysis of conflict co-operation have been the two major developments in the literature on international relations during the past ten
years is of more than passing interest. Hoffmann himself suggests that
there is a close connection between these two literatures. 'The explicit
ethical strand asks, in a variety of ways, for moral progress in international affairs; the scientific literature tries to prove that such progress is possible under certain conditions.'[10] The key term here, obviously enough, is 'progress', a term that perhaps more than any other
has come to affirm a positive stance towards modernity.

Thus many of those who root their analysis of international relations
in the epistemological claims of social science, can attempt – quite
properly – to resist the empirical inadequacies of state-centric realism
by developing accounts of interdependence and inter-state co-
operation. Yet they tend to do so through a powerful affirmation of a
modernist ethics, or at least ethos, whether as an account of human
action as the pursuit of instrumental rationality or of scholarly inquiry
as the formulation of empirical models and research techniques. In this
view, modernity brings not the clash between instrumental organisation and ultimate values but the effective reduction of all values to
the restricted visions of micro-economics and the theory of public
choice. In a rather familiar story, once passions are reconciled with
interests, it is not too difficult to move from the state of nature to the
wealth of nations.[11] And it should not be too difficult to see how this
story might be continued by way of Marxist critique of the ideological
character of class specific interests masquerading as universal reason.

The literature in which a concern with values is more explicit, on the
other hand, recognises that it is still not easy to affirm a clear connection between universal reason and international relations. Yet if we
look at the way that, say, Charles Beitz draws on Kant and John
Rawls;[12] or that Onora O'Neill, like many who are perplexed by the
seemingly intractable problems of global poverty, seeks to extend a
global dimension to our understanding of human rights and distributive justice;[13] or that Andrew Linklater draws on Kant, Hegel and
Marx;[14] or that W. B. Gallie thinks that even Kant alone has much to
offer once he is understood properly;[15] or that those interested in the
broad civilisational context in which relations between states can be
understood as a kind of society of states have become interested in the
internationalisation of the 'culture of modernity';[16] or that normative
approaches to world order have been able to preserve some space for a
critical discourse about world politics even in the United States;[17] or
that utilitarian forms of liberalism have managed to articulate influential accounts of international interdependence,[18] the identification of

the problem of ethics in international relations with the universalist promises of modernity is unmistakable.

Perhaps all is well. Perhaps the crisis of historicism to which Weber was responding has been effectively erased by more recent claims about convergence, development and the end of ideology that have been so often made in Weber's name. In any case, to situate theories of international relations in the context of a broader problematisation of modernity is to see that so many of the themes that are articulated in the form of an opposition between realism and utopianism, are not specific to international relations alone. Rather, theories of international relations reflect many of the primary preoccupations of social and political theory in general. Weber remains especially important in this respect. Weber offers a paradigmatic account of the contradictions of modernity, contradictions that have not, in fact, been erased. Platitudes about convergence, development and the end of ideology have, rather, been accompanied by continued militarisation, mal-development and the recourse to violence on many dimensions. Weber offered a particularly pessimistic account of these contradictions, and denied any possibility of dialectical resolution or transcendence. Stoic fortitude, a reworking of the Lutheran notion of a calling or vocation, a proto-existentialism, a decisionistic ethics, a power politics: these are all elements of Weber's sense of a new conception of political action demanded by new historical circumstances. Elements of this conception enter into the theory of international relations through his stress on the nation-state as a primary ground from which values are to be asserted. Here we enter into a different discursive universe, one concerned not with the fate of modernity, but with the nature and location of political community. In this context, many of Weber's questions fade into the background. His answers, by contrast, have been readily incorporated into a discourse arising not from the dilemmas posed by the trajectories of history, but from the dilemmas posed by an exclusivist articulation of political space.

Spatiality, sovereignty and the ethics of exclusion

From the perspective of most theorists of international relations, beginning with the general difficulty of speaking about ethics at all is to put the cart before the horse. The disjunction between ethics and international relations is disconcerting enough, it might be said, without questioning whether modern accounts of objective knowledge and universal reason are sufficient to save established ethical traditions from contemporary forms of scepticism. More significantly, for theorists of international relations the fate of modernity is already defined as a secondary matter, one that may well be of pressing concern for students of political theory, but not for those who seek to understand relations between the communities in which political theory may have some possible relevance.

To engage with questions about modernity is to work with accounts of history and time. It is to be concerned with the possibility of establishing and sustaining political community in time, with struggles to bring about better forms of political community over time. The problems of international relations, by contrast, are usually framed in terms of differentiations of political space. They emerge from the geo-political separation of territorial communities in space, a separation that may be taken to imply both the non-existence of a common community that may be improved over time and, consequently, the marginality of questions that presume the possibility of temporal progress within particular communities. Both the celebration of and scepticism towards modernity respond to well-established accounts of reason, progress and Enlightenment. These accounts already depend upon a prior claim that there is a political community in which reason, progress and Enlightenment might unfold. Theorists of international relations tend to regard such a claim as, at best, highly problematic.

From this point of view, therefore, the appropriate context in which to begin speaking about ethics and international relations is not the temporal agony of a socio-political theory torn between Enlightenment universalism and post-Nietzschean nihilism, but the spatial preoccupations of early-modern debates about where and what political community can be given the dissolution of medieval and feudal hierarchies. Here the relationship between ethics and universal reason is again at issue, but the relationship is posed not with respect to a single temporal process of modernisation but to a spatial dualism of life inside and outside the state.

In whatever way one understands the enormous complexities that are implied by phrases like 'the transition from feudalism to capitalism' or 'the rise of the states-system', the tension between the universalist claims of Christianity and Empire and the competing claims arising from participation in a particular statist community provides the unavoidable core of early-modern political thought. In the struggle to reconcile the claims of men and citizens, of a universalist account of humanity and a particularist account of political community, early-modern political thought both affirmed the primacy of the particular – the statist community, but also the individual – and attempted to legitimise accounts of political authority within particular communities through a reinterpretation and secularisation of claims to universal reason and natural law.

Machiavelli and Hobbes have come to represent the two key moments in this transition. Machiavelli is associated with an assertion of the primacy of temporal *virtù* within the *polis*/city-state against the universalistic claims of Christianity. Reversing the Augustinian valorisation of time and eternity, the possibility of establishing a community of *virtù* in time is read onto the spatial form of the principality and republic. Machiavelli's classical conception of *virtù* still emphasises the necessarily contingent and potentially corrupt character of all political communities, no matter how successful a prince or republic may be responding to the dangerous charms of *fortuna*. Hobbes, by contrast, has come to symbolise the attempt to fix the configurations of power within the state by an appeal to the universalist and eternal claims of reason. Where Machiavelli is concerned with the very possibility of establishing particularistic political communities at all, Hobbes is able to pursue questions about how authority and obligation within particular communities can be reconciled with the universalistic claims of Galilean science and/or Christian theology.

The primary resolution of this late-medieval and early-modern struggle to free accounts of political life from the hierarchical incorporation of particularity into an overarching universalism – while also preserving the possibility that particularity might still be reconciled with a reconceptualisation of what universality entails – appears with the principle of state sovereignty. As a principle, state sovereignty has come to seem quite uninteresting, the preserve of legal scholars and constitutional experts rather than the subject of heated exchanges among social and political theorists. Yet the principle of state sovereignty did not appear out of thin air. It embodies an historically specific account of ethical possibility in the form of an answer to questions about the nature and location of political community. Specifically, the principle of state sovereignty offers both a spatial and a temporal resolution to questions about what political community can be, given the priority of citizenship and particularity over all universalist claims to a common human identity. An extended analysis of what this involves will be developed in subsequent chapters, but an initial approximation can be sketched briefly as follows.

Spatially, the principle of state sovereignty fixes a clear demarcation between life inside and outside a centred political community. Within states, universalist aspirations to the good, the true and the beautiful may be realisable, but only within a spatially delimited territory. Consequently, modern political speculation is confronted with a double puzzle arising from the need to clarify the relationship between universality and particularity in two different spatial contexts. One part of the puzzle concerns life within states, and involves the difficulty of reconciling the pluralistic claims of people with the universalistic claims of state authority. In this context, the meaning of sovereignty oscillates both between unrestrained power and legitimate authority and between the primacy of the people and the primacy of the state as the locus of power and authority. The other part of the puzzle concerns the paradoxical dependence of all claims of universality within states upon the explicit but often silent recognition that such claims to universality are in fact particularistic, are made on behalf of a particular group of citizens, rather than of people as members of a common community.

The spatial resolution permits a temporal corollary. Within states, the possibility of universalist claims to the good, the true and the beautiful is opened up to actualisation in time. The received history of political thought, for example, traces the well-known path from the spatial rationalisms of Hobbes to the convergence of reason, history and the state in Hegel. Between states, however, the lack of community can be taken to imply the impossibility of history as a progressive teleology, and thus the possibility merely of recurrence and repetition. It is in terms of this temporal dualism, for example, that Martin Wight most sharply articulated his account of a contrast between political theory and international theory.[19]

The distinctive problematic of ethics and international relations arises directly from this spatio-temporal resolution of questions about political community. In fact, this problematic might be better expressed as the difficulty of even referring in any meaningful way to international relations as a form of *politics*. To refer to international *relations* is to suggest that what goes on between states is in principle quite different from what goes on within states. Relations between states do not offer the same basis of a centred political community for establishing a form of life that is subject to the guidance of established ethical principles. Rather, the lack of a centred community suggests – and here the distinction, and the ambivalence it permits, is crucial – either the difficulty or the radical impossibility of establishing ethical principles that are applicable to international relations.

From the perspective of international relations theory, then, the problematic suggested by references to ethics and international relations arises out of the spatial differentiations of the early-modern era, and especially from the formalisation of political space embodied in the principle of state sovereignty. Many have been content to let the matter rest there. The disjunction between ethics and international relations reflects the schism between community and anarchy, temporal progress and geopolitical contingency, politics and relations. As long as political space remains articulated in this way, it may be said, the disjunction between ethics and international relations must remain an unfortunate, even tragic fact of life.

Nevertheless, the analysis may be pushed a little further by enquiring more carefully into the ontological assumptions and discursive practices that permit the specific formalisation of political space offered by the principle of state sovereignty. Two broad themes are especially important. One arises from the double role played by the principles of state sovereignty as both an *answer* to historically specific questions and as a *question* that provokes the search for a quite different set of answers. The second theme arises from the conditions under which patterns of spatial differentiation can be taken to imply a radical schism between ethical community inside and contingent power outside. Taken together, these two themes permit a series of claims that ethical principles are both constitutive of and central to international relations rather than just a marginal after-thought.

The principle of state sovereignty is usually interpreted as a beginning, as a statement of an original condition that poses questions about how ethical claims may be established in the absence of political community. It is also obviously a continuation of a longer story, one in which the starting point is far from clear. As a continuation, the principle of state sovereignty may be read not as a question but as an answer. It is a very powerful, even elegant answer to the deeply provocative question as to how political life is possible at all. Building on a complex intellectual heritage that responds to the rearticulation of political life in the late medieval era, it offers an account of the spatial differentiation of political communities through a spatial resolution of the primary ontological question about the relation between universality and particularity. As an answer, the principle of state sovereignty already expresses a theory of ethics, one in which ontological and political puzzles are resolved simultaneously. It affirms that the good life, guided by universal principles, can only occur within particularistic political communities.

The possibility of two forms of ethical enquiry is then opened up depending on whether the principle of state sovereignty is read as a question or an answer. If the principle of state sovereignty is presumed to offer a satisfactory answer to questions about political community, then it is possible to seek some mitigation of the problems that are assumed to arise from the lack of any proper political community between states. If the answer is presumed to be unsatisfactory, however, it is possible to persist in asking the question to which the principle of state sovereignty has offered such a powerful and elegant response for so long. With the first option, we remain within the established traditions of international relations theory. With the second option, international relations theory becomes merely one aspect of a broader theory of politics. The selection of a point of departure is thus of considerable consequence in this context, as is the construction of a tradition of international relations theory in which a particular account of origins is specified and reified.

The second broad theme is relevant to each of these forms of ethical enquiry and concerns both the ontological assumptions that are encoded within the principle of state sovereignty and the interpretive procedures through which that principle has become reified within contemporary theories of international relations. Here it is perhaps helpful to reflect briefly on the relation between the principle of state sovereignty and the classical theory of the *polis*, and thus on the dangers of interpreting the consequences of the spatial differentiation of political communities through the polished prisms of the theory of the modern state.

Classical political theory is certainly introspective. It is preoccupied with *arête* and *eudaemonia*, with the virtu(e) and well-being of citizens. It is thus easy enough to draw parallels between classical political theory and the principle of state-sovereignty. In a text like the *Republic*, one might draw attention to the passing references to distinctions between Greek and non-Greek, and the celebration of differential standards of conduct appropriate to insider and outsider; or to the difference between the initial sketch of the self-sufficient city and the city of luxury, and thus the relationship between internal politics and patterns of inter-*polis* conflict; or to the explicit linking of a universalistic account of knowledge with the requirements for justice within a political community and thus, by inference, the linking of mere opinion with war outside. Given such a reading, it is also easy enough to treat Thucydides' rendition of the Peloponnesian War as an account of the permanent anarchy entailed by the absence of political community beyond the boundaries of the *polis*.

Still, the perils of anachronistic interpretation are never far away. The distinction between Greek and non-Greek may just as well reflect a pervasive indifference to outsiders as any sense of the need for defence against external threat. It would be difficult to argue that the classic texts of Greek political thought show the same sense of urgency about the dangers of inter-*polis* insecurity as do those texts that explain inter-state insecurity as a consequence of the primacy of the autonomous state. The construction of the outsider, of the Other as a radical negation of the Same, is by no means as clear cut as is implied by the principle of state sovereignty. In this sense, the differences between accounts of political life in classical Greece and early-modern Europe are much more interesting than the tenuous assertions of a continuity between Thucydides, Machiavelli and Hobbes as a tradition of international political theory. The writings of Herodotus, for example, might be just as instructive to theorists of international relations as anything to be found in Thucydides. As François Hartog has argued, Herodotus works with a complex rhetoric of representation in which Greek self-identity is defined in relation to non-Greek.[20] But this rhetoric of representation does not build upon the specifically modern metaphysics expressed by the principle of state sovereignty. The boundaries between inside and outside do not so sharply distinguish between a community within and an anarchy of difference without.

The principle of state-sovereignty specifies a rigorous distinction between politics and mere relations. But precisely how this distinction is to be interpreted, constructed and reproduced is open to considerable variation. It matters whether others are treated with relative indifference or as the negation of revealed truth and centred sovereign power. Framed within a spatial metaphysics of same and other, citizen and enemy, identity and difference, the principle of state sovereignty expresses an ethics of absolute exclusion. This same metaphysics has also informed other scholarly traditions concerned with life on the outside. In this respect, the theory of international relations is heir to many of the same metatheoretical difficulties as anthropology or comparative politics. In these other contexts, however, the primary difficulty occurs as a problem of comparison, of knowing the different in relation to the same. Moreover, this difficulty is prone to resolution through a theory of temporal process, or rather of Progress and its subsequent articulations in the theory of development. In the theory of international relations, however, Same and Other are differentiated spatially, and the possibility of temporal convergence towards a community of common identity is firmly resisted.

Hence the crucial significance of the distinction between difficulty and radical impossibility. Interpreted as an ethics of absolute exclusion, the theory of state sovereignty is an ethical principle that denies the applicability of ethical principles beyond a certain bounded space. But this is clearly to interpret the principle of state sovereignty in an extreme way. It does not help us to understand classical inter-*polis* relations, even though the classical theory of the *polis* articulated a superficially similar claim about the relationship between ethics and political community. Nor, most would admit, does it help us understand the construction of the international society that has in fact emerged since the seventeenth century. To speak of, say, an 'anarchical society' or a society of states is to refuse to take the exclusionist ethics of state sovereignty at face value. Not unexpectedly, the possibility of articulating ethical principles in international relations, even if the principle of state sovereignty is accepted as a satisfactory answer to questions about political community, depends on a capacity to construct an account of the relation between self and other that does not conform to a logic of universalist identity inside and difference and diversity outside.

The society of states and the ethics of cooperation

The principle of state sovereignty alone is sufficient to generate the characteristic problematic of ethics and international relations. The ethical and political claim to a statist monopoly on human identity, political community and legitimate authority is enough to justify a claim that human action in the specific spatial realm of international relations cannot be guided by ethical principles.

But everything is obviously not quite that simple. The principle of state sovereignty does permit a crucial ambiguity, especially if the extreme consequences of the logic of inclusion and exclusion are relaxed. In practice, and despite reiterated appeals to the formal logic of state sovereignty as the extreme or constitutive case, theorists of international relations have developed accounts of states-systems that do presume that ethical principles may be found even in the space between states. In fact the crucial ambiguity opened up by a relaxation of the logic of inclusion and exclusion turns out to be the sharp end of a very large wedge. To resist the logic of absolute exclusion, of Same and Other, is to open up the possibility of returning to an affirmation of the Same. Or, put slightly differently, to follow the attempt to re-establish the ground for ethics in international relations by healing the rift between community within and anarchy without is to return rather quickly to the dilemmas of modernity as a temporal rather than a spatial condition.

The exclusionist logic of state sovereignty is open to several secondary formulations. Three are especially familiar. One focuses on the presence or absence of a centralised power or authority. The anarchical condition of international relations may then be explained in terms of the absence of any mechanisms through which ethical principles might be enforced. A second formulation involves the transfer of a negative reading of ethical possibility in general onto the specific realm of relations between states. While it takes a considerable effort to read Machiavelli as anything but a theorist of political life within a centred political community, for example, it is in this context that his bad name has become largely synonymous with international relations. Similarly, generalised readings of human nature or a fall from grace find their most persistent expression in attempts to explain international conflict. In a third variation, life beyond the state is translated from a realm of temporal contingency into one of spatial structure. This usually takes the form of an analogy with the Hobbesian account of relations between equal and autonomous individuals in a state of nature. On this account, the absence of ethical principles is explained not in terms of temporal contingency but of structural necessity, of the structural determinations of the 'security dilemma'.

Relaxing the logic of inclusion and exclusion permits a more positive reading of each of these three formulations. First, it can be argued that the absence of a centred power/authority does not necessarily imply the absence of either order or ethical principles. The model of the *polis*, it might be said, offers only one account of what a political community might be. The analysis of pre-modern societies, for example, suggests quite different options.

Second, it is possible to give substantially different interpretations to those traditions of pessimism that have become localised in the theory of international relations. Machiavelli can be – surely must be – read as a theorist of *virtù* rather than as the enemy of virtue. Christianity can be read through the texts of, say, Aquinas rather than Augustine. In both cases, it then becomes easier to interpret the spatial resolution of inside and outside without the dubious benefit of a metaphysics of time and eternity or a theology of saved and damned.

Third, even if life beyond the state is interpreted in terms of structural configurations, Hobbes' account of the security dilemma among proto-bourgeois individuals is certainly not the only possible option. It is one that Hobbes himself explicitly rejected, suggesting instead that the clear differences between individuals and states imply both a less intolerable situation than arises among individuals and the possibility of ordering principles other than the fusion of freedom and necessity in a centralised sovereign.

Each of these more positive readings offers the beginnings of an account of relations between states as more than a mere anarchy. And if states-systems can be understood as a form of political life, then it should also be possible to conceive of practices of co-operation. While

the extremist expression of international relations as the radical negation of statist community has captured claims about a tradition of
orthodoxy, it is this insight – about the practices of co-operation – that
has probably been of greatest significance and influence in the history
of reflection about international relations. This is the insight pursued
most vigorously by Hedley Bull.[21]

Bull's position is difficult to pin down with any precision. This is so
despite his careful attention to the need for careful definitions; John
Vincent, for example, has suggested it 'may even be the case that Bull's
genius for making distinctions that went to the heart of a subject-
matter constituted the essence of his contribution to international
relations'.[22] Yet definitions and distinctions take us into the realm of
classification and typology. And in this respect, Bull's analysis is constrained by a familiar three-fold categorisation of approaches to international relations. Some of the many limitations of this categorisation
become apparent from the expansive capacities of the middle category. Introduced as a *via media* between the supposed extremes of
realism and revolutionism (or in other versions, idealism) Bull's analysis seems to be drawn in both directions at once. Moreover, this middle
position is amenable to a variety of names and associations. References
to Grotius loom large. Vattel, Montesquieu, Burke, Gentz and Hume
also manage to get in a word or two. Consequently we find themes
from natural law, notions about a broad cultural context in which
states can learn to get along, theories about the relation between
political practices and the creation of norms, and accounts of the
formalisation of norms in structures like the balance of power and
practices like international law.

Moreover, many of Bull's central themes are echoed in a wide range
of current approaches to international relations that combine a
concern for ethical principles with an analysis of the society of states as
a product of historical practices. Terry Nardin builds on Michael
Oakeshott's distinction between purposive and practical forms of
political association, the latter – concerned with establishing durable
relations among adversaries – Nardin considers to be especially important for international relations.[23] Friedrich Kratochwil's concern with
the establishment of norms builds on a post-Wittgensteinian analysis
of human action and hermeneutics.[24] Wittgenstein also plays an
important role in Nicholas Onuf's broad synthetic attempt to advance
a 'constructivist' theory of rules and rule in international relations.[25]
And with Richard Ashley's reading of the realist analysis of states-
manship[26] or James Der Derian's genealogical account of diplomacy as
the mediation of estrangement,[27] many of Bull's themes have even

been reinterpreted through an encounter with post-structuralist forms of social and political theory.

The expansive character of the middle category is kept under control in Bull's own work not only by the more extremist categories located on either side of it but also by two other persistent themes of Bull's analysis. One is the dichotomised formulation of the relation between order and justice. The other is suspicion of the domestic analogy. In both cases, the effect of the account of ethical possibilities given by the principle of state sovereignty is readily apparent. The possibility of justice is permitted within, the extreme difficulty of order is affirmed without. The danger of transferring assumptions about political life inside the state onto the analysis of relations between states becomes both a regulative principle of research and a normative prescription. Bull struggles to resolve the contradiction between order and justice, between inside and outside, and his analysis begins to open up a very broad terrain for exploration. Nevertheless, foreseeing the dangers of the domestic analogy, Bull constantly steps back to a position of profound scepticism, while at the same time remaining relatively open to more universalistic explorations.

There are no doubt reasons for this that are idiosyncratic to Bull himself, but in this respect Bull is caught within a broader conceptual horizon. Once one begins to analyse historical practices, to give an account of the emergence of norms and institutions and the constitution of a society of states, the temptation is to explain these processes as a move from anarchy to community, from difference to identity, from Other to Same. The road can be mapped as a spatial terrain. It goes from international anarchy outside to some kind of world order or global community predicated on the internal claims of the sovereign state. The road can also be mapped temporally, in which case we find ourselves engaged in the illicit trek from realism to idealism. The domestic analogy and idealism then come to serve as both temptation and prohibition.

The road is undoubtedly tempting and many have made the journey. Those who have ignored the prohibition invariably offer visions that are essentially modernist in inspiration. But the different articulations of the modernist vision that have been offered in this context are instructive. Again, three lines of thought have been especially influential.

The most explicitly modernist vision arises from the utilitarian liberalism characteristic of socio-scientific accounts of international co-operation, interdependence and regime formation. Here the domestic analogy is deployed with a vengeance, although the analogy is with a very narrow reading of domestic politics as the instrumental calculation of utilitarian individuals. In contrast with the strict ontological, epistemological and ethical dualism implied by the principle of state sovereignty, we find universalistic accounts of human action and scientific method. In this vision, questions about ethics tend to be framed either in terms of a dualism of the empirical and the normative or a dualistic account of the normative as a deontological pursuit of ultimate ends opposed to a consequentialist consideration of means.

In a second vision, the pursuit of ends is accorded a clear primacy, especially as these ends are articulated in relation to a Kantian account of universal reason. Here modernity is interpreted not in terms of a global space in which human action conforms to the efficient causalities of instrumental reason but of a divided space of sovereign states in which the categorical imperative gives rise to the two key demands of a perpetual peace. Internally, there must be the establishment of a perfect civic constitution. Externally, there must be a clear recognition that the use of coercion between states is irrational and unlawful. Both problems assign central importance to optimising the role of the state. In this sense, Kant offers an alternative resolution of the universality and particularity of political community to that offered by the principle of state sovereignty while retaining the same spatial differentiation between inside and outside. Under conditions of modernity, or Enlightenment, universal reason may be achieved internally so that the space between states might become an extension rather than a negation of the rational political community achieved within the state. The early-modern account of particularity, individuality and sovereignty is interpreted through an Enlightenment account of rational autonomy.

The third version is inspired neither by utilitarianism nor Kant, but by Weber. Autonomy becomes subject not to reason but to will. Modernity certainly brings instrumental reason, but not any universalistic foundation for an ethics of absolute ends. On the contrary, instrumental reason permits a rapid enhancement of the power of autonomous political communities, and thus an intensification of conflict between them. An ethics of consequences might mitigate a decisionistic appeal to some national interest, but modernity is more likely to bring about a resolution of the contradiction between instrumental and substantive rationality through war and imperialist domination. Confronted with the contradictions of modernity, statesmen might try to revive ethical traditions that emphasise a practical judgment or *phronesis* that owes more to Aristotle than to Kant. But again, as with Weber's ethic of responsibility, it is not clear that a classical conception

71

of practical judgment can be appropriately grounded in a statist account of political community given a convergence of the exclusionist logic of state sovereignty with instrumental capacities that threaten barbarism on an unprecedented scale.

Given these three visions, it is not difficult to see why Bull would resist taking an analysis of states-systems too far along this road. The attractions would no doubt be noted. Many of the insights of the utilitarians might be used to explain patterns of co-operation in the absence of a central authority. The global spread of a global culture of modernity might be used to explain the broad context in which the practices of a culturally specific political formation have come to be acceptable almost universally.[28] The relative lack of bellicosity on the part of modern liberal democratic states might be noted with some interest.[29]

But there is also enough in the Weberian version of modernity to act as a reminder of the tragedies that have given the claim to realism its continuing appeal. Utilitarian accounts of interdependence may be challenged by mercantilist accounts of new patterns of inter-state competition. Liberal accounts of the spread of democracy or the trickle down of economic benefits from global interdependence may be challenged by reminders that modernity has also been characterised by the unhappy experience of 'modernisation from above'.

With Weber, the road from the spatial logic of state sovereignty to the temporal trajectories of modernity leads to power politics, not away from it. The analysis of ethics and international relations begins with a spatial distinction between community and anarchy, is tempted by the possible erasure of this distinction in the name of a universalising modernity, but returns, with Weber, to a radical scepticism in which geo-politics meets nihilism in the glorification of the state. It is with Weber, not Thucydides, nor Machiavelli, nor Hobbes, that we find the most important expression of the 'realities' of international relations against which attempts to articulate an ethics of international relations are judged. With Weber, the temporal contradictions of modernity are resolved in favour of the spatial contradictions of state sovereignty. An account of the ethical irrationality of the disenchanted world of instrumental reason converges with an account of the possibility, or otherwise, of ethical life inside and outside statist political communities. Within the horizons constructed through this resolution, the search for a middle ground, for an ethical foundation for the society of states, must be a perpetual wandering on a road that is closed at both ends.

Taking the principle of state sovereignty as an adequate answer to questions about political community, it is possible to relax the exclusionist logic in which state sovereignty formalises a spatial differentiation of inside and outside, same and other, presence and absence, universal and plural. Once relaxed, the temptation is to reverse polarities, to move from the other to the same, from anarchy to community. The temptation is very difficult to resist. In most disciplines, the temptation takes an explicitly temporal form: progress, development, history as linear or dialectical progression towards the universal. In international relations, the spatial variation is more significant, although the continuing appeal of an historical move from realism to idealism shows the ease through which problems of spatial differentiation can be framed as the need for temporal convergence. Many have tried to resist this logic. The most important contributions to the discussion of ethics and international relations among those who have accepted the principle of state sovereignty have come from those, like Bull, who have attempted to analyse the historical practices through which states have learnt to co-operate in defining and resisting the intolerable.

Thus, one conclusion that might be drawn about how discussions of ethics and international relations are likely to develop is that there will be a continuation of already established traditions that have so far been understood as a middle road between extremes. The difficulty to be overcome – and the focus of critical attempts to rethink the future direction of such traditions – lies not with the search for ethical principles emerging from the historical practices of states but in the interpretation of those practices as merely a half-way house between anarchy and community, realism and idealism/revolutionism, war and peace. Here it will be necessary to inquire into the assumptions that are reproduced in the constitutive dichotomy between order and justice and the model of political community reified within accounts of the domestic analogy. This is why so much of the recent literature on the need for a more critical theory of international relations has emphasised the need to break with the discursive strategies that affirm a logic of same and different, inside and outside, pluralist and universalist, history and structure, theory/purpose and practice, friend and foe. But it is not enough to break with this logic in thinking about the principle of state sovereignty as a primary question or problematic that demands a resolution through some kind of international, or more accurately, inter-state society. It is also necessary to break with it in thinking about the more fundamental questions about political community to which the principle of state sovereignty has provided the conventional answer for so long.

Sovereignty, modernity and political community

I have so far cut into the problematic of ethics and international relations from three inter-related directions: in terms of the historical trajectories articulated by theories of modernity, of the spatial differentiations formalised by the principle of state-sovereignty, and of accounts of a society of states that try to mediate between geopolitical anarchy and temporal political community. Yet each of these three perspectives seems to marginalise what is perhaps the largest body of literature about ethics and international relations, a literature in which the difficulties of even beginning to speak about ethics are treated as relatively insignificant. This is, of course, the huge literature that insists that ethics must be grounded in a universalist understanding of both reason and political community. And it is this insistence that most powerfully informs the image of ethics and international relations as an intersection.

Such a claim is usually dismissed out of hand by theorists of international relations. Yet in one form or another, this claim has been constitutive of each of the three perspectives canvassed so far. In fact, it is precisely because of the presumption of universality that it is possible to use the term ethics, as I have done here, knowing that however pessimistic a Weber may be about the possibility of ethics in a disenchanted world, or theorists of international relations may be about the mitigation of violence in relations between states, most discussions of political life continue to assume the presence of some ethical standard against which either the fall from grace or the fall from community may be judged.

Interpreting goodness, truth and beauty in universalistic terms, accounts of modernity become torn between Enlightenment and despair, between a universalising progress and a relativistic nihilism. But it is the prior claim to universalism that permits the pluralistic negation. The possibility of Romantic subjectivity is already given by Enlightenment accounts of universal reason. The spectres of relativism are already defined by the master allegory of the cave.

Interpreting claims to universality through the spatial resolutions of the principle of state sovereignty, accounts of political community are torn between the possibilities of justice within states and the inevitability of anarchy between them. But it is the claim to community and justice inside that permits the negative claim to anarchy outside. Again, we are drawn to understand that the dominant theoretical tradition in international relations theory is not political realism but idealism, for it is the possibility of universality proclaimed by idealism that makes possible the discursive linkage between difference, relativism, anarchy, tragedy and violence.

Attempts to resist this dichotomising of extremes, this logic of identity and difference, same and other, embodied in the principle of state sovereignty, are easily caught up in the temptations and prohibitions generated by these extremes. If the problem is pluralism, the solution must be universality. If the problem is temporal contingency, the solution must be the progressive realisation of universality through time. Of course, it will be noted, human communities remain fragmented. Universal community can only be a distant aspiration. Therefore, theories of international relations must be cast in terms of pluralism, relativism, and, thus, cynicism and a resigned complicity with the necessity of violence. Again, this is not an easy logic to resist.

For some, however, resistance is already a lost cause. For them modernity is in fact a universal way of life. Utilitarianism explains all. For others, utilitarianism may explain the emergence of a global system, or help to explain the internationalisation of capitalist economic processes, but is hardly sufficient to inform the construction of a meaningful global community. Hence the attempt to recapture insights from Kant, Hegel and Marx, or to reinterpret the remnants of a universalist ethics surviving from earlier religious and philosophical traditions, most notably Stoic cosmopolitanism and Christian natural law.

There are thus many variations of the claim that any discussion of ethics and international relations must begin from a universalist presumption that the claims of people in general are prior to the claims of citizenship constituted through the principle of state sovereignty. Moreover, most tend to converge on a formulation of the problematic of ethics and international relations as a project of speaking universal truth to fragmented power.[30] The project then becomes preoccupied, predictably enough, with three main tasks. Two involve the subjection of the most troublesome consequences of state sovereignty to the demands of a universalistic ethics. Here there is a convergence with positions developed under the rubric of a society of states, but the temptation to affirm the universalising claims of modernity are felt more keenly. The third task involves a demand that questions about political community be answered by offering an alternative resolution to the relationship between universality and particularity to that formalised as state sovereignty.

The most troublesome consequences of state sovereignty, from this point of view, are the continuing legitimacy of the resort to war and the principle of non-intervention. The claim to at least some minimum universal standards of human decency has long been urged in relation to the laws of war. Hence powerful traditions of just war, discriminations between combatants and non-combatants, for example, or principles of proportionality restricting the resort to indiscriminate violence.[31] Similarly, as a constitutive principle of international order, the claim to non-intervention has long been subject to challenge on the ground of some higher principle. The classic case remains the argument that the traditions of European order were being threatened by the French Revolution. But it is now increasingly challenged in the name of the defence of oppressed peoples whose very existence is gravely threatened, or in the name of universal human rights as an historically established principle that transcends the claim to state autonomy.[32]

It is easy enough to understand the force of claims that, in the modern world, universalist ethical traditions must take increasing priority over those established through the spatial differentiations of state sovereignty. In an era of nuclear weapons, and the global reach of processes of production, destruction, distribution, exchange, and instrumental control, there is little doubt that the demand for a more universalistic account of ethics in relation to both war and the principle of non-intervention will continue to be voiced. The impossibility of establishing an ethic of responsibility in relation to weapons in which any proportionality between ends and means has become impossible to calculate (and thus the special challenge to accounts of just war arising from the regime of nuclear deterrence) is crucial in this respect. There is also little doubt that the demand for a more universalistic account of ethics in these two contexts will amplify the claim that a more universalistic account of human community is now called for. Hence the continuing importance of the questions posed by those concerned to make some sense of what can possibly be meant by terms like world order or world politics.[33]

Again, therefore, it seems safe to predict that new directions for research will involve a continuation of well-established traditions. But also again it seems safe to predict that the search for new directions will have to be substantially reframed. While it may be true that the modern world demands an account of ethical possibility that begins with the priority of people as people rather than as citizens, it remains quite unclear as to what this could possibly mean, despite the persistence of traditions that claim to be able to give it some degree of specificity. More significantly, but also more contentiously, the real difficulty is not the absence of universalistic accounts of how the problematic of ethics and international relations might be resolved, but quite the reverse.

Both the account of modernity offered by Weber and the account of political community offered by the principle of state sovereignty and, by extension, the attempt to resist the sceptical consequences of these accounts, arise from the prior claim that ethical principles are to be understood in relation to universalistic accounts of truth, beauty and goodness. Universalism, to put it bluntly and heretically, can be understood as the problem, not the solution. This does not imply any capitulation to an anti-ethical relativism or nihilism, though it clearly suggests a critical stance towards claims about what it means to be human and about how we should act that have achieved the official status of ethics in the modern world. Moreover, it underlines the possibility that explorations of what it can mean to speak of ethics under contemporary conditions might even be understood as elaborations of insights that are already expressed within the theory of international relations. Both the concern with historical practice and language which informs the society of states perspective and the claim that the principle of state sovereignty offers an inadequate answer to questions about political identity and community seem likely to be especially important in this respect.

The traditional objection to universalism in international relations will no doubt continue to be made on the ground of nationalism and national self-determination. For many peoples in the modern world, the establishment of a particularist identity against hegemonic forces remains the highest priority. But the assertion of this kind of counter-hegemonic particularity is likely to be pushed further than is implied by the limited pluralism established through state sovereignty. The continuing persistence of nationalism and self-determination does not necessarily imply the persistence of the nation-state. It is therefore possible to offer an alternative account of the plurality of peoples than is associated with the restricted pluralism of state sovereignty. Nor does the dissociation of nation from state imply any diminution in the importance of the state. As an historically constituted form of community, one that has been subject to considerable variation across time and space, the state does not have to be analysed in terms of the metaphysics of presence and absence demanded by the principle of state sovereignty. Where it has become conventional to equate state, nation and autonomy, and then to reify all three as the fundamental reality of international life, it now seems more useful to ask what states, nations, particularist identities and struggles for autonomy can now be under new historical conditions.

It will also become increasingly apparent that structural change in world politics will not take the form of a move from particularity to universality. The presumption that it will has been very powerful, informing diadic choices between the obstinacy or obsolescence of the state and the construction of both speculative and socio-scientific models of international interdependence, international institutions and world order. Yet if the principle of state sovereignty offers an inadequate account of contemporary dynamics, as I think it does, it is important to be clear about what state sovereignty is. It is not simply a formalisation of international fragmentation. It is, first and foremost, a spatial resolution of the relation between universality and particularity. International fragmentation is only one consequence of this resolution, the other being an account of political community and temporal progress within the state. It therefore seems more helpful to consider how universality and particularity might be rearticulated without capitulating to the modernist presumption that the different must always be resolved into the same. Moreover, to resist this presumption is to become increasingly wary of the extent to which the analysis of structural transformation remains caught within what are essentially seventeenth- and eighteenth-century conceptions of space and time, conceptions which are not obviously the most useful for understanding the implications of either contemporary military technologies or the global rearticulations and velocities of capital.

Third, the universalising claims of modernity will continue to be seen as inherently problematic on general philosophical and political grounds. The problems identified by Weber have not gone away, although both Weber's formulation of them and his response to it have come to seem quite unsatisfactory. That it is language rather than the relativity of values that has been at the centre of debate about modernity and late/post-modernity does not lessen the significance of such debate for the discussion of ethics and international relations. On the contrary, the critique of the logic of identity and difference that has informed general philosophical debate for at least the past three decades is especially applicable to the discursive politics that are anchored in the principle of state sovereignty. The problems raised by contemporary critical theories of international relations are not novel. They are already to be found in the mediation of Max Weber's quite inadequate response to them in the writings of the neo-Weberian realists. But the central philosophical issues are now more out in the open. And whether one opts to follow a Jürgen Habermas in the attempt to fulfil the dreams of Enlightenment through a universalist account of communicative competence or, as I would, to follow Michel Foucault in asking what political life can be once the 'blackmail of Enlightenment' is refused,[34] it remains clear both that the meaning of a universalist basis for ethics in international relations remains to be established and that the very possibility of something called ethics as we have come to understand it may well require fundamental reconsideration.

Each of these three themes points to questions about politics rather than to questions about ethics as traditionally conceived. This is as it should be. To invoke a problematic of 'ethics and international relations' is to presume that ethics is something to be applied to rather than constitutive of international relations, and that ethics is somehow separable from politics. Both presumptions are implausible, as is the converse claim that ethics is somehow reducible to some essentialist conception of politics. Theories of international relations must be understood as an integral aspect of political theory and practice. It is, moreover, the context in which some of the most interesting and most difficult problems of political theory are now posed. To raise questions about ethics and international relations is to raise questions that invoke the difficulty of speaking about *politics* in the late twentieth century, about what concepts like political community, obligation, freedom, autonomy, democracy or security can mean in the context of contemporary rearticulations of political space and time.

It is, therefore, necessary to be extremely cautious about the celebration of any revival of interest in ethics and international relations. A busier intersection is no indication of an escape from the routines through which attempts to speak of ethics are either marginalised or trivialised. These routines emerge from the way claims about ethical possibility are already constitutive of theories of international relations. Thus rather than focus directly on attempts to speak ethics to international relations, as if speaking truth to power, it is more helpful to interrogate those sites within the theory of international relations in which ethical claims are either encouraged or discouraged.

Specifically, I have suggested that it is possible to open up the site delineated by temporal claims about modernity on the one hand and spatial claims about political community on the other. Once opened up, it is possible to see how those moments of international relations theory usually associated with the refusal of ethics are in fact made possible through certain ethical claims. Again, therefore, political realism can be understood as a complex site of philosophical puzzles and contradictions, rather than as a banal tradition stretching from Thucydides to Morgenthau. It is in this sense also that it is possible to engage with Weber, as with Machiavelli, so as to clarify the historical connection between ethics and spatio-temporal transformations of political community. Once this connection is clarified, modernist resolutions of the relationship between universality and particularity, and thus between historicity and spatiality, appear to be inherently problematic. Given the degree to which these resolutions are entrenched in the prevailing conventions of contemporary social and political analysis, it is likely that the intersection between ethics and international relations made possible by these resolutions will become even busier. But it is also likely that the most interesting ways forward will be opened up by those who seek to speak of the possibility of new forms of political community while resisting the resolutions that have made the demand that ethics be applied to international relations seems so reasonable.

4 HISTORY, STRUCTURE, REIFICATION

Beyond hegemony, before epistemology

In some respects, claims about ethics or about the wisdom of perennial traditions of political realism have come to seem distinctly old fashioned. From at least the 1960s, explicit theoretical controversy has focused more insistently on the character and appropriateness of claims about social science. As with so many other disciplines that have been shaped by the broader ambitions of an empirically conceived social science, such controversy has occurred largely on the terrain of epistemology. Very often, the more far-reaching epistemological problems posed by those who seek to understand what is involved in making knowledge claims about social and political processes have been pushed aside in favour of even more restricted concerns about method and research techniques. Narrowing the range of potential dispute in this manner has undoubtedly enhanced an appearance of professional solidarity. It has also obscured many of the more troublesome and more important fractures now visible within contemporary debates about the general nature and possibility of social and political inquiry. Not least, many of the problems that I have posed in relation to claims to political realism and political idealism may also be posed in the context of continuing efforts to secure the analysis of international relations upon firm epistemological foundations.

The specifically epistemological claims of empirical social science have been challenged on many grounds, and there is little point in rehearsing the resulting controversies here.[1] Rather, this chapter develops an initial characterisation of the range of theoretical problems that have been systematically marginalised by repeated appeals to the epistemological stance and methodological procedures of empirical social science in the analysis of international relations. To begin with, I distinguish between some of the different philosophical contexts in which appropriate research strategies may be judged. Here I reflect on a recent influential assessment of these strategies offered by

Robert Keohane, who explicitly judges them primarily in the context of epistemological and methodological criteria. I then explore some of the broader ontological, ethical and ideological dilemmas that are at stake in the literature that Keohane discusses. I am especially concerned with the tension between the atemporal structuralism that informs currently fashionable socio-scientific approaches, especially theories of international regimes and what has come to be called structural or neo-realism, and approaches that stress the priority of historical interpretation. This specific tension is then taken up in greater detail in the following chapter.

While my primary intention here is simply to insist on the significance of themes that are played down in Keohane's analysis, I also argue in favour of three broad conclusions. First, I affirm the priority of history, and thus of approaches that stress interpretation, practice and the critique of reification. Second, I insist that differences between approaches to contemporary world politics must be addressed at the level of basic ontological assumptions: the possibility of empirical research strategies is a significant but decidedly secondary matter. Third, I again suggest that the contemporary analysis of world politics poses fundamental questions of political theory – questions that remain interesting and provocative despite socio-scientific attempts to reduce them to problems of utilitarian calculation and empirical testing.

Keohane's assessment of contemporary research strategies is a helpful starting point because it is relatively sympathetic to the considerable diversity of approaches now to be found within the discipline. Distinguishing between his own widely influential 'rationalistic' analysis of interstate cooperation and positions that he identifies as the 'reflective' approach, Keohane is especially sympathetic to the contributions of those who have criticised the rationalists for their reliance on ahistorical utilitarian presuppositions adapted from liberal microeconomics and public choice theory. Moreover, his claims for the explanatory power of the rationalist or utilitarian position are relatively modest, and the text as a whole is written as an invitation to a more constructive dialogue between what are characterised as potentially complementary schools of thought.[2]

Nevertheless, the central argument of the text is bold and blunt: the reflective school have 'failed to develop a coherent research program of their own' – coherent, that is, in the sense that it bears comparison with the paradigmatic research programme exemplified by the structuralist models of Kenneth Waltz or the utilitarian categories that constitute the theory of international regimes.[3] An encouraging opening towards a positive assessment of the plurality of theoretical perspectives is quickly closed off by privileging a highly specific – not to say philosophically contested – account of what a proper research programme should look like.

It is not difficult to find evidence of the continuing influence of similar – indeed even more forthright – claims that scholarly controversies should be resolved on the privileged terrain of empirical method. These claims have been especially tenacious in international relations, although even here they have begun to lose their grip. Invocations of the logic of explanation in the physical sciences have become relatively rare, not least because our understanding of what is involved in even the most precise sciences is sharply contested. The general lesson that seems to have been drawn is not that empirical social science is impossible or undesirable, but that its achievements and possibilities ought to be placed in a more modest perspective. This lesson is reflected in Keohane's emphasis on the context-specific character of generalisations, as well as in the emphasis on model building in the work of the utilitarian rationalists more generally. The hope, of course, is that the models offered for empirical testing can transcend their origins as analogical or metaphorical speculation. Whether the utilitarian images that have been deployed recently to explain interstate co-operation are successful in this respect will undoubtedly remain contentious. Moreover, some students of world politics will continue to be more fascinated by the philosophical, ideological, social and political conditions under which a liberal utilitarian account of human action can aspire to hegemony in a discipline that continues to raise far more interesting questions than it provides plausible answers.

Meanwhile, many scholars concerned with what it means to study social and political life have turned away from the largely discredited positivistic accounts of scientific explanation to a much broader arena of philosophical debate, one in which the explorations of literary theorists are treated at least as seriously as pre-Kuhnian dogmas about cumulative scientific knowledge.[4] Some have been impressed by the vitality of interpretive or hermeneutic procedures, especially where the old Cartesian assumption that language can be separated from the world in which it participates is resisted. Some have become immersed in controversies generated by the revival of political economy, controversies in which it has been relatively difficult to erase fundamental philosophical and ideological differences through the claims of universal method. Others have been drawn into forms of critical theory associated with the Frankfurt School or post-structuralism, and thus into long-standing controversies about modernity. Whatever one

83

makes of such trends, they undoubtedly reflect a different intellectual atmosphere than prevailed when the discipline of international relations became institutionalised as a major branch of social science some three decades or so ago. Keohane is clearly aware of these developments. But, in affirming a more socio-scientific account of what a proper research agenda should look like, he minimises much of their significance and complexity.

This is apparent initially from the very broad range of perspectives that Keohane groups together as exemplars of the reflective approach. They include the broad sociological influences on the work of John Ruggie, Hayward Alker's explorations of dialectical logics, Friedrich Kratochwil's concern with analytic philosophies of action and the post-structuralist approach developed by Richard Ashley. If we add all those who have resisted the charms of socio-scientific theories of international relations by drawing on neo-Marxist forms of political economy, theories of ideology and discourse, or critical and interpretive forms of political thought, the ranks of the reflective school could be made to swell considerably. And if we then think about the potential range of ontological, ethical and ideological commitments that are likely to be held by such a diverse group of scholars, Keohane's hope for some kind of convergence with the insights of utilitarian rationalism seems rather naive.

In this sense, much of Keohane's discussion is reminiscent of the quite misleading exchange in the 1960s between 'scientific' and 'traditionalist' approaches to international relations. In the earlier exchange, debate was explicitly preoccupied with contrasting accounts of what scientific explanation involves and how the more historical and even philosophical concerns of the traditionalists might be updated through the judicious application of appropriate method.[5] Yet, in initiating the debate, Hedley Bull offered a critique of the pretensions of scientific method that rested less on claims about knowledge as such than on arguments about the very nature of world politics. Scientific method was inappropriate, he argued, because of what world politics is. He was especially concerned with the dangers of the 'domestic analogy', that is, the transfer of philosophical and theoretical premises derived from the analysis of political community within states to the analysis of relations between states.

Unfortunately, Bull's underlying concerns about whether inter-state relations or world politics are in principle any different from politics within states were quickly translated into more limited epistemological questions about how research and analysis should be conducted. While initiated on the ground of an ontological dualism – statist community and the society of states, or in the unfortunately more common rendition, community and anarchy – debate quickly turned to the claims of an epistemological monism. Consequently, where Bull articulated a traditional claim that relations between states are distinctive enough to justify a separate discipline and different research strategies (not to mention an account of the relation between knowledge and power – or truth and violence – that would seem scandalous in the context of theories of political life within states) socio-scientific approaches have affirmed a fundamental continuity. Hence the possibility, so eagerly grasped by those searching for empirically testable models, of transferring assumptions, metaphors, research strategies and accounts of rational action from one context to the other.

Nevertheless, Bull's concerns cannot be made to disappear quite so easily. It may now be common to speak of 'interdependence', to analyse international regimes, or to enquire about the potentials of international organisation, but few would argue that we have moved from a world of statist communities to a global community. The early-modern European account of political life as the establishment of relatively autonomous political communities co-existing in territorial space has yet to be superseded by a coherent account of a common planetary identity or a cosmopolitan human community. The epistemological claim to a universally applicable scientific method thus co-exists quite uneasily with the contrary claim, articulated variously in ontological, ethical and ideological forms, that human life is essentially fragmented.

Keohane's more recent discussion poses similar difficulties. Many of the differences between the positions he examines arise far more from disagreements about what it is scholars think they are studying than from disagreements about how to study it. The latter depend in large part upon the former. To attempt to turn all theoretical disputes into differences over method and epistemology is to presume that we have acceptable answers to questions about what kind of world it is that we are trying to know. This is a rather large presumption, as Keohane partly, but only partly recognises. Moreover, even if Keohane's distinction proves useful at some level, it is not altogether clear why the methodological prescriptions of the utilitarian rationalists should be treated as the successful orthodoxy on whose terms the contributions of the reflective school should be judged. It might be argued, for example, that there are very strong continuities between the work of the reflective theorists – Kratochwil and Ashley especially, though quite distinctively – and the work of Bull and others who begin their work by attempting to come to terms with the historically constituted

85

distinction between politics within and relations between statist communities. Keohane's polarity might even be reversed by suggesting
that utilitarian rationalism merely adds some interesting analytic
models and a distinctive vocabulary to traditions of considerable
standing and achievement. Claims about what constitutes orthodoxy
in this respect can vary considerably depending on the cultural and
temporal horizons of the claimant.

In any case, the appropriate context in which to situate Keohane's
discussion is less the controversy about social science than the even
earlier opposition between political realists and political idealists.
While it is against the obvious limitations of that debate that the
promises of social science were articulated in the first place, the
categories through which that debate was constituted have remained
very influential. In fact, far from being merely one of a series of
debates that have characterised the history of the discipline, the
distinction between political realism and political idealism has provided the broad, but severely restricted context within which other
disputes about appropriate method or the priority of state-centred
accounts of world politics could occur at all. Framed within this
distinction, 'metaphysics', 'ethics' and 'ideology' have become the
names for roles in an old and obviously decrepit Manichean theatre.
Tamed in this way, it is hardly surprising that they have been
marginalised in favour of the louder and seemingly more up-to-date
claims of social science. Nevertheless, as Keohane moves closer and
closer to the primary themes that distinguish utilitarian rationalists
from historically inclined reflectivists, the echoes of this older debate
become much clearer.

To draw attention to the connection between current controversies
and this older debate is certainly not to suggest that the categories of
either realist or idealist can now offer much useful guidance. As roles
in a Manichean theatre, these terms have served primarily to close off
serious discussion in a manner that has helped to insulate the discipline of international debate ever since. Rather, the categories of realist
and idealist, as they were deployed in these debates – and as they have
since come to provide convenient labels and systems of classification –
should be understood as the primary sites at which the basic assumptions governing the study of world politics have been left to congeal in
forms that require little further exploration. As such they provide a
place to begin, and a place at which awkward questions may be
deferred.

Much of the literature that Keohane seeks to judge as if they are
contributions to empirical social science can also be understood as

attempts to re-engage with the philosophical and theoretical dilemmas that were packed away when the categories of realist and idealist were constructed as the appropriate arena in which dispute could be permitted to occur in an orderly and unthreatening manner. Unpacking these categories, it is possible to reformulate questions about, say, the relationship between claims to legitimate political community within states and the legitimacy of violence in relations between political communities; or the relative claims of people as human beings and people as citizens; or the tensions between universalist and pluralist ethical claims; or the relation between power and knowledge as this has been mediated by the claims of state-sovereignty.

Keohane rightly emphasises the significance of historical interpretation for all those who have challenged the structuralist tendencies of the utilitarian rationalists, and it is this theme that I want to dwell on here. For one way of reframing an account of current debates about approaches to world politics is to emphasise how contrasting perspectives have tended to privilege either history and time, on the one hand, or structure and space on the other. The tendency to privilege either history or structure rests upon historically constituted philosophical options. To emphasise one or the other is to generate distinctive theoretical puzzles. These options and puzzles explain part – but only part – of what is at stake in the opposition between realism and idealism. They also underlie many of the distinctive claims made on behalf of, and criticisms voiced against, socio-scientific forms of structural realism and regime theory. Moreover, the categories through which the privileging of either history or structure are sustained are themselves the product of distinctive historical conditions. They now tend to freeze or reify complex philosophical questions into a permanent problem: either an eternal debate between realists and idealists or a progressive struggle to establish a properly empirical social science against the recalcitrant metaphysicians, ideologists, historicists, hermeneuticists or critical theorists. Neither of these legacies seems likely to advance our understanding of the transformative character of contemporary world politics very far.

In exploring the tension between history and structure in the analysis of world politics in an introductory and schematic manner, I want to suggest that it provides a much clearer indication of what is at stake in many current debates in this context than is possible by fixing the discussion on the terrain of epistemology or method. Beginning with history, I move on to structure before returning to problems raised by Keohane's delineation of the options before us.

Historical departures

Once upon a time, according to a well-known story, the world was not as it is now. Precisely what it was like is not clear. Accounts vary, depending on when and where once upon a time is supposed to have occurred. Records and memories are notoriously deceptive, and require careful coding and interpretation. The skills of the story teller are judged more by the expectations of the audience than by the authenticity of the stamps in some time-traveller's passport. Even so, this particular story remains evocative. It tells of feudal modes of production, hierarchical arrangements of power and authority, and medieval forms of life and consciousness. This story can be told in many different versions and under many different titles. The version that is of concern here might be called 'Life Before International Relations'.

The telling of this story is often short and snappy, a preface to an equally concise denouement: feudalism gives way to capitalism, more modern forms of life and consciousness emerge, and political community gradually coheres around the sovereign claims of state. This story in turn has a sequel, full of plots etched deeply in the contemporary imagination. This sequel has come in two quite distinctive, but mutually interdependent variations.

One, especially favoured by those who refer to their stories as histories of social and political thought, impresses us with accounts of the progressive emancipation of statist political communities and the emergence of modern conceptions of freedom, justice and rationality. Another, favoured by an apparently more hard-bitten breed who refer to their scripts as theories of international relations, depresses us with tragic tales of violence, intrigue and the triumph of might over right. In both versions, however, the story about how the world was not as it is now easily recedes into the background, and we are gripped instead by seemingly more topical tales of the world that has become what it is.

References to accounts of medieval life, or of the complex transformations of early-modern Europe as mere stories may seem excessively flippant given the massive and erudite literature that has undoubtedly advanced our understanding of these phases of human experience. Nevertheless, this literature is not invoked very often in the contemporary analysis of world politics. Significant exceptions to this general rule are not difficult to find, but for the most part, influential strategies of analysis have been framed against a highly generalised story about when, where and how interstate politics emerged as an appropriate object for scholarly reflection. In this sense, the well-known stories continue to exercise a powerful hold over categories of analysis and methodological strategies. At least four groups of puzzles are implicated in these stories, puzzles that regularly enter into ongoing discussion about what the analysis of world politics ought to involve.

One set of puzzles arises from the rather sharp disjunction between the comfortable rhythms in which the best-known stories about the early-modern period have been reiterated and the untidy, even recalcitrant evidence that enters into the deeply contested accounts offered by contemporary historians. While old distinctions between ancients and moderns remain deeply entrenched in popular accounts of where we have come from, the role of these distinctions as a legitimation of modernity against the presumed darkness that came before is readily transparent. While the grand narratives of Marx and Weber continue to offer crucial insights into the conjunctures of forces responsible for the emergence of capitalism, modernity and the state, simple linear trajectories and unicausal theories have been sharply qualified by the details of multiple transitions. While we may remain impressed by the rapidity and scale of the socio-economic innovations of the sixteenth and seventeenth centuries or the spectacular intellectual achievements of the Renaissance, it is increasingly clear that the transformations of the early-modern period grew out of processes that had already been underway for a considerable period. Continuities have come to seem at least as important as ruptures. Complex interactions between mutually causal forces now seem more impressive than the residual prejudices of a self-celebrating modernity.[6]

In short, the simple story of life before international relations – a story of an absence against which the presence of contemporary international relations can be defined – has become quite implausible. Yet while often prepared to admit the inadequacy of the conventional stories, theorists of international relations are easily drawn into an affirmation of them as a convenient myth of origins. By identifying when interstate relations began and providing a sharp contrast with what came before, these stories offer a powerful account of what interstate politics must be given what it has always been since the presumed beginning.

Without such a myth of origins, of course, a number of rather basic questions from the philosophy of history begin to assert themselves. To what extent does our interpretation of contemporary interstate politics depend on particular readings of macrohistory? To what extent might these readings be challenged by, say, anthropologists, or by macro-historians who are more reluctant to place early-modern

European experiences at the centre of their analysis? To what extent are these readings caught up in unacknowledged assumptions about progress, or evolution, or eternal return? To what extent is our understanding of the possibilities of contemporary transformations constrained by our assumptions about the historical processes that have made us what we are now? Threatened by the implications of questions like these, a retreat to a clear point of origin from which contemporary trajectories may be delineated and continuities generalised, can seem very comforting. Nevertheless, it has rarely escaped the notice of the more astute political commentators that the capacity to construct a myth of origins signifies enormous political advantage.

Similar questions are at play in a second set of puzzles that regularly beset analysts of world politics, puzzles that arise from competing accounts of the most appropriate point at which to identify the origin of the modern states-system. Once we move away from the most caricatured accounts of life before and after the rise of the state, the variety of presumed points of origin can be quite striking.[7] Two options have been especially popular. One is to focus on the emergence of the state as a distinctive and relatively autonomous form of political community in late-fifteenth-century Europe. Another is to stress the period in which claims of state sovereignty became formalised and codified in international law. Here the Treaty of Westphalia of 1648 serves as a crucial demarcation between an era still dominated by competing claims to religious universalism and hierarchical authority and an era of secular competition and co-operation among autonomous political communities. But there are also analysts who would direct our attention to earlier periods. They may want to push accounts of relatively autonomous state authority back further into the feudal era, or more usually, point to analogies between early-modern Europe and the states-systems of antiquity. And others prefer to focus on later dates on the grounds that, say, only in the eighteenth century does the states-system generate recognisably modern procedures and 'rules of the game', or that only later still do we discover a system of relations between properly national states. Taking things to rather absurd extremes, it is even possible to derive the impression from some textbooks that interstate politics is an invention of the twentieth century.

This rather elastic identification of points of origin again raises very serious questions about what an analysis of world politics ought to involve. To engage with the literature on the emergence and development of the states-system is to be impressed by the transformative quality of both the state and the character of relations between states.

States can then appear to us as historically constituted and always subject to change. Distinctions between, say, the absolutist state, the nation-state, the welfare state and the national-security state become very interesting. Yet this historicity of states is at odds with a contrary sense that, whatever their historical transformations, states and states-systems exhibit certain regularities across time. Scholars do claim to be able to make plausible analogies between, say, the struggles of Athens and Sparta and our own epoch. Defence policies continue to be justified in the name of state sovereignty, a sovereignty that fixes a claim to permanence and continuity in the identity of the state as an ongoing political community.

In this way, the perspectives of history begin to give way to those of structure. Sometimes this takes the form of definitions of some sort of permanent essence, of accounts of the inter-state system as in principle always anarchical, for example, or of the state as always a maximiser of power, status or its own welfare. Sometimes it takes the form of the comparative analysis of various structural configurations, of the differences between multipolar and bi-polar systems, or of systems with and systems without a dominant actor. In either case, the historicity of states and state-systems recedes into the background, and world politics begins to turn into a permanent game, one that can appear to have conformed more or less to the same rules since time immemorial.

This apparent continuity, this sense of permanence or at least repetition, is particularly attractive to scholars who seek to develop an explanatory science of the politics of states-systems. Problems from the philosophy of history are difficult to negotiate. The historicity of states-systems leads to the contentious constructions of historical sociology or political economy. Discontinuity and historical transformation have long been viewed as serious threats to the accumulation of objective knowledge. One cannot step into the same river twice, say some. We have only managed to interpret the world while the point is to change it, say others. Against temporal flux, contingency, idiosyncrasy and revolutionary praxis, the identification of structural form offers an alluring possibility of a universalising objectivity.

This leads directly to a third set of puzzles, those that arise from claims that there is indeed a firm body of knowledge about the character of inter-state politics enshrined in the 'great tradition' of international theory. Whether as a permanent debate between realism and idealism, the repetitious monologue spoken by those who have somehow been conscripted into the army of realists, or the account of a tradition of international relations theory as a negation of a presumed

91

tradition of political theory, crudely anachronistic interpretive procedures have served to obscure another version of the contradiction between history and structure. Thucydides, Machiavelli, Hobbes, Rousseau and the rest appear to us as quite unproblematic figures, often in disguises that make them quite unrecognisable to anyone who examines the textual evidence we have of them. That each of these figures is open to sharply differing interpretations has mattered little. The history of political thought turns into an ahistorical repetition in which the struggles of these thinkers to make sense of the historical transformations in which they were caught are erased in favour of assertions about how they all articulate essential truths about the same unchanging and usually tragic reality: the eternal game of relations between states.

Following from this, a fourth set of puzzles arises from the historically constituted character not only of the state and the states-system, but also of the categories in which we seek to understand how the state and the states-system participate in the dynamics of contemporary world politics. This is perhaps the most disconcerting puzzle of all. It is always tempting to minimise the significance of the historical experiences through which crucial concepts and ways of speaking have been formed. The longing for timeless categories has exercised a profound influence on many of those we associate with rationalism in the more philosophical sense of this term. Yet it is possible to trace the history of the terms 'state', 'sovereignty', 'individual', 'culture', 'security' or many of the other terms we now take for granted, and in doing so we discover how they emerged in response to specific historical conjunctions and contradictions. Accounts of history as a sharp break between life before international relations and life since international relations easily detract attention from the historically specific meanings embodied in concepts and categories that can so easily appear to transcend their historical contingency. The categories and concepts we have learnt to use with such facility, almost without thinking, easily appear natural and inevitable. Their contested history is soon forgotten.

Structural proliferations

The story having been written, and sedimented into received accounts of origins, traditions and analytical concepts, attention may be turned to the architecture of structures. Grand structures having emerged, it is possible to inquire into their modes of operation, their mechanisms and determinations, their forms and their functions, their regularities and repetitions. Indeed, some of the most familiar analyses of relations between states have been facilitated by a certain forgetting of history.

In its more extreme forms, structuralist analysis tends towards universalism. It is associated historically with attempts to identify the universal principles of reason, or myth or language, the deep structures that inform the spatial variety and temporal variability visible on the surface of things. In practice, however, structuralist analysis is itself subject to considerable variation, partly with respect to the number of structural patterns that may be identified, and partly with respect to the way that under critical inspection, structural patterns always seem to mutate into processes of historical transformation.

It is in this context, for example, that it is possible to identify Thomas Hobbes as a paradigmatic thinker. Because individuals are autonomous and equal under conditions of scarcity, Hobbes suggests, they necessarily find themselves in a position of perpetual insecurity. Each individual's struggle to enhance his/her own security increases everyone else's sense of insecurity. Hence the imagery of both the 'state of nature' and the 'security dilemma'. On the other hand (and contrary to the usual direct translation of the fictive state of nature into an account of the security dilemma between states) Hobbes argues that precisely because states are both unequal and much less vulnerable than individuals, they are in a significantly different structural relationship to each other than are individuals.[8] Among (proto-bourgeois) individuals, Hobbes argues, structural relations of insecurity demand a superior sovereign power for an ordered polity to be constituted. Hence the powerful resolution of the relation between sovereign individuals and sovereign states through a contract that is both freely entered into and yet necessitated by structural conditions. Among states, by contrast, structural conditions of inequality suggest other ordering principles in what is nevertheless a 'state of war', although Hobbes himself does not much concern himself with what these principles might be.

It could be argued, of course, that in contemporary world politics, both the proliferation of nuclear weapons and the legal principle of sovereign equality have begun to make Hobbes' account of relations between individuals a more instructive guide to the dynamics of inter-state relations than Hobbes himself suggests. For the most part, however, despite continuing references to Hobbes as a theorist of international anarchy, most accounts of world politics presume that the equality condition is absent. Conflict there may be, insecurity certainly, but structuralist accounts of world politics are just as likely to show how insecurity arises from patterns of hegemony, hierarchy and penetration as from autonomy and equality.

The primary candidate for the most important structural form in world politics has been the balance of power, especially among those who identify the subject of world politics specifically as relations between states. Here we find the familiar themes of the consequences of different distributions or polarities of power, and of the presence or absence of great or hegemonic powers. These lead directly to a concern with, say, the nature of alliances or the transformations induced by the deployment of weapons of mass destruction and the regularised rituals of nuclear deterrence. When patterns of hegemony begin to seem especially significant, attention may turn to the difficulty of distinguishing the dynamics of states-systems from those of empires.

Other contenders for the primary structuring principles of world politics arise from those who situate the dynamics of inter-state relations within a broader account of an international or global political economy. Here the range of perspectives is particularly striking. Much of the literature on international regimes is often classified under this rubric. But the liberal categories of economic analysis deployed by this literature set it apart from more explicitly mercantilist or Marxist traditions that also inform contemporary political economy, especially outside the narrow ideological confines of the United States. Some, like Robert Gilpin, seek to combine liberal economic categories with a more mercantilist or 'realist' account of the state, especially in the context of contemporary disruptions and transformations in international trade and finance. Some, like Immanuel Wallerstein, echo Adam Smith in their stress on the determinations of a global division of labour and a world market, minimising the autonomous role of the state while stressing the relations between centre and periphery in a world system. Others, like Robert Cox and Stephen Gill begin – in my view more helpfully – with a concern for the global structuring of relations of production, and thus emphasise the transformation of state practices in response to the contemporary global reorganisation of production currently in progress.[9]

To canvass the range of structuralist accounts of world politics in this way is to become aware of the diversity of philosophical, theoretical and ideological assumptions that can be embraced under the heading of structuralism. In this sense, Keohane's category of rationalists is just as much in need of differentiation as his fusion of reflective approaches. But equally striking is the difficulty of distinguishing between structuralist and historical analysis.

Keohane recommends a greater openness to the reflective approach partly because it would complement the ahistoricism of the rationalists. Yet once we move away from the explicitly utilitarian models of regime theory, it is clear that accounts of the character of historical change are already built into many accounts of the structural forms of world politics. These accounts may not be entirely convincing, falling back, for example, on notions of change as alterations in the distribution of power in a system that remains essentially the same, or on accounts of history as either a sequence of repetitive cycles or a linear road from darkness to light. Nevertheless it is probably fair to say that few students of world politics would argue that structuralist analysis can be divorced from a concern with history and change. There is a 'plain common sense' view that both perspectives are obviously necessary. Some might argue, for example, that purely structural analyses of balances of power are intrinsically interesting, and that formal modelling or ahistorical ascriptions of utilitarian behaviour to states are entirely justified, as long as a complementary historical perspective is also encouraged. Even so, both the superficial tolerance of what passes for 'plain common sense' and the prevailing division of academic labour can easily obscure some of the characteristic difficulties experienced by structuralist analysis in understanding the historical political practices through which structural forms have been constructed.

Again it is helpful to reflect upon the supposedly paradigmatic quality of Hobbes' thinking for the analysis of world politics. Hobbes builds upon a fairly radical reworking of philosophical categories within the broad context of the scientific cosmologies associated with the early modern period. He is impressed, for example, with the unchanging character of reason, the spatial regularities of Euclidean geometry and the possibility of grounding the language of social explanation in a firm foundation of precise definitions. Unlike Machiavelli before or Rousseau after, he pays very little attention to history, at least not in the passages for which he has become a realist icon. Instead we find a classic expression of life before and life after the social contract, a shrinking of historical time and human practice to an ahistorical moment of utilitarian calculation informed by reason and fear.

Again, it is possible to identify a range of difficult puzzles that have beset those who have followed Hobbes in their privileging of structural form. Even if we try to avoid questions about whether structures can be said to exist, it is still necessary to engage with complex philosophical interrogations that converge on the question of what a structure is. Many of these arise from the contemporary emphasis on relationality rather than substance. Understood as part of a broader

95

challenge to Newtonian metaphysics, contemporary structural analysis conflicts with popular accounts of the world as an accumulation of things. Some people may kick tables to affirm the material solidity of the 'real world', but the demonstration is unlikely to be convincing to anyone familiar with categories and controversies of contemporary physics.

With a stress on relationality come questions about how one understands the distinction between parts of a structure and the 'emergent properties' that arise because, as it is often said, 'the whole is greater than the sum of its parts'. Hence the dilemma, especially familiar in sociological theory, of whether social explanation should begin with an account of 'society' or with the behaviour of 'individuals'.[10] Hence, also, some of the central dilemmas of the theory of international relations: the delineation of distinctions between individual, state and states-system in the so-called 'levels of analysis' typology, for example, or controversies about whether the states-system should be considered to have an autonomous logic of its own or to be part in a broader system of global political economy. The concept of causality also becomes problematic in this context, especially given that most popular accounts of causality are still informed by images of billiard balls colliding in a Newtonian universe. And with causality come questions about determinism, particularly about whether structural forms should be understood as constraining or enabling.

In pursuing questions like these, however, questions about the relationship between structure and history are never far away. Thus contemporary structuralism does not exhibit the same attachment to timeless universals as the earlier forms of axiomatic rationalism. On the contrary, as it has been used by anthropologists and theorists of language, structuralism has become more preoccupied with understanding the rules of transformation than with identifying patterns of continuity. More crucially, as a broad philosophical and theoretical movement, one associated with the work of Claude Levi-Strauss or Louis Althusser, for example, structuralism mutated rather rapidly into what has become known as post-structuralism.[11] And one of the central insights of post-structuralism, explored especially by theorists of language from Fernand de Saussure to Jacques Derrida, has been that structural patterns are constituted through historical processes of differentiation.[12] The emphasis on relationality is pursued in a temporal direction with the well-known result that post-structuralist analysis has come to be indicted for all the sins previously associated with those who insisted on the historicity of human existence. The indictment, of course, is invariably issued in the name of objectivity and universal standards, although it is the historically constituted nature of the capacity to issue the indictment in the first place that post-structuralism has sought to challenge.

As if this is not enough, questions about whether structures do, in fact, exist, will not go away. They are especially important for attempts to construct a theory of international regimes. The very term regime, like similar uses of the term governance, attempts to capture phenomena that seem to have a status that is somewhere between a concrete institution and a more or less invisible field of forces generated by structural determinations. The term international organisations is also quite problematic in this respect, caught as it is between accounts of specific institutional arrangements like the United Nations, and incohate attempts to forge an analysis of processes that are neither inter-state relations as conventionally understood nor readily grasped as precursors of some kind of world state.[13]

Interrogations like these lead into some of the most difficult conceptual terrain in contemporary social and political theory. They ought to give pause to anyone attempting to keep discussion of contrasting perspectives on world politics to questions about epistemology and method. Even those who adhere most rigorously to an empiricist conception of research discover that they have to struggle with interrogations of this kind. Kenneth Waltz's accounts of systemic explanation and the level of analysis typology or Robert Gilpin's attempt to reconcile modernist social science with an essentially historicist account of a classical tradition of theories of international relations clearly involve taking positions on these questions. Their positions may or may not be satisfactory, but their work has to be judged at least partially in terms of how far their more empirical work is both shaped and constrained by their prior ontological commitments.

A second set of puzzles follows directly from such considerations, for in practice answers to these more philosophical problems are often articulated in the form of metaphors, analogies and models derived from other areas of human experience. Here it is as well to remember that metaphors, analogies and models are a crucial aspect of theory formation, even in the more rigorous sciences. They assist in conceptual clarification and the development of systems of classification. It may well be that much of what we understand to be scientific analysis has been articulated against the dangers of misanalogy or the slippages in meaning that are intrinsic to metaphorical reasoning; that is, against the very possibilities that are often celebrated in the realms of literature and art. But, again, the conventional distinction between the sciences and humanities obscures more than it reveals. In the analysis of social and political life especially, textual strategies and literary devices are a characteristic part of even the most formalised modelling.

Two sub-themes are especially important here. One concerns the tendency to draw analogies between relatively simple structures in order to explain ones that are more complex. The role of images taken from Newtonian mechanics or Darwinian biology is relatively familiar and has generated long-standing debate about the reductionist character of so much functionalist explanation in sociology.[14] In the analysis of world politics, the concept of a balance of power itself clearly has an analogical quality, and leads to questions about whether, say, the notion of equilibrium it implies is sufficiently nuanced to comprehend the dynamics of great power diplomacy or the dialectics of nuclear deterrence. Similarly, many of the ideas articulated under the rubric of social choice theory or utilitarian accounts of substantive rationality have a distinctly reductionist quality. In part this derives from a methodological individualism, whereby it is assumed that social processes can be explained in terms of the behaviour of individuals, as if individuals somehow exist prior to society. In part it derives from literary inventiveness, as when something called a 'prisoner's dilemma' is presumed to bear some relation to what goes on under conditions of incarceration.[15]

A second sub-theme concerns the circulation of the metaphors and analogies used to analyse world politics within a broader cultural and political economy. Social and political explanation constantly draws on and collides with the imagery, prejudices and ways of speaking of the society being explained. To move, for example, from a structuralist account of a balance of power to one of nuclear deterrence, is to work within a cultural context in which the meaning of 'equilibrium' or 'security' or a 'nuclear umbrella' is mediated by complex cultural codes of which strategic analysts are themselves only partly aware.[16] Moving from structural analysis to metaphors and analogies, we quickly begin to understand how entangled we are in a complex politics of language or discourse.

This leads directly to a third group of puzzles, those which focus on the relationship between structures and human consciousness or practice.[17] Some of the most intense debates about structural analysis in modern social and political theory have occurred on this terrain, not least because structuralism has seemed to imply the erasure of human subjectivity.[18] In the context of world politics, versions of this problem have occurred in debates about whether a balance of power should be understood as an automatic mechanism to which statesmen simply respond appropriately or inappropriately, or whether it should be regarded as a practice or policy that statesmen have developed on the basis of long historical experience.

Something similar is involved in the different accounts of international co-operation and regime formation. In an extreme utilitarian approach, for example, human action is explained in terms of the rules of efficient conduct, rules that have a certain structural necessity. In this context, 'normative' behaviour is interpreted as following the prudential rules of utility maximisation. This is clearly not the only available account of human action, or of what normative behaviour involves. Even Max Weber, whose account of instrumental rationality is often invoked by utilitarian analysts, tended to see modernity not as a simple embrace of instrumental rationality, but as an intensifying clash between the meaningless rules of efficient action and a struggle to give meaning to life in a disenchanted world. And those who begin their account of human action in an analysis of, say, labour or language, are especially unlikely to be persuaded by the limited claims of utilitarian efficiency. To begin with the constitutive character of labour or language is to challenge the fundamental premises on which utilitarian accounts of social and political life are grounded. There is nothing very novel about this. It merely serves as a reminder that the distance between Keohane's categories covers some rather deeply rooted and enormously complex differences among those who seek to understand social and political life.

To make matters worse, it is always possible to raise a still further group of puzzles about how our prevailing understanding of terms like structure and history is itself informed by historically constituted accounts of the concepts of space and time. Here metaphysics enters with a vengeance. Questions about ethics and ideology cannot be far behind. For some, of course, this would be enough to bring on a bad case of positivist vertigo. In a discipline in which the reflections of, say, Machiavelli, Kant or St Augustine have not been entirely obliterated by the myth of a tradition, it should come as no surprise.

From international relations to world politics

While introducing his analysis of the relative merits of the rationalistic and reflective approaches, Keohane affirms his commitment to a socio-scientific analysis of world politics by explicitly marginalising the themes I have tried to sketch here. In his view, he says, it 'will not be fruitful ... indefinitely to conduct a debate at the purely theoretical level, much less to argue about epistemological and ontological issues in the abstract. Such an argument would only take us away from the study of our subject matter, world politics, towards what would probably become an intellectually derivative and programmatically diversionary philosophical discussion.'[19]

The problem, of course, is that Keohane's discussion is full of ontological and epistemological claims that are left abstract; his account of an empirical research programme is dependent upon ontological (as well as ethical and ideological) commitments; and in marginalising problems that have long been central to (non-empiricist) philosophies of social science, he diverts attention from the serious philosophical and political problems that are at stake in even postulating a subject matter called world politics. This is not, I should emphasise, to underestimate the importance of serious empirical research, although it does imply that empirical knowledge is a more complex and interesting process than it is so often made to appear. It is simply not enough to suggest that hermeneutic and critical concerns might be admitted as a secondary supplement to the privileged demands of empirical explanation, or that unless an ontological stance is stipulated, analysis will remain mired in philosophical controversy. Sharp distinctions between social science and socio-political theory, between empirical and normative, interpretive or critical forms of enquiry, simply cannot be sustained no matter how much they may have legitimated disciplinary divisions and claims to professional expertise. There is certainly a lot more involved in postulating concepts like interdependence, regimes, or international institutions than the formulation of an empirical research programme. As even conventional neo-Kantian philosophies of science have insisted time and time again, the appropriate conceptualisation of the problem already prefigures the solution. It is not a matter of arguing about ontological and epistemological issues in the abstract. Philosophical commitments are already embedded in concepts like state or state-system, utilitarian accounts of rational action, and, as I will suggest in greater detail in chapter 6, typologies like the so-called levels of analysis schema that has played such an important role in this discipline.

To advance concepts like interdependence or international regime is already to admit the significance of historical transformation. But to begin with history is to encounter problems that are usually encountered under the heading of the philosophy of history. Given the difficulty of some of these problems, it is perhaps not entirely surprising that they are so often marginalised and resolved in favour of ahistorical accounts of continuity and structural form. A sensitivity to history and time is always in danger of being undermined through reification. This *is* the essential complaint brought against the utilitarian or rationalist approach by those who are identified with reflection. Historical practices are analysed as ahistorical structures. Conscious human practices are erased in favour of structural determinations. But problems of temporality rarely disappear entirely. Attempts have even been made to analyse temporal process in terms of structural patterns. The flux of time has been portrayed as teleological or dialectical necessity. The history of human consciousness has been portrayed in relation to the generative structure of grammar. The logic of scientific explanation has been extended from the sciences of inert matter to encompass patterns of probability in historical practices. But such strategies have always encountered powerful opposition. The historicity of human experience remains deeply problematic.

These are not simply abstract considerations, to be deferred as somehow merely theoretical or philosophical. They are at play in the concrete practices of intellectual life. Claims about a point of origin, a tradition or an essentially timeless form known as the state have had an enormous impact on what world politics is assumed to be, and thus on what it means to participate in or offer a legitimate account of world politics. Questions about the relationship between reified structures and conscious human practices are at the heart of – though they are resolved in distinctive ways by – the dominant ideological forces of modern political life.

Just as these remarks do not imply that empirical research is unimportant, nor do they mean that structuralist analysis has nothing to offer. Still less that the questions pursued by the utilitarian rationalists are trivial. On the contrary. Questions about processes of inter-state co-operation and discord, the emergence of new patterns of interdependence and dependence, the appropriate conceptualisation of regimes or institutions, the globalisation of production, distribution and exchange or the changing character of state-formation in response to economic and technological transformations, functional problems and political struggles, are obviously crucial. Contemporary world politics is, as Keohane rightly emphasises, 'a matter of wealth and poverty, life and death'. Indeed, these questions should be understood in relation to the possibility of thinking about political life at all in the late twentieth century. They put in doubt the political categories that assume – with both Machiavelli and Hobbes – a fundamental distinction between political life within states and political life between states – the distinction that is constitutive of the discipline of international relations as we now know it. The questions are undoubtedly crucial, but the inherited categories of international relations theory do not necessarily offer the sharpest articulation of what they involve.

Structuralist analysis is also important, but so too are the persistent problems that structuralist analysis brings with it. A Kenneth Waltz has to wrestle with the relative merits of systemic and reductionist forms of explanation, choosing – contentiously – to resolve competing metaphysical claims through a reifying typology of the individual, the state and the states-system as the essential components of the 'real world'. Others try to reconcile conflicting accounts of the primary structure as either the states-system, on the one hand, or a more inclusive global political economy, on the other. In both cases, it is possible to see powerful tensions between the claims of structure and those of history.

These tensions have characterised much of contemporary intellectual life. They have been a familiar theme even within North American social science. Attempts to employ functional explanation or cybernetic and systems analysis, for example, have quickly attracted the charge of conservatism on the grounds that mechanistic and biological models systematically downplay the significance of human consciousness and political struggle. In a broader context, existential or phenomenological humanism was once challenged by the structuralisms of Claude Levi-Strauss or Louis Althusser; which were then challenged in turn both by reassertions of humanism and, more iconoclastically, by the non-humanist historicism of the post-structuralists and postmodernists. In the background lie all those complex yet stylised codings in which Hegel's universal history challenges Kant's universal reason, or Aristotelian teleology follows Plato's geometrically inspired account of unchanging forms. Yet if it is reasonable to urge the necessity of both structuralist and historical sensitivities, then it is also necessary to insist that empirical social science holds no monopoly on what this might bring. It might bring about a greater concern for the reifying practices that have been so powerful in accounts of a tradition of international relations theory, or in the more extreme presumption that a state is a state is a state. It might force open serious philosophical questions that have been closed off by the categories of realism and idealism, or by the pretence that neo- or structural realism is just an updated account of eternal realist principles. It might focus greater attention on the principle of state sovereignty as the crucial practice through which questions about human community are fixed within a spatial metaphysics that is sharply at odds with the historically constituted claims of the state. It might even focus attention on the deeply rooted categories through which we pretend to know just what space and time are.

All of which is to identify the analysis of world politics with a much broader account of social and political inquiry than is usual in the

specific discipline of international relations. If questions about interdependence, dependence, regimes and institutions are taken seriously
– that is as possibly putting into question the early-modern European
accounts of what political community can be given the passing of life
before international relations – then it is not clear that such explorations are any less significant than, in need of subsumption into, or just
a prelude to a utilitarian and empirical social science. Vague and
obscure hypotheses about the existence of something called world
politics involve a claim to historical and structural transformation that
throw historically derived concepts and disciplinary divisions into
rather serious doubt. The difficulty of analysing political life at this
historical juncture remains more impressive than the achievements of
theories of international relations. It is this difficulty, not the extrava-
gant presumptions of modernist social science, that demands our
attention.

5 REALISM AND CHANGE

Political realism and political realisms

In the early 1980s, the relative optimism of the previous decade receded in the wake of a harsher international environment, and many international relations theorists offered to console us with an old but appropriately mournful tune. This time pessimism came in a more thoroughly modern idiom, derived variously from structuralist social theory, hypothetico-deductive methodologies and utilitarian micro-economics. Since then, neorealism, as this idiom was quickly baptised, has had a profound and in some places even hegemonic influence on the analysis of contemporary world politics.

It is not surprising that in reflecting critically on this trend, Richard Ashley was reminded of the returning ghost of old revolutions: tragedy revived as farce.[1] Yet such reminders risk invoking a view of history that is deeply at odds with the historical narrative preferred by many of those who think of themselves as political realists. For them, the returning ghost merely reflects the inevitable return of tragedy itself. Against the view of history as qualitative progression they offer the claim that the 'realities' of international politics are enduring, and are consequently to be distinguished sharply from the politics of state and civil society. Yet the character of this enduring, of this sense of continuity that is also a form of change through time, remains highly problematic. It is even less surprising, therefore, that the reinvigoration of political realism has been accompanied by a renewed concern with the analysis of change in international politics. In fact, the conceptualisation of change – and thus the resolution of tensions between structuralism and historicism – provides a powerful point of entry into a critical analysis of claims to political realism in general and of recent forms of neorealism in particular.[2]

The most obvious difficulties that have arisen in this context are readily apparent in the writings of some of the most influential recent exponents of a realist position. Those, like Kenneth Waltz, who have clung most tightly to the promised certainties of atemporal structuralisms and positivist method, are taken to task for being unable 'to account for, or even to describe the most important contextual change in international politics in this *millennium*: the shift from the medieval to the modern international system'.[3] Those, like Robert Gilpin, who have shown a much greater sensitivity to the historicity of our existence, tempt us with the paradox that the world of humankind is in a state of constant flux and change, and yet a Thucydides reborn would have little difficulty in explaining our contemporary agonies.[4] Unfortunately, it is not immediately obvious that Gilpin's appeal to an ahistorical theory of rational choice, on the one hand, and a broad cyclical theory of hegemonic wars on the other, does much to confront this paradox in a sufficiently serious manner.

These difficulties underlie much of the recent debate about realism and neorealism in the theory of international relations. This debate has centred on a confrontation between defenders of various forms of structuralism, and several kinds of historicism – or rationalism and reflection, to use Keohane's terminology. The critics of neorealism have argued that the structures of the international system which neorealists treat as more or less universal and eternal are, in fact, the specific consequences of particular historical conditions. Against Waltz, for example, Ruggie has recommended greater attention to 'diachronic processes' as well as 'synchronic articulations'. Robert Cox has drawn on a variety of historicist writers to insist that the study of international relations itself, including the forms taken by realist theories in different eras, be analysed more critically in relation to the historical context in which it arose.[5] At a more general level, R. N. Berki's extended discussion of political realism considers a broad range of writers with strong historicist sympathies, which may explain why it has been almost entirely ignored in a discipline in which claims about political realism are so important.[6] Ashley himself saw in the more historicist or 'classical' version of political realism a more authentic, that is, more hermeneutic and practical approach to the study of world politics, an openness to history, meaning and action that had been piously effaced by constant appeals to instrumental rationality and social science.

Drawing on distinctions elaborated in the previous chapter, I am concerned here to explore the opportunities opened up by this specific confrontation between structuralist and historicist forms of political realism. Political realism, I suggest, must be understood less as a coherent theoretical position in its own right than as the site of a great many contested claims and metaphysical disputes. Whether situated against the early-twentieth-century crisis of historicism, analysed as a reworking of dilemmas originating between Judeo-Christian and Hellenic civilisational impulses, or taken as yet another benighted footnote to dualisms inherited from classical Greek philosophy, claims to political realism in the theory of international relations carry meanings and implications from a much broader discourse about politics and philosophy. In all these contexts, the conceptualisation of 'change', and the differential treatment of historicity and temporality inside and outside the sovereign state, has been crucial.

The interest in change among analysts of international politics[7] does raise a number of daunting theoretical and philosophical problems. John Vincent was undoubtedly right to warn us that the study of change in the abstract, without some idea of what it is that is supposedly changing, is a rather fruitless exercise. It does not help us to *know* very much, if anything.[8] Yet the plain common sense of this view depends primarily on an epistemological interest. Again, however, many other complex issues are at stake here, puzzles that have more of an ontological than an epistemic character. Moreover, to speak of change at all, whether abstractly or with reference to some particular social process, is to do so within historically specific theoretical and philosophical categories. We have become especially attached to treating stasis and change, being and becoming, or structure and history as mutually exclusive oppositions. These oppositions are central to the claims, metaphysical disputes and reifications around which our understanding of political realism has coalesced. Claims to political realism in international politics have drawn on quite different and fundamentally conflicting philosophical traditions. To the extent that such differences have been ignored, political realism has become less a hard-headed portrayal of international realities than a systematic evasion of the critical skills necessary for a scholarly analysis of those realities.

Contrary to the prevailing wisdom, therefore, I want to suggest that a renewal of realist interests does not necessarily have to result in yet another rerun of old tragedies. As there is no single tradition of political realism, but rather a knot of historically constituted tensions, contradictions and evasions, it is possible to reconsider the conditions under which certain realist claims might be rearticulated in a rather more critical and creative fashion. Just as it is not necessary to treat Machiavelli as a Machiavellian cynic, or to act on the basis of misleading dichotomies between ethics and international relations, or to delineate research options as a crude choice between rational science and less than rational interpretations and deconstructions, so also is it not necessary to accept the claim that prevailing forms of political realism offer a coherent codification of the conditions in which we must live.

To begin to analyse the problems posed by recent claims about political realism in the theory of international relations, it is necessary to consider how they have been produced within a specific disciplinary discourse. The substantive character of these claims is less significant than the processes through which these claims have been selected, shaped, articulated, legitimised and reproduced within a specific discursive economy.

While it is undoubtedly true that the theory of international relations can be portrayed as a web of fragmented discourses, a mosaic of analyses and commentaries on the global and international aspects of modern life, it is not difficult to identify an entrenched if opaque sense of historical continuity, of important texts, of great debates, of discontinuities with other forms of social and political theory, and so on. The most obvious way of understanding the overall coherence of the theory of international relations is in terms of a series of specific conceptual and philosophical differentiations, posed for the most part in oppositional form: politics and economics, high politics and low politics, science and tradition, rationalism and reflectivism, community and anarchy, ethics and power. All of these dichotomies converge in the grand opposition between political realism and utopianism. As something like a founding myth, this polarity has come to be treated as a relatively unproblematic ground on which major theoretical disputes can be, if not resolved, at least codified and left in peace. Yet this codification, this embalmed substitute for serious theoretical reflection and critical engagement, reduces a vast array of complex historical traditions and philosophical positions to a very simple opposition, as some of the more philosophically inclined theorists are quite aware.

To the extent that the meaning of political realism in the theory of international relations can be successfully specified in any clear way at all, it is less in terms of its substantive claims than as one pole of this reified antinomy. And just as the antinomy as a whole can be taken apart to reveal a much more complex texture, so also the realist pole is open to varying degrees of articulation. As it informs a rather large and influential literature on geopolitics and military affairs, for example, realism has often degenerated into little more than an antipolitical apology for cynicism and physical force. To the extent that deeper roots are sought, the search often comes to a rather abrupt halt with an arbitrary theory of the fall of man or the ritual invocation of some seemingly incontestable ancient text. But beyond this, there is clearly a much more serious struggle with important philosophical issues visible in some of the writings of some of the more prominent realists. The problem of change lies right at the heart of these struggles.

This was particularly the case with writers like Hans J. Morgenthau, E. H. Carr, John Herz and Raymond Aron who all wrote in the shadow of the early-twentieth-century crisis in German historicism. Similarly, in Berki's more recent analysis, the term political realism is taken to encompass a very wide array of themes, with classical, medieval as well as more modern formulations, but it is the general problematic of historicism that forms the main backdrop for discussion. Even the names of the theorists who are taken to be most important for the reconstruction of a more viable orientation – Aristotle, Augustine, Machiavelli and Hegel – are enough to remind us that political realism has to a large extent been informed by deeply rooted conceptions of time, change and history. There are, for example, a number of grounds on which one can dispute the claim that Hegel provides the 'still valid standpoint of political realism, in need only of marginal updating and some terminological revision',[9] but not the least of them concerns Hegel's transformation of earlier concepts of time and change into a particularly powerful vision of progressivist history.

Yet this continuity of historicism and political realism is obviously not all there is to it. Some of the most powerful forms of realist analysis in international political theory draw upon traditions that are less concerned with history and change than with stasis and structure. This should be especially apparent from the ambiguities that begin to emerge once one looks more carefully at those names that are so often linked together as a tradition. Although it is not difficult to find international relations textbooks that conflate a long litany of names from the history of political thought into a simple category of political realism, there is also a fair degree of disagreement about who ought to be included in this category. Even Thucydides is highly contentious in this respect. *The Peloponnesian War* has been mined both for its alleged lessons about the primacy of power over justice, and as a highly moral text, one which reflects a view much closer to that represented by Socrates than by Thrasymachus in Plato's theatrical characterisation of classical debate.[10] But it is with two other ritual authorities – Machiavelli and Hobbes – that ambiguities emerge most forcefully.

Superficially, Machiavelli appears as merely a theorist of cynical and pragmatic power politics, a codifier of maxims for the tyrant, the enemy of morality. In this guise he may be famous but he is without much theoretical importance. A closer analysis recognises a number of tensions that undermine this reading, not least the differences between the *Prince* and his other writings, and the distinction between *virtù* and wickedness in chapter 8 of the *Prince* itself. Hence the scholarly focus on Machiavelli's subversion of the universalistic conventions of his age, whether this is framed as a distinction between morality and politics, between two different but equally ultimate forms of morality, or as the assertion of the autonomy of politics, a fundamental reversal of priorities in the sundered world of St Augustine. Contrary to those who seek to flee from politics into the world of forms or the City of God, Machiavelli appears as someone who is prepared to take seriously the world of fleeting impressions, of flux, becoming, and illusions. Political reality is then seen to have been rescued from its subordination to eternity and transcendence. It becomes redefined in terms of time: time as the context of political life; temporal images as the source of new vocabularies of political thought within a discourse dominated by universals; and maxims about how to cope with time, change and illusions as the distillation of political knowledge. Even where he appeals to the possibility of fixing political life within a spatial form – *lo stato* – it is a spatial form with its own temporal contingency. At best, he appeals to the possibility of establishing a temporary home for man, one that even the greatest efforts of republican *virtù* are unable to insulate from inevitable decay over time.

In taking its cue from such a reading of Machiavelli, political realism resonates with all those other discourses that have also given priority to temporality, to difference through time, and which have also attracted the indictment of relativism. The Sophistic movement has become paradigmatic in this respect, but it is the historicists of late-nineteenth-century Germany who have been most important for the specific forms of political realism that have been influential in modern international relations theory. Temporality became history. History became the cunning of reason. But by the late nineteenth century, the cunning of reason no longer seemed persuasive. History collapsed into historicism, and the stress on temporality and process once again generated the spectre of relativism. Whether in terms of the Nietzschean challenge to prevailing theories of progress, or of the barbarities of a war to end all wars, the seminal sources of realism in international political theory were acutely aware that the clash between philosophies of history grounded in Enlightenment optimism and their radical rejection constituted the starting point for almost any serious discussion of politics. International relations provided a particularly compelling case for despair, but the general problematic had a much wide application.

Resistance to this trend took many forms, including the various attempts to re-establish the ground for epistemology in different genres of neo-Kantian natural science. From the point of view of international relations theory, however, the most interesting move was to take the nation-state – the German nation-state in particular – as the absolute value by which the dilemmas and mysteries of relativism could be resolved. As I have suggested earlier, the most important figure here has been Max Weber. Morgenthau did not explicitly acknowledge his debt to Weber until late in life. Aron's writings are rather more explicit, and reflect his own influential interpretations of Weber's nationalism and power politics. Similarly, Carr's influential formulation of the realism-utopian polarity is strongly influenced by Karl Mannheim's struggles with historicism, which in turn drew on the quite different responses to this issue made by Weber and Georg Lukacs.

In short it is not difficult to trace the Machiavellian thematic as a major current in contemporary international political theory to the crisis of German historicism. The sometimes visible angst and despair that in part elevates the classic realist texts to something more than tracts for the times flows from a rich and complex heritage. Their attack on idealism and utopianism is to be understood not only in terms of the limits of universalist aspirations in foreign policy and world affairs, but also, and perhaps even more fundamentally, in terms of the wholesale challenge to Enlightenment thought that historicism represented. Of course, this particular form of historicism must be understood within its own specific historical (Cold War) context. But there is also some kind of continuity here with the challenge to universalist pretentions represented by a Machiavelli.

If it is *this line* of continuity that is understood to be the core of the realist tradition in international political theory, then the problematic of change, time and becoming is in fact constitutive of the realist position itself. In fact, this is not the only line of continuity that can be identified. A rather different set of ideas is often implied by an appeal to political realism, one linked less to Machiavelli than to Thomas Hobbes. Hobbes has been the subject of a rather large recent literature in international political theory, and there is a commonly identified 'Hobbesian tradition' in this field, even though Hobbes himself wrote very little explicitly on international politics as such.

The usual focus is inevitably on the proposition that relations between states are analogous to the relations between individuals in Hobbes' state of nature. Hedley Bull, for example, has reiterated the feeling that we are 'entitled to infer that all of what Hobbes says about the life of individual men in the state of nature may be read as a description of the condition of states in relation to one another'.[11] On this account, states are led to war because of competition for material possessions, mistrust, fear, and the pursuit of glory, with fear being the prime motive in that it supposedly leads to a concern to secure what we already have. In this 'international state of nature', there is, therefore, only the natural right of self preservation among equals.

But Hobbes has not been accepted as an authentic realist without considerable equivocation. To begin with, there are the general problems that there is a good deal more to Hobbes than his evocation of a state of nature, and that his overall position is susceptible to radically different interpretations. But even those who are content to stress the state of nature argument acknowledge that there are some problems in applying it to international politics. After all, Hobbes does remark that war between sovereigns is relatively tolerable: 'there does not follow from it, that misery which accompanies the liberty of particular men'. Indeed the institution of the contract itself implies that relations between states are *necessarily* quite different from relations between individuals. Thus it can be argued that states are less vulnerable than individuals and cannot be so easily removed with a single blow. The sovereign is able to make reasonable calculations about relative strategic forces, and can at least ensure some security from the subjects for whom he is the source of justice and right. The state of war can even stimulate the domestic economy and thus in some way 'improve' life in civil society. Furthermore, the central assumptions of Hobbes' state of nature concern the autonomy and equality of the individuals in it, an assumption which makes little sense in the international context where inequality and hegemony, in the form of the prerogatives and obligations of 'great powers', is itself seen as a principle of order.

It is possible to go even further with this line of reasoning. Given that states are not as vulnerable as individuals, prudence and fear suggest not the necessity of a global Leviathan but the need for some rules of co-existence; principles of sovereignty and non-intervention, for example, or mechanisms like the balance of power. In teasing out these themes, Hobbes begins to slide out of the realist camp and becomes a prime example, like Bull himself, of a theorist of interstate society, rather than of interstate anarchy. But there is more to it than even this degree of ambiguity. In moving away from the early chapters of *Leviathan*, away from the predicament of fallen man in a competitive proto-capitalist universe, it is the discontinuity with the position associated with Machiavelli that becomes most striking. It is perhaps enough to recall only his nominalism, his contractarian legalism, and his concern to distinguish between legitimate and illegitimate power in order to come to the position that Hobbes offers a vision of politics

111

which is in many ways directly opposed to that offered by Machiavelli.[12] To place them both in some undifferentiated category of political realism is seriously misleading, particularly with respect to the issue of change. For here Hobbes has become an archetype of those thinkers for whom time and change constitute a problem to be overcome, not by learning to live with the times as with Machiavelli, but by attempting to abandon time entirely. The image of the state of nature does draw on a view of politics posed in terms of the despair of man in time. But the geometrical method, the appeal to reason and to artifice based on reason, the concern with order, the archetechtonic impulse which gives the *Leviathan* such rhetorical power, are all informed by a spatial and structuralist consciousness. The historicity of the contract is one of the perennial puzzles associated with Hobbes' argument. It is even possible to trace Hobbes' gradual abandonment of history, the contrast between the introduction to his translation of Thucydides and his treatment of memory and the past in the early chapters of *Leviathan* being particularly interesting in this respect.

The interpretation of writers like Machiavelli and Hobbes is a notoriously difficult enterprise, and the contrast being drawn here is admittedly rather crude and schematic. The intention is merely to suggest that *if* both Machiavelli and Hobbes are still to be understood as archetypal realists, then it is at the very least necessary to recognise that the issue of change enters into their analysis in quite distinct ways. This is not just a specific contrast between Machiavellian *fortuna* and a mechanistic or inertial notion of movement, although this is important. Nor is it just a contrast between a pre-modern and an early-modern cosmology, although it is certainly necessary to try to understand both writers in their historical context, both intellectual and political. It is more that where Machiavelli's conception of politics depends on a view of the world as essentially changing and becoming, Hobbes' view is constructed primarily around a metaphysics of being. In this sense the realist tradition of international political theory has managed to encompass one of the deepest rifts within Western thought since the classical period. This rift underlies many of the contrasts that are to be found in the recent literature on realism in international relations. It lies at the heart of the debate about the poverty of neo-realism. The appropriate response to this debate, therefore, is neither to insist on some reified catechysm of classic texts nor to engage in polemics as to who is the legitimate heir of the more 'authentic' tradition. It is rather to begin unpacking the assumptions and contradictions which lie buried in the claim to political realism itself.

112

Realisms, histories, structures

There is hardly a theoretical orientation in the modern human sciences that has not been chastised for its conservative bias, for its neglect of change and its consequent reification of the status quo. The argument has usually turned on the inadequacy of some particular understanding of the nature of change, especially those which have been rooted in analogies drawn from the physical or biological sciences. The history of modern social and political thought can be partly written as a review of how specific images, metaphors and models from, say, physics or theories of biological evolution have guided analyses of social and political change. International relations theory has been particularly susceptible to mechanistic analogies, not least in balance of power theories and in the versions of systems analysis that have been influential in this discipline. In other contexts, contention has centered on the explicit stress on continuity and gradual evolution found in so much functionalist sociology and its derivatives.

In the more recent literature on social and political theory, the problem of change is increasingly posed in a much more general manner. Here the distinction between Machiavelli and Hobbes may be understood at least partly as one aspect of the broader contrast between history and structure. The debate is framed not around the merits of any particular model of change, but around the underlying metaphysical principles of being and becoming from which our conceptions of structure and history have been derived. In one form or another this contrast has come to dominate recent thinking about socio-political phenomena.[13]

The main themes that are at play here are complex, but they can be approached, at least initially, as variations on the general problematic of identity and difference as this has come to be framed in our conventional understanding of the philosophical legacy of classical Greece. Things in a class are different, but as a class they are similar. Hence the problem of universalism and pluralism. From the paradigmatic formulations of Athens to the recurring rationalisms that have dominated so much 'Western thought', this antinomy has provided the most fundamental criterion for distinguishing between truth and error, reality and illusion, beauty and ugliness, or good and evil. The general problem has a more specific version: all things become other than they were, yet remain somehow enduring. The problem of identity is raised in terms of time and change. It is with Plato in particular that we conventionally locate the crystallisation of a fundamental difference between metaphysical universals and a realm of becoming, between being and being-in-the-world, the latter having identity and reality only through participation in the former.

This momentous formulation of a radical opposition between eternity and history, between identity and difference in time, continues to haunt contemporary social and political theory in its search for new horizons. Here structuralism, like the great Cartesian and Kantian rationalisms before it, has inherited the claim to transtemporal, transspatial abstract universalisms. Structural invariants are distinguished from the mere succession of events. In the more extreme versions we then get a vision of the synchronic structure of universal mind in which the lived meaning of history is excluded. Not surprisingly, it is just this lived meaning of history that is then championed as the alternative ground on which to construct, and reconstruct, a more appropriate account of human affairs. In some forms, history itself becomes the antithesis of structure; Hegelian or post-Hegelian temporality opposes the atemporal structuralisms of Kant. In other forms, the stress is on the historically constituted *meaning* of human experience, and hermeneutics or understanding comes to oppose the reifying methodologies of positivistic science. In some variations on this theme, accounts of lived histories are articulated as theories of conscious human actions, of a realm of greater or lesser degrees of freedom circumscribed by more or less determining structural conditions. More recently, structuralism has mutated into post-structuralism. The absolute priority of universal structure has given way to the priority of spatio-temporal process, of 'trace' and *'différance'*, to use Jacques Derrida's terms.[14] Whether on the ground of history, meaning, praxis, or the deconstruction of Western 'logocentricism', modern social and political theory has become intimately concerned with the dilemmas and horizons set up by a discourse about change organised as a specific form of an opposition between identity and difference.

Neither the more arcane intricacies of contemporary debate about structure and history, nor even the more familiar problems of interpreting long dead political thinkers are usually of much interest to analysts of modern world politics. Both enterprises seem, and in some senses certainly are, remote and abstract, divorced from the pressing concerns of state policy and global conflict. Yet in another sense, the very refusal to take the issues that arise from these two contexts seriously is of at least some minor significance in the processes through which the 'reality' of modern international politics has come to be constituted, and continues to be reproduced. The key themes here are usually addressed in relation to the concept of ideology, a notable and telling absence from almost all theories of international relations except as a simple descriptive synonym for 'doctrine'.

Insofar as it is a critical category, rather than a descriptive term, our understanding of ideology is also rooted in the underlying problematic of identity and difference. The truth of the one is opposed by the illusions of difference, whether of the many or of the realm of becoming. Hence many of the characteristic moves of ideology-critique. From one direction, the standpoint of the one, of identity, can be used to judge the illusory nature of the plural world of change. This is the typical pose of rationalism, structuralism and positivistic science. Here the analysis of change tends towards a reification into ahistorical and universal laws. From another direction the claim to universality is itself challenged as a mere parochialism, whether in space or in time. Here the many critiques of Enlightenment conceptions of science or Marx's critique of the pretentions of the bourgeois economists are fairly typical. These moves are central to the tension between structuralism and historicism in modern social and political theory. Structuralist positions generally aspire to scientific status, to ahistorical laws and explanations. Historicist positions lean towards the categories of hermeneutics and practice. For post-structuralists, of course, the real problem is the prior framework in which truth and illusion are assumed to guarantee each other.

Structuralism and neorealism

These issues are crucial for current controversies over the latest revamping of political realism in the analysis of international affairs. For all that Ashley's critique of neorealism appealed to some of the most recent currents in modern social and political theory, the underlying themes are quite old. And for all that Ashley's position has become highly controversial, most of the points he made draw on familiar conventions.

Ashley objects to the newer forms of realism on a variety of grounds, but the main ones have to do with the 'structuralist turn' that informs writers like Waltz and Gilpin. It is not only that an appeal to structures has been used to overcome perceived problems with older traditions informed by historicism, 'the subjectivist veils and dark metaphysics of classical realist thought'. It is also that this structuralism has come in highly specific forms. These either compromise the coherence of structuralist principles as such, as with the ontological priority given to the state, which results in an 'atomist' or 'reductionist' style of structural analysis. Or else they reenforce the static and reifying potentiality of structuralism, as with the use of various kinds of utilitarianism and rational choice theories.

It is fair to say that as a general movement, structuralism has demonstrated considerable difficulty in dealing with diversity and difference. It has been guided by a fundamental attachment to the principles of identity and resemblance. By ignoring diversity and particularity, it is possible to establish uniformity and universality in, say, all human myths. But this has led, for example, to Claude Levi-Strauss' alleged failure to account for the diachronic, and thus the difference between, say, Homeric and Theban myths. The suppression of difference in time is a special case of the suppression of difference in general. It is not that the classic structuralist writers ignore the dimension of change as such. In Ferdinand de Saussure's conception of language, for example, change is something that affects the elements of a language and can thus only indirectly affect the whole, which would then reorganise itself to accommodate disturbances. In this way, even diachrony can be studied synchronically. The history of a system is itself treated as a system. History is turned into structure. Becoming is subordinated to being. Or else, change becomes a radical discontinuity, a leap from structure to structure without any benefit from the cunning of reason. This latter conception of change and history is indeed not without interest, especially insofar as it challenges the familiar stories of progressive historical development and the cumulative nature of science.[15] But it is interesting precisely because it focuses on the highly problematic nature of the relationship between structure and history. It generates a philosophical puzzle rather than a scientific posture.

Kenneth Waltz's approach to international systems is resolutely concerned with structural continuity. Diachrony is studied synchronistically; process is a matter of ongoing relations constrained by structure. As long as the analysis is primarily concerned with the abstract modelling of continuity, this is perhaps as it should be. Critical attention can then be directed to the substantive contributions of the particular structural models that are employed. Except, of course, as John Ruggie correctly – but rather politely – points out with specific reference to Waltz's work, what can be a useful methodological principle turns into a rigid ontology.

The most decisive part of Ruggie's critique is that the structures that Waltz treats as continuous are in fact a product of historical discontinuity. For Waltz it is the structures of differentiation that are themselves understood as having identity through time. For Ruggie on the other hand, it is the form taken by this differentiation that has changed

116

radically. On this argument, the pattern of political differentiation in post-Renaissance Europe is historically specific. It took the form of a double movement of territorial exclusion. In the political theory of civil society we can find a fairly sharp textural expression of this in the chapter on property in John Locke's *Second Treatise*. In the theory of international relations, a parallel appears in the consecration of secular sovereignty in, say, the Treaty of Westphalia or the writings of Emmerich de Vattel. Each of these reflect moments in a longer process. Each participates in a restructuring of political space, a transformation in the mode of differentiation, a reconstruction of the relationship between universal and plural. Legitimations of identity gave way to legitimations of difference, with difference here becoming a matter of absolute exclusions. The principle of identity embodied in Christian universalism was challenged by the principle of difference embodied in the emerging territorial state. This was perhaps not much more than a change in emphasis. But this change in emphasis had enormous repercussions. From then on, the principle of identity, the claim to universalism, was pursued within states. International politics became the site not of universalistic claims but the realm of difference itself. Here lies the essential ground of the relationship between the political theory of state and civil society and the theory of relations between states ever since. Here also lies the point at which it becomes possible to understand the specific emergence of the modern state as the crucial mediator between the claims of identity and those of difference.

Not the least of the implications of this double movement in Renaissance and early-modern Europe is the emergence of the modern form of the state. And not the least significant characteristic of Waltz's analysis is the absence of any serious theory of the state. It offers merely something like a theory of the structures of oligopolistic competition in which states become 'units' and units become synonymous with firms operating within some kind of market. This analogy may affirm an understanding of the state as little more than a territorial entity possessing some kind of 'capability', but it is not a convincing portrayal of the central feature of modern political life. It is precisely because of a refusal to come to terms with the historical specificity of the state, and particularly with its participation historically in both political and economic activity, that structuralist forms of realism are so prone to portray the state in such an empty fashion. Waltz, and all those who would understand such phenomena only from within a structuralist analysis, confront historically specific patterns of identity and difference on the ground of identity alone. Moreover, it is the pattern of differentiation that is treated as having identity through

117

time. Difference itself is elevated to a permanent ontological principle. Structuralism becomes a philosophy of eternity, and eternity becomes history as a form of forgetting. The most appropriate critical image here is less the returning ghost of old revolutions than the 'unimaginative conceits of the eighteenth-century Robinsonades'.[16]

To understand how structuralism reflects the heritage of the philosophy of identity is thus to grasp the close connections between the structuralist emphasis on continuity, the typical critique of structuralist theories on the grounds of difference in general and difference through time in particular, and the critique of structuralism in terms of its capacity for ideological mystification. Much of the debate about the 'poverty of neorealism' is then appropriately understood as yet another replay of a venerable theme. This debate is important not for its novelty but for its potential for opening out this knot of reified metatheoretical controversies. It is not that these controversies have been entirely ignored within the theory of international relations. Rather, they have been subjected to partial resolutions through which the need for further consideration is put into abeyance. Two strategies have been particularly important here. They might be called the strategy of ambivalent juxtaposition and the strategy of reductionism respectively.

One form of ambivalent juxtaposition has characterised much of the literature that has been heavily indebted to positivistic and behaviouristic conceptions of scientific method, especially in the context of claims about 'ethics and international relations'. On the one hand, claims are made about pluralism, difference and conflict as the characteristic values of the modern interstate order. On the other, we find an epistemology that, in its claim to a universalistically designated model of science, affirms the principle of identity. The desire to resolve this rather fundamental contradiction can be traced back at least as far as Weber. But where Weber struggled with this dilemma, the neorealist or systems-analytic emphasis on the identity of structures of difference through time becomes an effective way of ignoring it. The pluralist or historicist moral theory then becomes a mere backdrop to theories framed in quasi-positivistic terms. Moral relativism is resolved in epistemological certainties. As with the Hobbesian model of the state of nature and utilitarian models of rational choice, an appeal to science legitimises the transformation of radical pluralism into an eternal theory of human behaviour.

Some of Robert Gilpin's work provides a particularly interesting example of ambivalences of this kind. While it shares some of the structuralist predispositions of Waltz, it is also full of historical insight, is deeply influenced by writers associated with historicist traditions, and is quite modest in its appeal to positivist method. Difficulties arise not only from the invocation of a particularly narrow conception of micro-economic theory and rational choice and the resigned 'pessimism regarding moral progress and human possibilities'. He also tends to define realism so as to reify it into a single (and even arbitrary) category and thus to rule out any serious discussion of the assumptions and contradictions which are thereby covered over. This is particularly the case in his response to Ashley's critique.[17] Here Thucydides, Machiavelli and Carr all miraculously become 'scientists', as if neither the highly problematic nature of our understanding of science nor the methodological intricacies of anachronism are of any real concern. That Morgenthau's writings exhibit two quite distinct tendencies – historicist and structuralist-positivist – in different texts is seen not as raising any problems about the intellectual coherence (and ideological consequences) of Morgenthau's work, but precisely as evidence of the unproblematic nature of the category of realism. Treated in a more limited way -- as specific hypotheses about specific historical structures – many of Gilpin's analyses are quite suggestive. But they do not by themselves necessarily lead either to an Augustinian metaphysics of earthly despair or to a thesis about international politics as a realm of inevitable, though cyclic recurrence. Where Waltz exhibits a fairly consistent attachment to various forms of structuralism, Gilpin exhibits an eclectic attachment to both structuralism and historicism. Contrary to his explicit appeal to a single realist tradition, his own intuitions and commitments point to a complex set of problems and the need for a much more critical appraisal of what these commitments entail.

The strategy of ambivalent juxtaposition slides easily into the strategy of reduction. One value is reduced to the other. The transformation of forms of realism that begin on historicist principles into structuralisms of one kind or another is particularly interesting in this respect. The flux of human existence is turned into an ahistorical human nature. The groundlessness of human values becomes a Manichean choice between two absolute alternatives: the City of Man or the City of God; the state of nature or state sovereignty; idealism or realism. It is in this context that one can also locate the characteristic resort to the leap of faith. Where the dilemmas of historical contingency have often been at least partly resolved by the appeal to the prince (Machiavelli), the proto-existentialist hero and the nation-state (Weber), or a class (Lukacs, Mannheim), the final paragraphs of so many realist texts in this century simply resort to an appeal to hope itself.[18]

Stated in this way, the tensions *within* realism are clearly related to the issues at stake in the claimed opposition *between* political realism and idealism or utopianism. Realism defends a variety of positions rooted in the affirmation of difference, whether of the plurality of competing units in a fragmented world or the constant flux of becoming. Idealism, by contrast, encompasses a variety of universalistic claims, whether in terms of the essential unity of humankind or the possibility of establishing an ordered global community at some future time. Beyond all the dubious propositions about the national interest, realism does express the important ontological principles of pluralism, becoming and difference. Historicist forms of realism thus confront two temptations. They may try to eternalise the structures of difference in the manner of Waltz, or they may hope for the future abolition of difference and the ultimate priority of the moment of identity. In taking this latter move, many realists simply imitate their idealist critics despite the greater degree of pessimism with which their hopes are tinged.

This formulation of the available alternatives has had a tremendous impact on our understanding of what 'change' in international politics might mean. The either/or choice between the same old game played again and again, on the one hand, and some version of the move towards world government, the centralisation of power and the integration of previously autonomous units, on the other, still seems to provide the most prevalent way of formulating the options before us. Change, in short, has come to be understood in terms of the desirability or the impossibility of a move from difference to identity, from pluralism to universalism, from conflict to peace. This certainly provides a powerful and familiar ground on which to argue that because universal human community is not in sight, the world remains more or less the same. It is an understanding that has been re-enforced by the abandonment of temporal sensitivities in favour of categories that are primarily spatial in nature, as has been the case where the state has been understood mainly in territorial rather than political terms. It underlies much of the ritualistic character of so much contemporary public debate about peace and security.

In the strategy of reduction, time can be turned into space, history turned into structure, pluralism turned into the hope for universalism. Ambivalence is cancelled, and the central insight of historicist forms of realism is lost. The temptation to abolish the moment of difference can thus be understood as part of a larger project of escaping from history; and from politics.

The ambivalences of historicism

These considerations suggest that there is rather more to political realism than might appear from the rather crude doctrine into which it has often degenerated. In fact, the renewed claim to realism must be understood as less a return to a simple uncontested tradition of thinking about world politics than a renewed encounter with complex philosophical and political difficulties. The apparent eclipse of the optimistic or pseudo-idealistic tendencies of the 1970s does not render the analysis of world politics any more coherent. It merely shifts attention to contradictions within the claim to political realism itself. From this it follows that we cannot usefully make any simple essentialist appeal to the given 'realities' of international politics; nor to an anachronistic tradition of great texts; nor engage in yet another 'great debate' between realists and idealists; nor focus only on more purely epistemological and methodological problems. Something more than these conventional refusals of critical analysis is called for.

The most persistent line of constructive thinking about the revitalisation of political realism has been to stress insights associated with historicism, and thus with the acknowledgment and even celebration of difference in political affairs: of pluralism and diversity, of change and becoming. Nevertheless, it is at just this point that the most pressing problems begin. After all, the structuralist movement of the post-war era arose in the context of widely perceived limitations of a purely historicist orientation. The historicist critique cannot simply end with the indictment of structuralism's failure to deal with change, for its innate conservatism masquerading as science or perpetual tragedy. But it is far from clear on what grounds history and historicism can provide an adequate alternative to the structuralist turn. Whether caught between twin historicisms – the cunning of reason and the despair of contingency – or pitted against its supposed opposites – structuralism and positivism – our understanding of history as a concept is, to say the very least, essentially contested. The attempt to place history at the centre of the analysis of international politics, whether as the appropriate ground on which to understand 'change' empirically, or as the key moment of a properly realist orientation, has to come to terms with the terrain on which the dilemmas of historicisms have been framed.

One line of approach to this problem has been taken by R. N. Berki in what is undoubtedly the most sustained attempt to reinject political realism into contemporary political theory. It is especially concerned to preserve realism both from a false bifurcation with idealism and from kinds of realism that themselves turn into various kinds of false idealism. He envisages a more authentic realism not as counterposed to one simple idealism, but as somehow located between an 'idealistic nostalgia' for the past, and an 'idealism of imagination' that sees the future through the abstract possibility of eliminating a pernicious and contingent present in favour of a world that is somehow more 'natural'. The key theme is distinctly historicist in flavour: the importance of preserving a sense of contingency, possibility and necessity in time from the false reifications of the past, on the one hand, and the future conceived as a radical transcendence of politics, on the other.

This historicist emphasis is perhaps even clearer in a subsequent more specialised treatment of the problem of communism in Marx's writings[19] in which Marx's entire project is analysed as riven with a tension between 'insight' and 'vision'; between insight into actual events, secular histories and a communism understood as a concern of actual existing people with worldly secular aspirations, on the one hand, and a vision of moral perfection and finality, on the other. Again, Berki comes down on the side of the temporal, the existential, the dynamic and plural. But in this text Berki also makes a further very telling move that, although advanced in a more tentative and speculative manner, illuminates the central thrust of his overall analysis of political realism. The original ground of the tension between insight and vision in Marx is sought in the 'largest appropriate canvas available, namely in the Western intellectual tradition as such'.[20] The problem that arises here, or course, concerns how that large canvas, how those founding fathers and their message, are to be identified and interpreted.

Berki's interpretation is fairly conventional and focuses on 'the original, primal duality of Western civilisation, namely its *Hellenic* and *Judeo-Christian* components'.[21] In this Hegelian contrast, it is the Judeo-Christian tradition that is identified with the eschatological view of history as the working out of God's purpose, while in the Hellenic view history is identified with mere cosmic movement and eternal return. There is no doubt that many realist approaches to international politics have been defined *against* the eschatological view of history, whether in its theological or secular versions. Machiavelli is often analysed in these terms; it can be seen behind Weber's distinction between an ethic of responsibility and an ethic of ultimate ends; and there has been a very significant neo-Augustinian school of realism that has treated international politics more or less explicitly as a consequence of the 'fallen' nature of life on earth.

Although this distinction between 'Heaven and Hellas' is conventional, it is particularly suspect in its essentialising of the Hellenic option. It obviously clashes with another conventional reading of the larger canvas – the one that has been followed in this chapter, for example – that stresses dualisms within the Greek heritage itself, with the tension between identity and difference playing the central role. To argue that is is necessary to avoid the eschatological transcendence of politics is one thing. To suggest that the Greek heritage offers a more appropriate anchorage is quite another. The return to classical Greece involves not a decision on behalf of politics as against transcendence, but a recognition of the way that this polarity was itself central to the problems posed within the Greek context. The return to Greece, whether to Aristotle, Thucydides or the Myth of Prometheus, offers not so much a path to the solution of problems posed by political realism as a clearer recognition of the historically constituted nature of those problems.

Within a discourse that pits universalism against pluralism, structure against history, identity against difference, the counter assertion of one against the other makes considerable sense. The key mystery remains why this discourse is itself treated as the great unchanging given. After all, the categories of classical Greek philosophy did not spring out of thin air; and our understanding of them is mediated by the interpretive categories of our own history.

However one comes to terms with these large and perhaps intractable questions of historical interpretation, one fairly prosaic lesson can be drawn. The real problem confronting the reinvigoration of political realism in historicist terms is that in opting for difference rather than identity, it is in danger of retaining the prior framework in which identity and difference are counterposed as mutually exclusive opposites in the first place. The major insight of political realism does lie in an emphasis on pluralism, change and difference. This does not imply that an understanding of structures is unimportant; on the contrary, one can readily affirm that much of human existence, international and otherwise, is constrained in highly deterministic structures of one kind or another. But it is to insist on the priority of the historical human practices through which such structures came to be. Difficulties arise not from an insistence on difference as such, but from how this principle has been formulated as the simple negation of the principle of identity. This is why it has been so easy to turn history into structure, pluralism into a projected universalism. More seriously, once difference is assumed to be the simple opposite of identity, a theoretical universe of Manichean dualisms ensues: order *versus* justice; national interest *versus* human interest; international politics

123

versus civil society; community *versus* anarchy. Whether we think of E. H. Carr's formulation of Realism and Utopianism, John Herz's Realism and Idealism, Reinhold Niebuhr's Children of Light and Children of Darkness or Hans J. Morgenthau's Scientific Man and Power Politics, the most influential formulations of the realist position in international political theory all depend on the negation of identity. Whatever insight the classic historicist realist texts offer on particular themes, the overall framework in which these insights are cast offers little guidance for the future. Not only are they texts that are caught within the temporal and ideological interests of their own era. They are also texts in which the essential insight of the historicism of that era is surrendered.

6 THE TERRITORIAL STATE AND THE THEME OF GULLIVER

States and spaces

Although the state has long been the central category of almost all theories of international relations, specifications of the character and practices of states remain especially enigmatic in this context. The worst caricatures of the state are readily familiar here: the billiard ball or black box operating within determinist mechanical systems; the proliferating categories of early decision-making theory; the identification of politics only with the more or less formal institutions of government or the uncritical conflation of the categories of state and nation. At the other extreme, there are finely detailed analyses of the foreign policy-making processes of individual states in which the state is dissolved in the particularity and specificity of institutions, personalities and events. Even apart from these extremes, it would be difficult to argue that theories of international relations possess anything like an adequate account of the nature of the state or the diversity of state formations, or even that they show much concern for questions about the relative autonomy of states from civil society or economic determinations. After all, these are things that are supposed to come from those who are concerned with life within states rather than with relations between them.[1]

This division of labour between political theory and theories of international relations has had important consequences for theories of the state, not least through the reduction of complex historical structures to little more than a point of transition between internal and external activities: between defence and foreign policy conceived as the limits of domestic politics within and the mere relations in which states are engaged without. Despite all the attempts to overcome the institutionalised gaps between, say, foreign-policy analysis or comparative politics, on the one hand, and the analysis of particular societies, on the other, the state still looks different when viewed internally or externally. One consequence of this division of labour has been particularly significant for the analysis I have been pursuing so far. It has especially encouraged accounts of the state within specifically spatial categories, categories that are in principle incapable of supporting a plausible analysis of historical transformation in any context.

Most accounts of the state follow Weber's classic definition of it as the human community that successfully claims the monopoly of the legitimate use of physical force within a given territory.[2] This definition permits and even encourages a twofold emphasis: either on the exercise of power or on the territory in which power is exercised. Most accounts of the state do stress both aspects to some extent, and both are implicated in concepts like sovereignty and property to which the concept of state is closely linked. Nevertheless, there is a relatively clear contrast between the stress placed on the territoriality of states in the analysis of international relations and the more socio-economic traditions that have dominated discussions of the internal practices of states and their relation to civil society. In the international context, the state has come to be viewed almost geographically or spatially. In extreme form it has been subsumed into the cruder determinisms of geopolitics. By contrast, speculations about the state in the context of civil society have tended to take an undifferentiated territorial space as given unless unusual pressures of regional diversity have been strong enough to warrant a specifically geographical perspective on, say, federal institutions or cultural conflicts.

This distinction between spatial and temporal emphases among theories of the state is both fairly straightforward and dauntingly complex. It especially draws attention to both the philosophically contested and politically constructed character of claims about space and time. Without attempting to engage with anything like the full complexity of these claims here, I do want to underline the continuing importance of historically specific spatial metaphors in the conceptualisation of the state, and the incongruity between such metaphors and persistent claims about the speed and accelerations of contemporary world politics.

Most specifically, I will suggest that the familiar realist assertion that the state will obstinately remain the only central actor on the world stage and the counter-assertion, usually attributed to political idealism or utopianism, that the state is becoming obsolete, share the same spatial imagery, an imagery rooted especially in seventeenth- and eighteenth-century ontological traditions. 'Obstinate or obsolete' is a phrase popularised by Stanley Hoffmann in an influential analysis of the literature on the state in the theory of international relations in the

1960s.[3] In a related manner, John Herz initiated considerable debate by making and then quickly retracting predictions about the coming demise of the territorial state in the face of powerful innovations in military technology.[4] Many, if not most contemporary theorists of international relations would now undoubtedly repudiate such formulations. They would certainly hesitate to suggest that states are about to wither away in the forseeable future, although they would also be willing to qualify claims that states are the only relevant fact of life in contemporary world politics. Yet the oscillation between the continuing presence and imminent absence of states is difficult to shake off. It is difficult to shake off not because of any lack of empirical evidence about the complex and multidimensional character of contemporary historical transformations but because a specific metaphysics of presence and absence is so thoroughly entrenched in the spatial assumptions that inform modern accounts of life inside and outside the sovereign state. Even theories of the state that take their cue from theories of history are sharply constrained by the image of the state as a spatial container that is so familiar to theorists of international relations. In fact, the affirmation of the principle of state sovereignty, a principle that expresses an account of the character and location of political community in explicitly spatial terms, has clearly set the conditions under which accounts of historical possibility within states have been possible at all.

Political life occurs in space. So much is at once both obvious and obscure. For ideas of space, like those of time, express many of the greatest mysteries of human existence.

There are many concepts of space. They range from the absolutes of Euclid, Newton, and Kant to the relativities of Leibniz, Einstein, and Lao Tsu, or from territorially derived notions of personal space to the abstract intellectual edifices of contemporary physics. Some conceptions of space are examined at a wide cultural level, others are claimed to be more subjective and to differ from individual to individual. Moreover, there are many different approaches to the concept of space. Geographers, mathematicians, artists, architects, philosophers, cosmologists and mystics all approach the issue from different directions.

Especially difficult problems are involved in disputes about the ontological status of space. We may pose questions as to whether it exists or is mere illusion, whether it is finite or infinite, or two-, three-, or n-dimensional. We can inquire into its relationship with concepts of time and matter, into its intrinsic relation to the epistemological perspectives that have developed in the history of philosophy, into the relation between abstract multidimensional constructions of the human mind and the spatial context of everyday existence, or into the nature and importance of the paradoxes which emerge whatever one's position with respect to almost any given problem concerning claims about it.

Such problems are not the province of philosophers and cosmologists alone. From the phenomenology of perception[5] and the poetic imagination[6] to the sociological and geographical analysis of social structures and practices,[7] it is clear that the analysis of concepts of space cannot be constrained within established disciplinary procedures. Moreover, as Henri Lefebvre has put it, 'space has been shaped and moulded from historical and natural elements, but this has been a political process. Space is political and ideological. It is a product literally filled with ideologies.'[8]

The precise historical development of the most influential conceptions of space is a very long and complex story, one which goes to the heart of the interplay of science and philosophy from the sixteenth to the eighteenth centuries.[9] One key theme is the re-emergence of the neo-Pythagorean elements of Platonism, and the consequent stimulation of a mathematical formalisation of space. Galileo, for example, constantly affirmed that his work was written in the language of mathematics, without a knowledge of which one 'wanders in vain through a dark labyrinth'. In Galileo, moreover, we can find a particularly clear articulation of the connection between the formalisation of space and the formalisation of the subject–object dualism that has been so crucial to the constitution of modern philosophical discourse. The troubling gap between the finite and the infinite that had so preoccupied the medieval theologians finally turned into a straight line between autonomous individuals and the external world.[10] Modern epistemology especially, that patch of puzzles about how the autonomous knower is able to know the known, has been constructed on the basis of an ontology of spatial separation.[11] Galileo himself distinguished between 'primary and secondary qualities', between those qualities that are absolute, objective, immutable and mathematical and those that are relative and subjective. But whether in the categories of Galileo, Descartes or Kant, modern philosophy has since been defined very largely as a sequence of attempts to live with or to overcome a metaphysic of distance, a dialectics of here and there, the delineation of presence and absence in the stately measures of eternal geometry.

This dualistic ontology informs Isaac Newton's basic distinction between true space and apparent space, between absolute homogeneous space and the space of ordinary experience which is treated as merely apparent and relative. For Newton, true space was absolute, 'always similar and immovable'. It was the final expression of the old atomists' void, having been refined along the way by Bruno, Campanella, Pierre Gassendi and Henry More. Moreover, as a homogeneous medium it was describable in terms of the axioms and theorems of Euclid, for the basic assumptions of Newtonian absolute space and the postulates of Euclidean geometry are neatly coextensive. The first postulate, which requires the possibility of drawing a straight line between any two points, assumes the homogeneity of space. The second postulate, by which it is always possible to extend a finite straight line, assumes the limitlessness of space. The third postulate removing any restriction on the size of a circle assumes both the continuity and infinitude of space. The fourth postulate on the equality of all right angles is a direct consequence of the principle of the invariability of figures. The fifth postulate admits the possibility of constructing similar figures on any scale of magnitude. Consequently, and this is the point that I want to stress here, all of the classical postulates of Euclid 'expresses various aspects and consequences of one fundamental feature – the homogeneity of space'.[12]

The spatial constructs associated with Euclid and Newton played a decisive role in determining the cultural forms of European civilisation. This is perhaps most vivid in the one-point perspective system of late fifteenth-early sixteenth-century Italian painting: the beginning of the mechanisation of aesthetic expression later castigated by William Blake as 'single vision and Newton's sleep'. It is no less apparent in the cartographic revolution which accompanied the expanding commercial interests of Europe around the rediscovered spherical earth; indeed, Gerhard Mercator's sixteenth-century projection still provides a popular image of the world in terms of the mathematical space of Euclidean geometry.[13] It is in precisely this historical–intellectual context that we can see the emergence in post-Renaissance Europe of the linkage between ideas of state sovereignty and a sense of inviolable and sharply delimited space. This context is often stressed by geographers, particularly those given to cross-cultural comparisons. Edward Soja, for example, once wrote about the Western bias of rigidly compartmentalised political space and has also linked it to the treatment of pieces of territory as commodities in a marketplace, a linkage that finds its paradigmatic textual expression in John Locke's legitimation of private property on the basis of a labour theory of value.[14] As Soja describes it, the conventional Western political map is highly linear, incredibly precise (at least in appearance), partitioned into distinct parcels, and continuous in the sense that, with only a few exceptions (generally involving unpopulated areas), it is entirely 'filled'. Moreover, the separate compartments are perceived as being imbued with a sense of independent integrity and internal homogeneity. The world becomes, in the popular Western image, a rigid mosaic resembling not only local property patterns but suggesting what are understood to be the well-defended and clearly demarcated cells identified in some studies of animal territoriality.[15]

Similarly it is rather striking that Ernest Gellner, whose explanations of nationalism focus almost entirely on its social rather than its cultural or territorial roots, has nevertheless been drawn to spatial metaphors taken from different styles of modern painting. The age prior to the rise of nationalism is compared with the works of Oskar Kokoschka:

> The riot of diverse points of colour is such that no clear pattern can be discerned in any detail, though the picture as a whole does have one. A great diversity and plurality and complexity characterizes all distinct parts of the whole: the social groups, which are the atoms of which the picture is composed, have complex and ambiguous and multiple relations to many cultures; some through speech, others through their dominant faith, another still through a variant faith or set of practices, a fourth through administrative loyalty, and so forth.

By contrast, the political map of the modern world is said to resemble more the work of Amedeo Modigliani:

> There is very little shading; neat flat surfaces are clearly separated from each other, it is generally plain where one begins and another ends, and there is a little if any ambiguity or overlap.[16]

Spaces and hierarchies

Observations about concepts of space, or of time, are likely to seem far removed from the contemporary analysis of world politics. They are necessarily much too general and much too vague, saying little about deployments of power, expressions of self-interest or the materiality of states and states-systems. Conversely, however, the extent to which concepts of space and time do seem so far removed from the concerns of most theorists of international relations might be treated as an indication of the kinds of assumptions that are too easily taken for granted, of the silent ontological claims that permit the confident proclamation of epistemologies and methodologies in the name of empirical science and responsible scholarship. Yet, as historical and social constructs, conceptions of space and time cannot be treated as some uniform background noise, as abstract ontological conditions to be acknowledged and then ignored. Kant may have treated the spatio-temporal postulates of Newtonian mechanics as a guarantee against subjective scepticism, but the bankruptcy of the great Newtonian insurance company in the late nineteenth century has been crucial to claims and counterclaims about the character and achievements of modernity ever since.

The spatial character of modern theories of international relations is most obvious in the context of the territoriality of states and geopolitical articulations of military strategy. It is less obvious but no less apparent in what is undoubtedly the most important categorisation of theoretical options available for the analysis of contemporary world politics, the so-called 'levels of analysis' schema.

This typology is puzzling on several counts. On the one hand, it seems all-pervasive, with hardly a textbook or research programme omitting some reference to its distribution of phenomena that might provide the primary focus for substantive analysis: in Kenneth Waltz's paradigmatic formulation, 'Man', 'state' and 'international system'.[17] On the other, it has been subjected to very little critical appraisal. It seems that the categories are entirely straightforward and uncontentious: after all, what other categories could there possibly be? Moreover, this elegant distribution of obvious categories is usually put forward precisely as a simple typology, and not as a statement of causal explanation or theoretical sophistication. Despite the label, it does not refer to, say, levels of abstraction. Nor, tellingly enough, does it explicitly invoke a metaphysics of natural hierarchy. Waltz himself may be famous for his dismissal of anything except the 'level' of interstate structures, but the typology does not obviously privilege any 'level' over any other. Its purpose is usually understood to be the prevention of analytical confusions that might be introduced by misleading cross-category hypotheses.

Like most simple taxonomies, however, this one has indeed often transcended its humble status to become an affirmation of theoretical and ideological claims. After all, it might be asked, what exactly is a 'level' in this context? The affirmation of the modern state involved a fairly protracted struggle against the hierarchical claims of church and empire. Autonomous sovereignties have successfully subverted the Great Chain of Being. The flat territorialities of states have replaced overarching claims to hierarchical authority. And, in any case, what, precisely, are we to make of all those categories that this typology manages to ignore so effectively, categories of class, nation, gender and ethnicity, or categories based on region and locale? Are they in fact all simply subsumable within accounts of individual subjectivity, or statist community, or international anarchy? Where is there room for an analysis of, say, capitalism as a globalising mode of production or of Islam as a transnational cultural identity? And how can such categories help us to capture any sense of historical discontinuities or temporal accelerations?

The ambiguous sense of hierarchy invoked by the notion of 'levels' is especially interesting. It seems to resonate, for example, with another well-known hierarchical typology through which theorists of international relations have sought to capture the dynamics of contemporary world politics, the classification of approaches to the management of power in international relations developed by Inis Claude in the same post-war epoch that generated Waltz's schema.[18] Claude distinguished between the concepts of balance of power, collective security and world government, all characterised as 'successive points along a continuum, differing most fundamentally in the degree of centralisation of power which they imply'. Balance of power represents the extreme of decentralisation while world government represents the extreme of centralisation: 'an institutional system involving a "monopoly of power", comparable to that alleged to exist in a well-ordered national state'. Within this framework, change is conceivable in one of two ways: either in terms of adjustments within one of these categories, most obviously a re-equilibriation in a balance-of-power system; or in terms of a movement from one category to another, that is, as a movement towards a system of world government. When put this way, this second alternative is easily dismissed. It seeks to create a system that requires co-operation in order to eliminate the evils of a system supposedly characterised by non-co-operation. If it is attainable, then it is unnecessary, while if it is necessary, then it is, of course, unobtainable – a dilemma familiar from the before-and-after scenarios of Hobbesian contract theory.

This way of approaching the idea of change in international politics may retain a considerable popular adherence, but few professional analysts would now admit to taking it very seriously, certainly not as a guide to historical developments. Yet its influence should not be dismissed too easily. It remains most conspicuous in the more institutionally oriented approaches to the study of international organisation. The history of the brief but intense flurry of analyses of international integration in the 1970s could also be written in terms of their gradual and perhaps only partial emancipation from just this delineation of available options. At one point, for example, Ernst Haas was led to comment 'that we lack clear dependent variables because we have followed the practice of erecting these terminal states by treating them as ideal types reconstructed from our historical experience at the national level and then of observing the types of behaviour that contribute – or fail to contribute – to the attainment of that condition'.[19] Much of the proliferation and indeed fragmentation of theories of international politics over the past decade or so might also be understood in terms of attempts to escape from these categories, whether through claims about 'interdependence' or through theories about the establishment of international regimes. In either case, we may have merely acquired new bottles from the vintners of the status quo.

In Claude's admirably clear and paradigmatic formulation, two major features of this centralisation–decentralisation typology take on special significance. First, it simply assumes the traditional distinction between the anarchy of the international system and the sovereignty of the state/civil society. Second, both historical and structural transformations, other than the simple readjustment between competing powers in a quasi-mechanical balance, are conceptualised as a return to the image of the sovereign state, but on a grander scale. The domestic analogy is fixed within precise ontological coordinates. Any movement towards supranationality, or any structural alteration that implies a slight undermining of the state, comes to be interpreted and evaluated in relation to a magnified image of the state.

Again, the fundamental limitations of this typology have been recounted often enough, but one source of its power and influence has generally gone unremarked. For its most significant underlying assumption is precisely that of spatial homogeneity, or what, following Pierre-Maxime Schuhl and Milič Čapek, can be called 'the theme of Gulliver'.[20] At the core of Claude's typology lurks the remains of the classical homogeneous conception of space which is so brilliantly captured in Swift's satire.

Lilliput resembles our human world in everything but its smaller size; Brobdingnag likewise is merely bigger. This theme reflects the conception of the microphysical world which came with classical mechanics, together with its associated Euclidean–Newtonian–Kantian conceptions of space. Microphysical space was assumed to be just like the space of the commonsense world, merely reduced in magnitude. Both this micro-world and the macro-universe being revealed through astronomy came to be viewed within the context of an absolute homogeneous space continuing on without limit. Man, as Pascal and others felt, was assumed to be floating somewhere between two infinities.

Where the age of Newtonian science subscribed in large measure to a preformation theory of human development – the embryo being the same as a fully developed person except for its smaller scale – the modern age has adopted a parallel account of the development of a future world order. Conventional accounts of world politics have implicitly assumed a classical conception of homogeneous space. Structural change has thus been conceptualised either outside time and history, or in terms of a notion of time and history which is essentially spatial, the future being merely a straight line to a macro-version of the present. To the extent that more sophisticated recent research on change in international politics has tried to avoid the seductiveness of Claude's categories, it has of necessity, if only implicitly, been led to elude the classical conception of space upon which that model depends.

Waltz's three categories are clearly at odds with this typology in several respects. Claude's three options are all variations on the theme of power distributions in relations between states, and thus work within only one of Waltz's categories. Moreover, Waltz's own extreme structuralism is not conducive to accounts of historical transformation conceived as an increasing centralisation of power. In fact, by contrast with Claude's schema, Waltz's version seems to both confirm and resist attempts to think in terms of levels and hierarchies at all. The term 'level' is entirely inappropriate, and even seriously misleading in some respects. While there is an important hierarchical dimension to the relation between the categories of individual, state and interstate system in that it suggests a sequence of more and less encompassing categories – many individuals, a few states and one states-system – the categories are more appropriately grasped on a horizontal rather than a vertical axis. They are, in fact, no more than an apparently vertical or hierarchical rendition of the spatial distinction between the state and the international system. Inside, the possibilities are reduced to the usual liberal options: the sovereign state and the sovereign individual. Within this ideological universe, categories of culture, class and gender have been repeatedly excised, and Waltz's typology merely confirms the excision. Outside, there are states in a states-system, the anarchical distribution of forces in space, amenable to structural rearrangement but not to historical transformation. It is left to the middle category of 'state' merely to confirm a line of demarcation. In effect, Waltz is able to both insist on a sharp distinction between politics within states and relations between them and to deploy a universalising account of instrumental rationality that he believes to be equally applicable to states systems, tribes, oligopolistic firms and street gangs. Once again, the privilege of having one's cake and eating it is preserved by smothering ontological contradictions with epistemological platitudes.[21]

Oscillations and continuities

The spatiality of the state conceived as a territorial entity has always been fairly obvious and has consequently allowed for a strong geographical component within theories of international relations. The significance of the Theme of Gulliver, of the construction of typologies and the depiction of historical possibilities informed by concepts of homogeneous space, has been more obscure. But the connection between statist territorialities and this particular understanding of spatiality is important. The homogeneous conception of space has come to have both a 'horizontal' and a 'vertical' dimension in the theory of international relations: horizontal in relation to claims about the relationship between political life inside and outside the sovereign state and vertical in the sense that it permits a distinctive account of both supranationality and future possibility. Consider, for example, the relationship between claims about the fate of the territorial state as a consequence of contemporary technological transformations and the invocation of Kantian conceptions of universal peace as a plausible response to contemporary dangers.

Herz's analysis of the rise, demise and reconfirmation of the territorial state is developed mainly around the relationship between military technology and the basic political unit that is able to provide security and protection in any given epoch. On the one hand there is an analysis of the technological changes accompanying the transition from the small, weak units of the medieval era to the hard, relatively impermeable sovereignty of modern states. On the other, there is a claim that from the nineteenth century onwards, military technology has rendered the territorial state less impermeable and more penetrable. Thus, he has written in retrospect, it seemed that 'the world had become too small for traditional territoriality and the protection it had provided'. The implications seemed obvious: 'only a radical change in attitudes and policies could, in the long run, save the world from disaster'. That attitude would have to be 'universalist'. Consequently, 'that which in earlier periods had to be considered utopian, namely, to subordinate national interests to internationalist ideals, now, with the total threat of demise to all, had itself become an overriding interest'.[22]

In a subsequent essay, the prediction of radical change was severely qualified. The proliferation of new states in the post-colonial era, together with the paradoxical 'unavailability' of the huge force of nuclear weapons as a consequence of the dynamics and prohibitions of nuclear deterrence, led Herz to speak of a re-strengthening of the territorial state.[23] But then, less than a decade later, the original thesis received renewed support. A new analysis, he suggested, 'would have to take into consideration the whole gamut of nonstrategic and non-nuclear factors that now imperil the functioning of states big and small, from food and energy crises to the pollution of the environment in which we live, threats that do not respect either boundaries or the sovereignty of states'.[24]

The oscillation is both familiar and instructive. Technological innovation and the other factors to which Herz refers are clearly very important in contemporary world politics. Technological determinism in the development of modern weapons systems has become a particularly worrying issue. But the tendency to move so quickly from theories of transformation to theories of continuity and back again says quite a lot about the discursive construction of our understanding of the state. It expresses a wider disciplinary ambivalence – both empirical and normative – about the status of the most fundamental category of our political experience. And it illustrates in greater or lesser degree several consequences that seem to follow directly from viewing the state in essentially spatial terms. First, threats to the territorial integrity of the state are immediately interpreted as necessarily implying the decline of the power and autonomy of the state as such. Secondly, alternatives to the state are posed in terms of a simple movement towards more universalist political organisation. Precise institutional structures may not be specified, but universalisation clearly seems to imply centralisation. Thirdly, novelty in the structure of the international system becomes translated into theses about the radical transformation of the system in the immediate future. Fourthly, the fact that universalist forms of organisation do not materialise as predicted, or that the system does not change either radically or rapidly, is taken to mean that everything remains as it always has been. Either Thucydides and Hobbes merely require a few footnotes to bring them up to date, or the globalist millennium is just around the corner. Other alternatives – collective security for Claude, the re-establishment of détente and some kind of minimum deterrence and arms control for Herz and many others – are again locatable somewhere in between, either as the extreme limits of statist co-operation or as holding operations until a world community can be established. The analysis of the state as a particular spatial form turns into the analysis of structural change through a particular spatial metaphor.

136

Herz is a particularly good example of this tendency because of the great significance he gives to the territorial aspects of the state. One might expect Kant to have shown similar tendencies. After all, he is often portrayed as an exponent not only of cosmopolitan universalism but even of world government. And Kant is the philosopher who perhaps more than anyone else appropriated and formalised the Euclidean–Newtonian conception of space for his own purposes, as a pure form of *a priori* intuition. Moreover, despite the impression created by so many commentaries on Kant's politics, and despite the rather fragmentary nature of his explicitly political writings on war and peace, there is a close connection between his general philosophical position and his observations on international relations. His analysis of the movement from war to peace parallels his more general philosophical discussion of the movement from diversity and conflict to unity.[25]

In Kant's moral philosophy, the problem emerges as the realisation of reason through a cosmopolitan order on the one hand, and the realisation of individual freedom on the other. Hence the idea of the categorical imperative, that one should always act as if the principle of one's action were to become a universal law of nature. Hence also Kant's ideal of the republican state, a civil society of freedom and law. It is his rationalist universalism that is central to all this. It seeks to go beyond the earlier positions of Pufendorf and Vattel which accepted the absolute rights of sovereign states, the separation between public and private morality, and thus a pragmatic view of international co-operation. It also provides the ground from which Kant attempted to escape from Rousseau's pessimism about the possibility of transcending the international state of nature. This rationalist universalism is also central to Kant's idea of freedom as the only original right that belongs to each human being by virtue of his humanity. For Kant, the growth of uniquely human capacities through reason allowed for the gradual development of a universal kingdom of ends and the eventual replacement of legal constraints by freedom and morality alone. Thus just as individual men have a duty to move from a state of nature to civil society, so nations also have a duty to pass out of their state of nature into a relationship that is somehow analogous to that which joins individuals in civil society.

It is easy to see how Kant has so often been understood as making an argument for the centralisation of authority in a universal state. Yet he clearly recoils very strongly from any such suggestion in view of its potential for despotism. For Kant, freedom is something that occurs within the state. Consequently, his speculations on the practical problems of international politics lead to a vision of a federation of states, one that presupposes the development of a republican order in all states concerned. It is, to stay with Waltz's categories, a solution at the second level of the state itself, although in this case it is a state that is less a simple line of demarcation than the ground on which the competing claims of microcosm and macrocosm, of the autonomous individual on the one side and a universalising humanity on the other, might be resolved in conformity with the demands of universal Reason. Kant's speculations about alternatives to the territorial state do not lead, as the theme of Gulliver might have suggested, to the need to replace the state with a macroscopic version of the state. Instead, the territorial state itself remains to be perfected as the realm of human freedom. Reason itself retains its identity at the level of the individual, the state, and the international system. The move is from the perfectibility of the individual to the perfectibility of the species, a move that can be understood both as history and as progress, although Kant himself was not particularly optimistic about the prospects and had to resort to the idea that war might be the indispensable means of progress and peace.

Herz oscillated back and forth. Kant aspired to the continuities of universal reason from the perfectible individual to the perfectible species. Within this play of presence and absence, temporal possibilities are fixed within a metaphysics of homogeneous space. The horizontal extension of community within and the absence of community without turns into an apparent hierarchy of eternal categories from which there is no escape. The static character of Waltz's structuralist treatment of interstate relations is already prefigured in the spatial metaphysics of his tripartite categories.

An instructive recent example of the consequent banging of heads upon conceptual walls is provided by Barry Buzan's recent attempt to articulate a more coherent account of security in the modern world.[26] The project itself is undoubtedly important. Contemporary claims about security are notoriously imprecise. Buzan refers to the concept of national security in particular as underdeveloped and he cites five eminently plausible explanations for this. It involves complicated and ideologically laden ideas, although no more so than, say, 'freedom' or 'state'. It overlaps with the concept of power, particularly in the conflation of means and ends typical of so much supposedly realist literature. It was largely ignored rather than analysed seriously by those pursuing methods of empirical social science. It was also ignored by the policy driven sub-discipline of strategic studies. Finally, conceptual ambiguity has been useful 'as a justification for actions that would otherwise have to be explained'. All five forms of explanation under-line the 'intensely political' character of the concept, a character that is readily apparent from the discursive and ideological routines in which it has become so firmly embedded.[27]

Buzan's response to this conceptual mess is to appeal to Waltz's typological strategy of 'levels'. Dispute about national security, he argues, has hinged on which 'level' is chosen for emphasis, contrasting concerns with the state and the interstate system being most important in this respect. Buzan argues, convincingly, that security cannot be divided up in this manner. Rather, it requires a reintegration, a holistic conception in which 'national security' is understood within the broader context of 'systemic security'. In making this argument in detail, Buzan undoubtedly offers a persuasive critique of the fetishi-sation of the military postures and capabilities of states in the formula-tion of contemporary security policies. Yet for all its claimed holism, the analysis remains almost entirely preoccupied with the security of states, albeit a security of states understood within a broader context, as part of some kind of interstate order: Waltz's tripartite categories remain but, on the one hand, his characterisation of the international 'level' is challenged in favour of something more like a society of states and, on the other, some attempt is made to treat the distinction between the national and international levels as more than a simple line of demarcation.

Consequently, but not surprisingly, Buzan manages to by-pass most of the harder questions about the possible meaning of security in the contemporary world. Proclaimed intentions to the contrary, he does not address the concerns of those worried by, for example, ecological breakdown, unequal development within and between states or the manner in which states continue to be the primary threat to people's security in many places. Or rather, to the extent to which these are recognised to be legitimate concerns, they are simply translated into the familiar even if modified routines marked by claims about national security. While there are no doubt persuasive grounds on which to argue that contemporary attempts to rethink the meaning of security must come back to the sovereign claims of state, the categories that Buzan uses in order to introduce greater coherence into contemporary discussions of security are precisely those categories that have pro-duced incoherence in the first place. Oscillating between presence and absence, between inside and outside, between realism and utopianism or between peace and power,[28] the Theme of Gulliver permits no middle ground on which Buzan can build a sensible alternative to contemporary confusions. Taking historically constituted categories

139

for granted, with no semblence of an attempt to understand how these categories have been produced historically, Buzan is left with no option but to rearrange and revalorise categories which gave rise to the problems he is trying to resolve.[29] If the categories are indeed assumed to be adequate, to express the continuing resolution of all political options through the spatial metaphysics of the territorial state, attempts to make them more coherent, as Buzan certainly does, can only be encouraged. In fact, of course, many analyses of contemporary insecurities suggest that such resolutions are very far from being persuasive. Not least, they suggest that attempts to reconstruct the practices of security require urgent attention to just who it is who is to be made secure.[30] If this is so, then the categories that Buzan takes for granted seem likely to be a primary source of the intensely political contestation that he would prefer to clear up. The spatial limits of the state become the limits of theoretical reconstruction.

These limits are no less apparent if approached from the inside, from the perspective of those concerned with the horizons of theories of political life within states. Claims about democracy under contemporary conditions seem as fragile as claims about security. It is to these claims that I turn in the next chapter. The limits of theories of international relations I will suggest, can be read in relation to the characteristic contradictions expressed by theories of democracy, and thus to assumptions about the nature and location of political community on which those theories depend.

7 ON THE SPATIO-TEMPORAL CONDITIONS OF DEMOCRATIC PRACTICE

Cosmopolitan charm and cultivated cynicism

'We are all democrats today', wrote John Dunn in his wide-ranging interrogation of the limits of 'Western political theory in the face of the future'. And beginning the interrogation with the claims of democratic theory, he immediately reminded us of the broadly acknowledged double role of democracy as both a rhetoric of great 'cosmopolitan charm' and a practice that is, to Dunn's sceptical eye, 'pretty thin on the ground'.

> Democratic theory is the moral Esperanto of the present nation-state system, the language in which all Nations are truly United, the public cant of the modern world, a dubious currency indeed – and one which only a complete imbecile would be likely to take quite at face value, quite literally.[1]

Just over a decade into the future horizons that Dunn was trying to scan in the rearview mirror, democratic practices came to seem rather more prolific. Democratic achievements were celebrated in many places over that past decade, but the linking of democracy with the shattering of rigidities crystallised at Yalta seemed especially exhilarating. Entrenched geopolitical platitudes and the rhetoric of infidels began to shrivel – or at least to be redirected – before that most fundamental of all political insights: things change. Amidst the swirling events of contemporary European politics especially, the cosmopolitan charm of democracy became more seductive than ever. After the demolition of the Berlin Wall, the mood was suddenly upbeat, victories were celebrated, and even the most sceptical eye was forced to blink – to blink, but not to avert its still cold gaze.

The great charm of democratic theory – the singular label, of course, should not be allowed to obscure the multiplicity of specifications – undoubtedly lies in its cosmopolitan pretention. It has come to be articulated as the ambition of people everywhere; a relatively recent ambition, to be sure, but one that has become an indispensable component of most claims to legitimate authority and progressive practice. Yet the familiar dissonance between rhetoric and reality (to employ what perhaps should be dismissed as a misleading metaphysical conceit) is amplified by the contradiction between cosmopolitan ambition and the articulation of democratic practices within the particularising and distinctly chauvinistic parochialisms of territorial states. The literature on democracy now assumes gargantuan proportions. Yet to search this literature for insight into what democracy can possibly be given the structures of modern *world* politics is to come up with exceptionally meagre pickings.[2]

We may be aware that international processes have a significant impact on democratic possibilities in particular places, or that particular struggles influence what goes on elsewhere in the world.[3] To take the cosmopolitan pretensions of democratic theory seriously, however, seems to suggest that the term 'world politics' does indeed mean something of consequence: that it is more than a convenient synonym for interstate or international relations. In fact, leaving aside those still familiar attempts to reduce all political life to a universal struggle for power, and despite the prevalence of the easy synonym, modern political analysis is predicated on the assumption that interstate politics and world politics have a radically different character. Something is missing from mere relations between states or nations that ought not to be missing from the more authentically political life within them. Presence and absence, politics and relations, community and anarchy, historical progress and eternal return: such are the spatial conditions under which the possibility of change and transformation can be envisaged and sustained. It is not surprising, therefore, that Dunn's scepticism about democracy is amplified by his even more sceptical reflections on nationalism. 'Even at its most ideologically pretentious', he writes, 'the species has not yet conceived a practical form in which to transcend the nation state.'[4]

One is left to conclude that all the universalising ambition and cosmopolitan charm that characterises modern theories of democracy must be reconcilable with the particularistic forms in which democracy has been articulated in practice. And the character of this reconciliation, one is led to suspect, is not unconnected with the double role of democracy at both cant and achievement. Despite the upbeat mood, the sceptical eye must continue to be puzzled by the current revitalisation of appeals to democracy everywhere given that principles of democracy have been worked out with any degree of conviction only in relation to a particular somewhere – to the contained and territorialised community of the supposedly autonomous and sovereign state.

From one direction, this puzzle might be expressed simply as the contradiction between universalist aspiration and particularist realisation. Consequently, attention may be directed towards the claim of states to be able to resolve this – or any other – contradiction. From another direction, however, it might appear as a rather different contradiction – or perhaps it is just an incongruity – between structures of power that seem to be increasingly internationalised, globalised, in some sense universalised and processes of participation, representation, accountability and legitimation that remain rooted in the institutionalised apparatuses of states. Cosmopolitan charm there may be but, in either case, a democratic process that is cosmopolitan in anything other than charm is altogether more elusive.

The sceptic must therefore wonder precisely how the universal appeal of democracy has been reconciled with the particularistic character of states. If 'we are all democrats today', the evident contradiction between universalising pretension and particularising realisation must lead us to wonder about who this 'we' is that is, today, democratic. It must lead us to wonder about precisely how states have been able to claim to resolve all contradictions so that universal ambitions for democracy have become so easy, so compelling, and yet so intangible in anything but the rhetoric of a world divided against itself.

In this chapter, I seek to explore these contradictions in relation to the spatiotemporal framing of claims about political community and political identity that has begun to emerge from the analysis so far. I am especially concerned to focus in more closely on the principle of state sovereignty and its specifically modern resolution of the relation between universality and particularity. As expressed in the principle of state sovereignty, this resolution already articulates a claim about cosmopolitan pretension and outlines the kind of cultivated cynicism required by a realistic appraisal of the limits of democratic practice. As such, I shall suggest, it constrains our understanding of the possibilities of contemporary democracy. Specifically, it constrains our capacity to imagine the potentials of local, grassroots and marginal practices, as well as our ability to understand those practices in relation to what is going on in other locales and marginal places. Some of the most interesting forms of democratic practice, in fact, depend on a persistent refusal to conform to the spatiotemporal assumptions that have informed the most influential traditions of democratic theory, traditions that invoke a cosmopolitan universalism while cultivating the familiar scepticism, the cultivated cynicism, and the blind eye.

Democracy and political community

To say that we are all democrats today is to recognise that we have not always been so. To try to understand how it is possible to speak of democracy in what are, ambiguously, global or universal terms, while recognising that most accounts of what democracy can be simply refer to particular territorial *spaces*, it is helpful to reflect on the *temporal* trajectories that are assumed by and reflected in contemporary debates about democracy. Democracy confronts us not only as a universal ambition and the partial achievement of particular places but also as an interpretation of history. In this context it is useful to reflect on three interrelated temporal attitudes through which the critique of democratic achievements and possibilities has been persistently effaced.

To begin with, one may be tempted to respond to the immediate moment, the recent event, the momentous breakthrough. The difficulty here is that one can never respond to the immediate moment without inserting it within some broader reading of temporal direction and potential. Most recently, for example, the relative, and remarkable, lack of blood on the streets seemed to induce a massive flow of blood to the head. Seemingly unthinkable events in Europe and the Soviet Union undermined nearly half a century of structural rigidities, thereby scrambling scholarly categories, rhetorical gestures and cultural identities. Among more circumspect commentators, of course, certain reservations are urged. Enormous difficulties remain, as even Gorbachev the virtuoso quickly discovered. Eyes cast on other places perceive the contradictory struggles and uneven developments as usual. Among the more light-headed, however, the interpretation of specific events affirms a triumphant philosophy of history: the conversion of Them into Us (or U.S.), the final admission that freedom and democracy are to be gained only where the magical logics of capitalism and modernity are allowed to cast their spell over time and space.

Thus the second attitude is already at work in the first. Instead of being swept away by the passing moment, accounts of democracy become scarcely indistinguishable from grand visions of Enlightenment and Progress. Once there was a beginning, an origin. In this case the spotlight is usually trained on the mysteries of the Greek *polis*. From this beginning may be traced the seemingly inevitable progression from tyranny to freedom. Once upon a time ... and they all lived happily ever after.

Even so, the usual scholarly objections are never entirely suppressed. The Greek *polis*, most concede, was a rather special, even peculiar place which harboured rather odd ideas about what democracy was supposed to be and distinctly uncharitable ideas about its value. Whatever lines of continuity may be drawn between it and the Renaissance city-state, let alone modern national and bureaucratic states, the discontinuities are considerably more striking. Rousseau, for example, may be understood partly as an expression of nostalgia for a *polis*-like participation of citizens in a civic community, but also as a recognition of the difficulty, perhaps impossibility, of reconciling such nostalgia with the demands of modern society, and not least with the consequences of private property.

Even within modern European political thought, notions of democracy are relatively recent. It may be easy enough to read certain ideas now indelibly associated with democracy back into the classic texts of, say, Locke, Hobbes, or even Machiavelli, but these ideas are usually associated first and foremost with specifically modern accounts of statist political community and individual identity, on the one hand, and to specifically capitalist accounts of property and self-interest on the other. That glib hyphenisation 'liberal-democracy', for example, obscures a complex historical convergence of ideas about the sovereignty claims of state and the right to private property that were anything but democratic in their initial formulation.[5] In a world of prickly, even if only quasi-autonomous states, and of a globally organised capitalism, disputes about whether the hyphenisation is even now anything more than a rhetorical ploy remain central to contemporary political debate.

By forgetting these warnings about anachronism, it is possible to slip from grand philosophies of history into a third temporal stance, one in which democracy is interpreted as a more or less achieved condition rather than as a continuing and very difficult problem. Here the temptation is to forget that questions about what democracy can possibly be remain no less urgent than questions about how it might be achieved in particular places. Ironically, but crucially, the meaning of democracy has become even more obscure and contentious at precisely the moment when democratic breakthroughs are being celebrated so widely. Or, to put this slightly differently, the prospects for an historically specific understanding of democracy seem brighter than ever – to some commentators at least – at precisely the moment when that understanding seems increasingly dissonant with rapid transformations in the structural context in which people struggle to exercise some control over their own lives.

The meaning of democracy has become more obscure and contentious because the interpretation of specific events, claims about grand philosophies of history and accounts of what democracy has now

145

become are all caught up in fundamental uncertainties about the direction and significance of contemporary temporal trajectories. We do want to interpret recent events as historically significant, as evidence of progress towards human emancipation. Yet while victories are celebrated, the sceptic continues to remind us that even if it is true that democracy is becoming a meaningful condition in more and more places, we still understand very little about what democracy could mean as an ambition of humankind in general. Generalising references might be made to 'the people', and brave theorists may try to make some sense of economic, cultural or technical processes that might be encompassed under terms like 'global' or 'planetary'; but to ask what democracy could possibly be in relation to 'the people' in general or to structures of global power is to engage with the great silences of contemporary political discourse. To say that we are all democrats today is to recognise not only that we have not always been so, but that the 'we' that is supposedly democratic remains a very strange being.

Thus, if we are all democrats today, even if more convincingly so in rhetorical flourish than in routinised practice, then we are all engaged in a problematic, in an ongoing struggle rather than a finished condition. Given the enormous literature that seeks to explore this struggle, it is doubtless brazen to attempt to characterise it in any short form. Nevertheless, it may be useful to indicate how some of the most familiar themes that are canvassed in the literature may be framed in relation to what I have so far sought to sketch as the central contradiction expressed by most forms of contemporary democratic theory – the contradiction, or disjunction, between universal aspiration and particularist practice.

Such a framing can be envisaged in three stages. First, we may remember the seemingly perennial contradictions that now characterise most debates about democracy, at least within Western political thought. I think especially of the competing claims to liberty and obligation, on the one hand, and to liberty and equality on the other. Second, we may examine a variety of contexts in which these contradictions have been resolved either as unstable dualisms or as attempted monisms. I think here especially of the familiar pairings of public/private and state/civil society, as well as corollary accounts of governmental institutions and the relation between policy and economy. Taken together, a very large proportion of the literature on democracy can be accounted for in this way.

Third, we may examine the conditions under which these contradictions and their at least partial resolution have become possible. Here, in the most neglected, but possibly the most important contemporary explorations of democracy, I think especially of the treatment accorded to those boundary conditions, those marginal situations through which the contradiction between universal aspiration and particularistic practice is affirmed: the external limit framed spatially as 'security' and 'international anarchy' and temporally as 'development'; the internal limit framed most tellingly as the 'local'; and all those accounts of difference that affirm the sovereign identity of 'rational man', an identity that has, since the European seventeenth century, found such a comfortable home in the great Leviathan that still dominates our understanding of what democracy, indeed politics in general, can possibly be.

A large part of the difficulty in thinking about democracy without falling back into the ruts of obsolete ideological confrontation involves the degree to which democratic theory is indebted to distinctively modern accounts of individual identity as both autonomous and equal. Few people have captured the implications of this radically innovative feature of early-modern thought as incisively as Thomas Hobbes. Precisely because he assumed that individuals are both autonomous and equal (assumptions supplemented by accounts of inherent psychological motives, a bounded competitive arena, and the consequent absence of natural obligations between individuals), he was drawn to conclude that they will be driven to assure their own security in whatever way they can, thereby making everyone else insecure in the process. Thus, as so many other early-modern thinkers were forced to recognise, if individuals are assumed to be autonomous, and not connected to a wider world through the grand hierarchical schemes of feudalism, empire and scholastic metaphysics, the status of their being in the world is radically problematic. The conditions of autonomy and equality, Hobbes saw, lead to anarchy, to a war of all against all: not a happy conclusion to contemplate if autonomy and equality are seriously taken to be the cardinal virtues that democratic practices must celebrate and sustain.

Hobbes' own attempt to resolve this dilemma on the terrain of a contradiction between individual freedom and natural necessity quickly came down on the side of natural necessity. Hence the architectonic legitimation of the sovereignty claims of state. But hence also the attempt to pry open the space that Hobbes left between necessary obligations to the state and the equally necessary 'natural right' of individuals to ensure their own survival at any cost. Hobbes' solution, quipped Locke, merely offered a direct line of escape from pole-cats and foxes into the lion's jaw. In any case, said others real sovereignty must lie with 'the people'. Hence the accounts of consent, participation,

147

and representation that came to be articulated as a way of holding apart, yet also reconciling, the claims of supposedly autonomous individuals with the claims of obligation to a broader collective, the community of citizens, the people, the nation, the state.

Not the least difficulty in judging whether these attempts have been successful, however, is that they tend to shy away from the stunning radicalism of Hobbes' starting point. That is, they tend to privilege the demands of autonomy over those of equality. Moreover, just as claims to individual autonomy have had to be reconciled with the demands of participation in a broader political community, and especially with claims to the sovereign authority of the state, so also claims to equality have had to be reconciled with the dynamics of a specifically capitalist mode of production. It is in this context, of course, that Locke has become synonymous with both an account of popular consent and that brutally elegant legitimation of inequality known as the labour theory of value. Whence we are led not to the antinomies of individual and state but to the problems of reconciling claims to individual autonomy with the concrete consequences of a capitalist political economy. For some, the reconciliation is already effected by the magic of the market, the play of plural interests, the transformation of autonomous passions into a rational collective welfare. For others, such a reconciliation is impossible given the extent to which the labour theory of value both explains and legitimises processes of capital accumulation. Where a Hobbes announces modern political life as a universal condition of equalitarian individuals, a Marx is able to dissect its inner workings as a process of alienation, commodification and class conflict: a process that is merely obscured by the universalising claims of bourgeois reason in general and by the antinomies of liberal democracy in particular.

Torn between the competing demands of capital and state, theories of democracy remain preoccupied with attempts to either stabilise or transcend contradictions that were already articulated with considerable clarity in the seventeenth and eighteenth centuries. For all the contemporary sense of novelty and historical achievement, perhaps the most striking recent trend has been the extent to which hopes for transcendence have been gradually abandoned in favour of those for stabilisation. It is in this context that it is possible to understand much of the general character of many recent democratic struggles. It is in this context also that it is possible to understand the gradual dissolution of the grand opposition between representative and participatory forms of democracy, an opposition which had in turn been incorporated into the even grander but perhaps now even more tenuous opposition between liberalism and socialism.

Instead, three other themes have come to the fore: a plea for democracy as a double process involving both state and civil society;[6] a plea for greater attention to the routinisation of institutional procedures;[7] and a plea for something that goes under the name of radical democracy.[8] While the first two of these are perhaps easy enough to understand and encourage, precisely what it means to call for some other – radical – form of democracy remains troublingly unclear.

The distinction between state and civil society has been subject to all the usual privileging strategies that have become familiar from the ideological struggles of the past century: maximise the state or maximise the market. More recently, the need for processes of democratising both state and civil society has become a pervasive theme in many parts of the world, especially in Eastern/Central Europe and Latin America. Attention is focused especially on the need to ensure the autonomy of democratic processes within civil society from state interference; on the reconstruction of civil society so as to mitigate the worst consequences of economic and social inequality (as with schemes for economic democracy in the workplace); and on the reconstruction of state power so as to maximise accountability to representative officials. Similarly, concerted efforts are now being made in many places and from many ideological perspectives to recover what usually have been construed as specifically liberal or bourgeois accounts of representative institutions. In fact, part of the widespread appeal of democracy, it might be said, stems from the extent to which it expresses much of the most attractive residue left over from scepticism towards both liberalism and socialism as these have been understood for most of this century.

There is little doubt that this new-found confidence in the value of both state and civil society will play an important role in democratic struggles for some time to come. But it is a confidence that begs some rather difficult questions, questions that have been too easily ignored by most of those who are content to understand democracy within established categories, and not treated seriously enough by most of those who understand – in my view correctly – that contemporary conditions call for a radical rethinking of what democracy must involve.[9] Most crucially, the distinction between state and civil society was elaborated rather late in the development of European accounts of political life and depends on the prior affirmation of a specific account of political identity and community. Attempts to trace theories of democracy back into the remote past may be fraught with anachronism. But it is certainly necessary to focus on those early-modern attempts to construct an account of political life in a world of autonomies

149

and separations out of the ruins of a world of hierarchies and continuities as the context in which it became possible to envisage modern forms of democracy at all.

There is thus some irony in the extent to which democracy is now being asked to resolve all contradictions despite the fact that contemporary accounts of democracy express the historically specific contradictions – those grasped by the political theorists of early-modern Europe – that are increasingly resolved in other (postindustrial? global-capitalist? postmodern?) ways. For even if it is exceptionally difficult to say quite what these other resolutions might be, it is clear enough that, in affirming a specifically modern account of political community, aspirations for democracy cast within established accounts of state, civil society and representative institutions also affirm a specific account of the limits of democracy. It is at this point that we confront that awkward and distinctly unfriendly confrontation between democracy and international relations, that queasy confrontation between democracy and development, and that entirely nebulous confrontation between democracy and world politics.

Again, consider Hobbes. Given his current reputation as one of the great figures in an imagined tradition of political realism in the theory of international relations, it is useful to recall once again why he did not offer any account of the international anarchy that is so often invoked in his name. The condition of war of all against all was a situation that Hobbes thought must arise, logically, from his assumptions about the autonomy and equality of atomistic individuals. The state of war between states, however was depicted in significantly different terms: as conflictual, yes, but also as a condition of inequality and hegemony, a condition, moreover, that he thought might even lead to the greater welfare of states, not to a quick and violent end. What is crucial about Hobbes' formulation is not the depiction of an international anarchy but the further sharpening of the distinction that had been already delineated in relation to both the *polis* and the Renaissance city-state: the distinction between an authentic political community within and an absence of community between states. Within, the problem is posed as the possibility of moving from anarchy to community in a moment of contract. Without, neither the problem nor the solution is of much concern at all. In this context, therefore, Hobbes becomes especially interesting as part of a broader attempt to reconcile claims to political community with claims to a more broadly conceived humanity. With Hobbes, the reconciliation is developed internally. The hope that it might be developed externally is largely abandoned to the moral philosophers, to all those who would speak the truth about the universal integrity of humanity to the fractured politics of citizens and states.

In effect, the legitimacy of the modern state depends in the final instance on the claim that it, and it alone, is able to allow the citizens of particular states to participate in a broader humanity, no matter whether this participation is understood to be a product of mere utilitarian prudence or some more elevated ethical or communitarian principle. The conventional history of Western political thought can then be told as a tale of the different ways in which this participation has been construed: a tale in which reason, history, property, nation and, not least, democracy, have featured as prominent heroes. The conventional theory of international relations, by contrast, is told as a tale of tragedy and power politics, a story that delineates the very precise limits within which claims to citizenship can be reconciled with claims to humanity. The state itself may be understood as a site of potentially perfect rationality, but as a Hegel or a Rousseau sometimes suggested very clearly, such an account of universality within the particular community implies the acceptance of the necessity of violence and war between particular communities struggling to survive in a states system that is simultaneously universal and particularistic.

This double reading of the canons of Western political thought is itself one of the most interesting features of contemporary political discourse. It is a feature that has attracted remarkably little attention. Yet the construction of each part of the canon depends on some tacit acknowledgment of the other. All too often this takes the form of silence or caricature. Silence is especially characteristic of much political theory, though it is often broken by loud claims that principles of political conduct worked out in relation to communities within states can be simply transferred to the wide world beyond. Caricature is more characteristic of theories of international relations, and is especially visible in claims about a tradition of political realism and the depiction of the state as a remarkably featureless surface.

Any more useful reading of this double canon must begin by acknowledging the mutually constitutive complementarity of these internal and external renditions of the modern state. The 'anarchy' of international relations might then be read as the tacit condition that makes all claims to universality within states possible. Violence outside permits peace and justice inside. Hence the very special character of 'defence policy' or 'national security' as somehow beyond the limits of politics as usual. Defence policy is usually understood in relation to the securing of boundaries from external threat. It is at least as important to understand it as a practice intended to inscribe the boundaries of 'normal' politics, a patrolling of the borders at home, a disciplining of claims to sovereign authority and national identity within.[10] Hence, especially, the points at which restraints on democracy are most easily applied: the invocation of dangerous infidels; the stipulation of official secrets; the delineation of loyalty and treason, citizen and alien, the properly rational or productive member of the community and those rendered unfit by age, gender, race, creed or psychic health.

Conversely, the claim to universality within states becomes the ground against which a tradition of international relations theory may be constructed through a discourse of negation. Against order, anarchy; against peace, war; against justice and legitimate authority, mere power and rules of accommodation; against progress and emancipation, mere contingency and eternal return. The only alternative to negation, of course, turns out to be an affirmation of the hope that someday, somehow, all that is presumed to be possible inside may be extended to the outside – a hope that is constantly deferred, and indeed can only be specified as a condition of its own impossibility in anything other than the bounded space of the sovereign state.

From this, it is not too difficult to understand the slide from the limit constructed spatially as 'international anarchy' and the 'enemy' as absolute Other to the limit constructed temporally as the 'primitive', the 'oriental', the 'Third World' and the 'underdeveloped'. In this sense, the modern academic disciplines of international relations and anthropology can be understood as the twin – spatially and temporally deployed – guardians of the discursive boundary between the 'normal' and the 'pathological': the authentic community in which democracy might be possible and the world of strangers and dangers beyond.[11]

The denigration of otherness also has an internal dimension in the privileging of the state as the authentic voice of reason and efficiency through which the 'local' may be absolved of its responsibility and power. In a curious, but even more curiously neglected inversion, the history of democratic practices has involved the celebration of grass-roots participation – much like the celebration of universal aspiration – and the effective erosion of the locale as a place where serious politics can occur.[12] Consequently, in all the great debates about representation and participation or about liberty and equality, attention has been focused on those two abstract sovereignties of the modern world, the state and the individual. The character of the community in which people actually live, work, love and play together has seemed unproblematic and uninteresting, of peripheral importance to the serious business of capital and state. To engage with the local is to be sidetracked into the trivial; to aspire to some broader and more universal conception of humanity is to recede into the mists of utopia. It is not possible to be 'realistic' or 'practical' or 'relevant' in such places. Nor, of course, should one think seriously about constructing a meaningful democracy in such places either.

All of which is to engage in a cautionary reading of what, in so much recent debate about democracy, has tended to emerge as a celebration. To affirm the statist account of political community that was given such a sharp articulation in early modern Europe, and which lingers in the divisions and discursive rituals of contemporary scholarly disciplines, is to anticipate the fulfilment of statist promises through the mechanisms of democratic struggle. In its most recent manifestations this affirmation has permitted renewed hopes for the simultaneous democratisation of both state and civil society. But it also gambles rather heavily on an account of democracy that seems especially problematic under contemporary conditions. What can this account say about democracy in relation to 'world politics' or to 'development' or to the significance of the 'local'? The easiest answers to these questions are still informed by the cold gaze of scepticism, and it is very difficult to see how any other responses can be envisaged.

Affirming and challenging state sovereignty

The problematic character of contemporary understandings of democracy, then, must be situated in relation to prior accounts of the nature and location of political community. The limits within which accounts of democratic possibilities are constrained are the limits of the particular community set among a system of other particular communities. The characteristic contradictions between representation and participation or liberty and equality have been articulated for the most part as if it is enough simply to assume the spatially defined autonomous community, and thus to forget about the broader setting in which self-righteous communities find themselves co-existing uneasily with other self-righteous communities. This is why contemporary thinking about democracy cannot go much beyond the attempt to sustain or revitalise practices that have been associated with at least some states for a significant period without coming to terms with the limits of that historically specific understanding of political community under present historical conditions.[13] If democracy is to be understood as having something to do with 'the people', let alone with the conditions under which the people might be able to exercise some control over their own lives, then it is necessary to ask what the concept of 'the people' has come to mean in practice, and what it might conceivably

153

mean in the future.[14] This is why rethinking the meaning of democracy cannot be separated from a fundamental rethinking of the principle of state sovereignty as the key practice through which a specifically modern reification of spatiotemporal relations affirms a specifically modern answer to all questions about who we could possibly be.

The principle of state sovereignty is less an abstract legal claim than an exceptionally dense political practice. As a response to the problem of proliferating autonomies in a world of dissipating hierarchies, it articulates a specifically modern account of political space, and does so through the resolution of three fundamental contradictions. It resolves, in brief, the relation between unity and diversity, between the internal and the external and between space and time. It does so by drawing on the philosophical, theological and cultural practices of an historically specific civilisation driven by the need to realise yet also control those moments of autonomy that emerged in the complex transitions of early-modern Europe.

As a response to questions about whether 'we' are citizens, humans or somehow both, state sovereignty affirms that we have our primary – often over-riding – political identity as participants in a particular community, but retain a potential connection with 'humanity' through participation in a broader international system: thus we are the peoples of the United Nations. As citizens, we may aspire to universal values, but only on the condition that we tacitly assume that the world out there is in fact a realm of particular states, of other communities each aspiring to some notion of goodness, truth and beauty. The crucial difficulty, obviously enough, concerns whether these notions are different (in which case we get international conflict or, at best, pragmatic rules of accommodation) or the same (in which case there may be reason to be, like Kant, mildly optimistic about a perpetual peace among autonomous republican – or liberal, or democratic – states). Moreover, until such a condition is realised, it is still possible for citizens of states to cultivate a home, a space for politics in which temporal processes might unfold as they should, in which the cosmopolitan charms of democracy may be displayed as ambition, achievement, rhetoric and, sometimes, as problematic.

The resolutions expressed by the principle of state sovereignty have proved to be remarkably durable. But it is becoming more and more difficult to claim that they offer a very convincing portrayal of the conditions that now force people to try to reconstruct the world(s) in which they live (and not, it should go without saying, under conditions they would prefer to choose themselves).

States, it is often observed, have not disappeared. Nor have they lost their capacity to deploy violence on a frightening scale. But this says very little about the continuing capacity of states to resolve the contradiction between citizenship and humanity through claims to absolute authority. Whether we examine the proliferation of cultural identities or the reconstruction of state instrumentalities in relation to global patterns of 'interdependence' and the internationalisation of production, early-modern accounts of inclusion and exclusion, autonomy and obligation, or authority and participation have a distinctively unconvincing feel.

Capitalism has certainly not disappeared either. To change the emphasis in one of Dunn's formulations,[15] the political universality of Marx's proletarians may not have worn very well, but his analytical universality, his insistence that capitalist social, economic and political processes will reconstitute human life in all parts of the world, remains as incisive as ever. Problems of inequality consequently remain with us also, and have to be grasped in relation to global processes that nevertheless seem to elude even – or perhaps especially – the most holistic and totalising categories of analysis. Given that most theories of democracy have in effect attempted to respond to problems of inequality through the mediation of the state, the meaning of democracy in relation to emerging rearticulations of global capital seems especially obscure.

Contrary to those who insist that a state is a state is a state or that it is still possible to respond effectively to capital through the mediation of the (welfare, nationalist, revolutionary) state, the most interesting forms of contemporary analysis begin with the observation that both states and capital participate in spatiotemporal processes that are radically at odds with the resolutions expressed by the principle of state sovereignty. Defence policies may still focus on geopolitical borders, but contemporary military strategies are now characterised by a concern with contracting response times rather than the logistics of extended territorial spaces. Discourses on political economy are concerned with the enhanced mobility of capital in relation to the territorial constraints on governments and labour. Late capitalism is characterised by a culture of postmodernity, says Frederic Jameson. We live in a world of speed, says Paul Virilio. All that is solid melts into air, said Marx: but contemporary accelerations and dissolutions seem to elude the categories of even those who have been most sensitive to the temporal dynamism of modernity. It is no longer a simple matter to know *where* one is politically. Simple distinctions between inside and outside may still provide a basis for rhetorics and chauvinisms but the hope that temporality may be tamed within the territorial spaces of sovereign states alone is visibly evaporating.

Thus, in the very broadest terms, contemporary thinking about democracy seems to be directed both towards the realisation and perfectibility of accounts of political community fixed within the spatiotemporal coordinates of state sovereignty but also towards the reconstruction of what we mean by political community under novel spatiotemporal conditions.

In the first case, we remain within a distinctly modern universe. The options before us are those delineated by Kantian hopes for a universal peace. The early-modern contradiction between progressive politics at home and conflict abroad is translated into an Enlightenment reading of statist *virtù* conforming to the universal moral law. Hence the significance of attempts to defy radical scepticism both about the capacity of states (let alone a system of states) to realise the universalising ambitions of Enlightenment. Here, to take some currently prominent examples, one might evaluate the significance of attempts to salvage a neo-Kantian aspiration for a 'universal speech situation' in the manner of Habermas; or attempts to salvage the humanism of the young Marx's notion of 'species being', perhaps as in some readings of global interdependence or world order; or attempts to do for international relations what eighteenth-century political economists did for the Hobbesian state of nature by translating autonomous passions into a rational collective welfare, as with the recent literature on competitive interdependence and international regimes.

Even so, in all these cases, it is still possible to glimpse memories of Weber's *macht-staat*. In Weber's rendition of statist power politics, the autonomous Kantian community is driven not by universal reason but by the charismatic (and distinctly counter-Enlightenment) *virtù* of the politician who knows – even better than Machiavelli – that political life and universal reason were severed irrevocably by the proliferating autonomies of the modern world. Far from being the grand opposition between two schools of international relations theory, the supposedly utopian aspiration for a Kantian peace and the supposedly realist submission to a Weberian power politics are merely the twin offspring of modernity, parallel readings of autonomy either saved by universal reason or damned by particularistic will.

In this context, the lure of democracy understood as the struggle to make the state accountable and to revitalise the public sphere is certainly understandable. And it is difficult to think of any society in which dissonance between rhetoric and practice is insufficient to generate serious forebodings in this respect. In this context, also, it is possible to be encouraged not only by recent events in some places, but also by revivals of interest in, say, regularised procedures of accountability, the extension of democracy to the workplace and refusals to equate politics with government. On the other hand, it is especially difficult, from this point of view, to see any clear connection between aspirations for democracy and emerging structures of global power, or what might be called – but only in a very tentative manner – world politics.

Kant's understanding of a universal peace, it must be remembered, speaks to a world of states. And the crucial consequence that has to be drawn from the principle of state sovereignty is that a system of states, or international relations, is not synonymous with world politics. If the cosmopolitan charm of democracy is to be anything more than the moral Esperanto of the present states-system, therefore, the Kantian aspiration which now guides so many attempts to enhance democratic practices must be seen as both a possibility condition of but also a severe constraint on the contemporary political imagination. Explorations of the meaning of democracy must be driven to consider other options.

If the framing of the problem developed here makes any sense, it is already clear what this must involve, at least in very general terms. It must mean, first and foremost, a refusal to reify the three resolutions through which our identity as both citizen and human is simultaneously affirmed and denied. It must lead to the most fundamental questions about the relation between unity and diversity, self and other and space and time. This is a crucial common theme of emerging literatures on global political economy, especially in relation to emerging forms of international capital and communications technology;[16] the proliferation of cultural and ethnic identities;[17] the explorations of at least some kinds of social movements;[18] struggles over the contemporary meaning of 'security',[19] 'development',[20] or 'gender';[21] the revalorisation of both the 'local' and the 'global' as places/movements of simultaneity rather than as synonyms for 'parochial' and 'cosmopolitan';[22] and attempts to reconstruct 'modern' conceptions of, say, 'freedom',[23] or 'toleration'.[24] It is also why many of the currents that have come to be known under the labels of the postmodern and the poststructural have been able to resonate so easily with attempts to specify what it might now mean to speak of a 'radical democracy'.[25] But the key resonance here is less the critique of the grand narrative as such, or the celebration of indeterminacy, than a radical scepticism towards those resolutions of identity and difference which, as expressed by the principle of state sovereignty, have become the primary context in which it has been possible to speak of democracy at all.

To dichotomise so sharply between accounts of democracy that affirm and challenge the resolutions of state sovereignty is necessarily to oversimplify. Most accounts of democracy attempt to take some account of changing structural conditions. Moreover, the diversity of settings in which specific struggles for democracy occur is almost enough to discourage analysis entirely. Nevertheless, this formulation does focus attention on two final puzzles, one posed temporally and one posed spatially.

Temporally, we may ask whether this dichotomisation affirms a clear philosophy of history, a move from the modern to the post-modern, for example, or from relations in the states system to some kind of authentically world politics. My sense is that it does not, and that the most interesting accounts of democratic practices are those that have learnt to refuse the modernist choice between evolution and revolution, immanence and transcendence, the rendition of political struggle as the preservation or transformation of all that is.

Spatially, we may ask whether this dichotomisation might become articulated as a choice between centre and periphery, the included and excluded, the serious politics of modern states and global capital and the marginal politics of the weak and oppressed. This, it seems to me is a more difficult and more important matter. The overthrow of authoritarian regimes and heavy-handed bureaucracies does not say very much about it. If modernist and statist resolutions of the relations between citizenship and humanity seem increasingly inadequate, it is certainly easy enough to imagine worse possibilities. Celebrations of democracy may have managed to finesse the problem of inequality for rather a long time, but no serious account of democracy can now avoid coming to terms with the reconstruction of disparities and exclusion on a global scale.

Nevertheless, to continue even to pose questions on the basis of a dichotomisation of spatial and temporal modalities is, of course, to work within precisely those assumptions that are so comfortably entrenched in the claims of modernity. It is here that the silences of modern political discourse become so radically problematic. Any account of democracy that seeks to treat these silences seriously turns out to be a web of barely theorised possibilities and tentative struggles, hardly the stuff of mass movements and startling headlines. However, it does not take too much courage to predict that democratic struggles that do not respond to fundamental rearticulations of spatiotemporal relations, rearticulations now marked more by accelerations and simultaneities than by reifications and separations, can only turn out to have an increasing ratio of cant to achievement.

8 SOVEREIGN IDENTITIES AND THE POLITICS OF FORGETTING

Sovereignty and repetition

The careless embrace of acute ontological antagonisms in the deceptively simple name of political realism. The attempt to fix origins in texts that problematise all origins. The insistence that something called ethics be inserted into politics at an intersection that is already constituted as the paradigm of modern political ethics. The disciplining of scholarly procedures by constant appeals to epistemological privilege. Oscillations and continuities informed by pervasive spatial metaphors. Typologies translating horizontal territorialities into apparently hierarchical levels. Articulations of cosmopolitan aspiration for principles that celebrate the virtues of particularity. Such strategies, I have argued, delineate some of the distinctive limits of modern political discourse in an era perplexed by temporal accelerations and historical/structural transformations. These limits are especially apparent in the categories and debates of international relations theory as the discipline most explicitly constituted as a limit of authentically political life within the territorial container of the sovereign state.

To read theories of international relations in this manner, I have also suggested, is to understand them less as an explanation of contemporary world politics than as an expression of processes they are claimed to explain. As such, I have sought to interrogate the assumptions, reifications and textual strategies of international relations theory not because I hope to contribute to a better explanatory theory, at least not one about international relations, but in order to problematise theoretical and practical horizons that continue to be taken for granted. Better explanations – of contemporary political life – are no doubt called for, but they are unlikely to emerge without a more sustained reconsideration of fundamental theoretical and philosophical assumptions than can be found in most of the literature on international relations theory. Modern theories of international relations mark a site at which critical political reflection has conventionally come to a stop but also one – among many – at which such reflection might now be taken up differently.

Perhaps the most obvious characteristic of the readings developed here is their repetition. Starting with quite diverse literatures and debates, the discussion has kept returning to several key themes: identity and difference, inside and outside, space and time. In this respect, the analysis parodies the binary oppositions that have been so evident in the most familiar texts of the discipline. In part, this parody is intended to draw attention to the extent to which claims about realism and utopianism, or community and anarchy, have been so easily naturalised in those texts, and treated as the inevitable ground from which necessities and possibilities must be engaged. However, rather more is at stake in the constant reappearance of these three themes. Like the reified categories of international relations theory themselves, they give some indication of how contemporary political thought and action are governed and disciplined by a specifically modern account of political identity, the account expressed most crucially by the principle of state sovereignty. While it is perhaps all too easy to criticise the banal dichotomies that inform the discipline's classic texts, it is rather more difficult to respond to the questions to which state sovereignty has offered such a powerful and elegant answer for so long – questions about our political identity as political actors in space and time, about who 'we' are in the space/time of late twentieth-century planet earth.

For all that theories of international relations have attempted to make sense of historical/structural transformation through concepts of international integration, complex interdependence, international regimes, hegemonic stability or hegemonic decline, they demonstrate a marked disdain for critical reflection on the historically constituted claims of state sovereignty. Insofar as the interests of political theory are invoked at all, it is as the familiar repository of already established principles waiting to be applied: hence not only the canonical caricatures but also the kitsch Kantianism that so often lurks behind expressions of faith in modern social science in this context. Yet an uncritical appropriation of established political principles is precisely what cannot inform an account of world politics. The established principles of modern politics are founded on the assumption that a world politics is impossible by definition. The extent to which world politics and international relations have come to be treated as easy synonyms simply indicates how readily this assumption has been forgotten, even among those who are so keen to remind us of the realities it entails.

If theorists of international relations are serious in their claim that interdependence, regimes and the rest do suggest the emergence of a qualitatively different 'world order', then attention to what it means to challenge the constitutive principles of modern political life must be a first priority. The uncritical affirmation of these principles, whether as kitsch Kantianism or empirical social science, as the utilitarian taming of passions by rational economic interests or the high ground of a modern, and modernising, virtue, is conspicuously inadequate in this respect. If it is true that contemporary world politics is characterised by profound challenges to the principle of state sovereignty, whether these challenges are characterised through concepts of inter-dependence and globalisation or, as I prefer, by reference to (late- or postmodern) processes of temporal acceleration, then the theoretical and philosophical assumptions that are themselves constitutive of all claims to sovereign identity are not likely to provide much critical perspective on what these challenges might bring.

It is in this context that I want to conclude with yet another replay of state sovereignty as a discourse that constantly works to express and resolve all contradictions arising from a specifically modern account of who 'we' are. In this replay, I want to pay closer attention to how this historically specific account of political identity is affirmed as inevitable, how other identity claims are marginalised, and what it might mean to suggest that the claims of state sovereignty can no longer effectively resolve all political contradictions in space and time.

Questions about political identity are undeniably difficult. The usual categories and valorisations – of cultures and nations, of passions and Balkanizations – remain with us. Even so, a sense of novelties and accelerations is also pervasive. More significantly perhaps, contempo-rary struggles for particular identities occur in the context of reiterated claims about the forging of a common identity, of a sense of connection in some shared enterprise of production, distribution and exchange, perhaps, or of modernity as a universalising cultural condition, even of rights attributed to humanity as such.

Claims about some common identity convey a great deal about our capacity to imagine particular identities, for a common identity is precisely what we do not have, at least in any politically meaningful sense. Modern political identities are fractured and dispersed among a multiplicity of sites, a condition sometimes attributed to a specifically postmodern experience but one that has been a familiar, though selectively forgotten, characteristic of modern political life for several centuries. This specifically modern proliferation of spatially delimited identities has had sharp limits. The presumed anarchy among states has been an anarchy of the select few. But it is this proliferation, affirmed by accounts of the modern state as institution, container of all cultural meaning, and site of sovereign jurisdiction over territory, property and abstract space, and consequently over history, possibility and abstract time, that still shapes our capacity to affirm both particular and collective identities. It does so despite all the dislocations, accelerations and contingencies of a world less and less able to recognise itself in the cracked mirror of Cartesian coordinates.

Whatever avenues are now being opened up in the exploration of contemporary political identities, whether in the name of nations, humanities, classes, races, cultures, genders or movements, they remain largely constrained by ontological and discursive options expressed most elegantly, and to the modern imagination most persuasively, by claims about the formal sovereignty of territorial states. As both principle and practice, as an expression of a specifically modern articulation of political identity in space and time, state sovereignty is something we can neither simply affirm, nor renounce, nor gaze upon in silent admiration. The Cartesian coordinates may be cracked, identities may be leaking, and the rituals of inclusion and exclusion sanctified by the dense textures of sovereign virtù(e) may have become more transparent. But if not state sovereignty, and if not the anachronistic ambition to perfect its spatial autonomies in a condition of perpetual peace among nations, what *then*? It remains exceptionally difficult to renounce the security of Cartesian coordinates, not least because they still provide our most powerful sense of what it means to look over the horizon.

Sovereignty and historicity

For most of this century, if not longer, social and political theorists have been predicting, describing, analysing and advising policymakers about the emergence of global processes and even institutionalised global structures. They point to the increase in the number and significance of international organisations. They recognise how difficult it is to understand economic, cultural, technological, social or political processes anywhere without some grasp of the international or global scale of the most important forces that affect people's lives. There is obviously nothing strikingly original about, for instance, an international division of labour, or global patterns of trade and communication. But in this century, and especially since 1945, the scale and vitality of globally organised structures have begun to raise questions about the character and significance of the state as the primary focus of political identity, community, authority and power. Multinational corporations have global reach. Information can be flashed to all parts of the world simultaneously. What were once simply nightmares of species extermination have turned into plausible consequences of routine military policies. Whether expressed as cliché or statistic, as computer simulation or graphic image of a vulnerable planet spinning in cosmic drift, contemporary political discourse has absorbed vivid expectations of profound structural transformation and global integration.

Unfortunately, the powerful sense of change apparent all around us is not matched by an equally clear sense of how evidence of change is to be interpreted. Evidence is not in short supply, but neither is controversy about what it signifies. Analysts and even policy-makers use terms like common security, interdependence, international integration, international regime, world economy, world order, or global civilisation to suggest that rules of the game devised in relation to the structural dynamics of the European states system and a world of nationally organised economies offer only a partial or even seriously misleading account of contemporary trajectories. Even where they are more than surface rhetoric or subjected to close theoretical scrutiny and analytical rigour, such terms are much more plausible as evocations of the unknown than as precise concepts of scholarly analysis. As gestures, they signal a widespread dissatisfaction with more conventional terminology and a constant search for more helpful ways to delineate events. Despite reiterated claims about the overriding need for more strictly empirical modes of investigation, many of the most pressing difficulties of interpretation involve gnawing problems of a more theoretical and philosophical character.

To begin with, it is impossible to speak about emerging global processes or the reconstruction of political identities without some sense of what it is we are supposedly moving away from: enter all those troubling questions sheltering under the rubric of the philosophy of history. Most specifically, it is necessary to engage with the politics of origins, with the fixing of a temporal moment as a source of power, authority and ambition, and specifically with the tendency to treat claims about state sovereignty as the initial point from which all contemporary trajectories can be measured and controlled.

Despite all appearances, sovereignty is not a permanent principle of political order; the appearance of permanence is simply an effect of complex practices working to affirm continuities and to shift disruptions and dangers to the margin.[1] Nor can it be said that sovereignty is simply passé as if it were here today and gone tomorrow. It is true that to work with the principle of state sovereignty is to engage with deeply entrenched discourses about political life in which the analysis of contemporary structural change is often formulated as if sovereignty must be either permanent or defunct. But this is to work with philosophies of history that are themselves constituted through claims about sovereign identity. These discourses necessarily place firm limits on how we understand contemporary trends and future possibilities. They inscribe implicit limits in time to complement explicit limits in space.[2]

Second, to speak about emerging global processes is to engage with a realm of conceptual rarefaction. The languages available for discussion of life within states seem to be exceptionally rich. Most prevailing ideologies and political aspirations can – and do – take established ways of speaking about statist forms of political community for granted. By contrast, conventional languages that refer to relations between states are conspicuously barren. This is largely because the character of international relations has been understood as a negation of statist forms of political community, as relations rather than politics, as anarchy rather than community. This pattern of affirmation and negation, presence and absence, identity and difference or universal and plural has left its traces in the sharp distinction between theories of political life within states and theories of relations between them. Again, the conceptual rarefaction that greets any attempt to speak of political identities other than those affirmed by the modern state is a specific effect of the metaphysical resolutions that the principle of state sovereignty works so effectively to sustain. Silence is thereby affirmed in space, in the realm of otherness beyond the authentic political community of the state, just as it is affirmed in time through philosophies of history that forget the conditions of their own possibility.

In some ways, focusing on the principle of state sovereignty may seem like a way of avoiding a more direct confrontation with the literature on the concepts of state and nation. By contrast with these, the principle of state sovereignty has received relatively little analytical attention. Yet this lack of attention is itself interesting. Though relatively silent in contemporary social and political analysis, the principle of state, sovereignty has become indispensable to our understanding of what a state, nation or political identity can be. Indeed, the silence depends largely on the presumption that sovereignty, state and nation are more or less interchangeable terms, terms, moreover, which also give other crucial concepts – like power, authority, community and obligation – much of their contemporary meaning. This presumption is less and less plausible, not only because it conflicts with so many claims about empirical tendencies but also because it has become more and more obvious that it effaces our understanding of the historically constituted character of political life, and of the specific articulation of spatiotemporal relations we have come to treat as the *a priori* condition of all political existence.

The modern principle of state sovereignty has emerged historically as the legal expression of the character and legitimacy of the state. Most fundamentally, it expresses the claim by states to exercise legitimate power within strictly delimited territorial boundaries. This claim now seems both natural and elegant, although it continues to generate familiar and seemingly intractable problems.

Most significantly, perhaps, the principle of sovereignty stands in an ambiguous relation to the claims about power and authority. On the one hand, there remains a strong tradition, associated with Thomas Hobbes and John Austin, among others, which insists that sovereignty is to be equated with supreme power. On the other hand, it has also been conventional to follow Hans Kelsen and H. L. A. Hart in equating sovereignty with political authority. Despite the evident difficulty of attempts to reconcile power and authority within the modern state, however, the most common understanding of state sovereignty presumes that terms like sovereignty, state, power, legitimacy and supreme authority can be treated more or less as synonyms.

It is because of the presumed convergence of such concepts, for example, that it has been so easy to string certain names together as another (sometimes loose) canon of textual reference: Bodin, for whom sovereignty referred to the supreme power over citizens and subjects, unrestrained by law; Hobbes, and the conceptualisation of the sovereign Leviathan within a determinist/rationalist metaphysics, one that definitively fixes a conception of the sovereign state in direct opposition/identity to the sovereign individual; Austin, for whom the sovereign obeys no superior and receives habitual obedience from a specific society; Kelsen, for whom sovereignty consists in a logical role as the supreme norm or source of validity within a legal system; the Wimbledon case, which refers to the state that is subject to no other state and exercises full and exclusive powers within its jurisdiction; Georg Schwarzenberger, for whom sovereignty signifies either supremacy over others (omnipotence) or freedom from control by others (independence); Max Weber, for whom the conventional concept of sovereignty echoes in his account of the state as having a monopoly on the legitimate use of violence in a given territory; and Carl Schmitt, for whom sovereignty involves the capacity to decide on 'the exception that legitimates the norm'.[3] The canon may admit a certain degree of controversy about relations between power and authority or the sovereign state and the sovereign people, but the degree of controversy

165

also affirms the limits within which controversy can occur. Not surprisingly, the most perplexing problems associated with the concept of sovereignty arise precisely when this convergence on a monopoly of power and legitimate authority in a specific territory is challenged, whether on the basis of externality (by other competing sovereignties, which, by definition, are not supposed to be in the same place at once) or of hierarchical conceptions of authority (against which the exclusive claims of sovereignty were articulated in the first place). Not surprisingly, also, these problems tend to become more pressing in the context of theories of international relations, in accounts of a world beyond the secure confines of territorial jurisdiction, rather than of theories of political life that assume that these secure confines can be taken for granted.

Despite the ambiguous relationship of state sovereignty with concepts of power and authority, and the untidy realm of impinging jurisdictions and hegemonic practices in which clean-cut claims about it have been made, sovereignty has been subjected to continuing attempts to give it precise definition. Most would-be definers have fixed upon claims of monopoly. A few, more bemused by the ambiguities of power/authority or the empirical slipperyness of hegemonies and competing jurisdictions, have concluded that no clear definition is possible at all. In either case, however, and like the construction of a canon of classic theorists of sovereignty, the very attempt to treat sovereignty as a matter of definition and legal principle encourages a certain amnesia about its historical and culturally specific character.

The principle of state sovereignty contrasts sharply with concepts of state and nation in this respect. It is obvious enough that the concept of state has developed historically in response to the rise of industrial societies, and thus to the interaction between state institutions and particular socio-economic processes. Nationalism also is usually grasped as an historical occurrence, one linked particularly to the nineteenth and twentieth centuries. Claims about history are also usually indispensible to claims about nation. By contrast, claims about state sovereignty suggest permanence; relatively unchanging territorial space to be occupied by a state characterised by temporal change; or a spatial-cum-institutional container to be filled by the cultural or ethnic aspirations of a people. Governments and regimes may come and go, but sovereign states, these claims suggest, go on forever.

This suggestion of permanence makes the concept of sovereignty appear to be comparatively unimportant in contemporary social and political thought even though it is the crucial constitutive principle of modern political life. Moreover, this affirmation of permanence is enhanced by the paradox that the principle of state sovereignty as a claim to particularity is most frequently expressed in a universalist manner. All states are now assumed to be able to claim sovereignty; sovereignty has become the most basic norm of the international system, however much this norm may be qualified in practice by messy patterns of hegemony and interdependence.

Yet like the concepts of state and nation, the principle of state sovereignty did not appear out of thin air. Though it has become the initial ground of all constitutions of state, it was itself constituted through complex processes which, despite libraries of scholarship, we still understand only imperfectly.[4] Though it continues to inform our familiar world of common sense and political realism, it was once bizarre and radical, even nonsense.

As an historical construct, the principle of state sovereignty has been clothed in a widely accepted story. This story generally begins with tribes; progresses to the Greek city states; becomes complicated with the age of empires, especially in the case of Rome; becomes muddied with the strange geography of European feudalism; flares into life with the emergence of the Renaissance and the early-modern struggle for autonomy from empire; then becomes increasingly refined as the principle of sovereignty is codified, and as the state meshes with the organisation of capitalist economic life, on the one hand, and with the fusion of cultural and social differences into national solidarity on the other. As a story, it is not clear whether it will just go on and on, in which case boredom is tempered with a sense of tragedy; or whether it will come to a sudden – glorious or catastrophic – end when patterns of fragmentation give way to those of integration.

This story is both conventional and controversial, and it is important to remember the usual objections to it. First, it is said to celebrate a reading of history centred on the West, thus buying into the broader tale of progress, modernisation and the rest. While it may be true that states systems have existed before, and that familiar patterns of inter- action and conflict can be traced comparatively, it is also true that the sharp delineations expressed by the modern claim to state sovereignty have little precedent. Superficial references to Thucydides, Kautilya or Machiavelli typically obscure much more than they reveal in this respect.

Second, the story presents a statist reading of the history of sover- eignty and the state. It builds on and reproduces the claim to a great tradition of Western political theory, a tradition at whose core are all those writers from Plato and Aristotle to Machiavelli, Hobbes, Rousseau, Hegel and beyond who celebrate the *polis*, the centred political community, as the model of proper political life. To the extent that more cosmopolitan traditions have been considered relevant, for example, it is only because they have been adapted to the particularistic ambitions of statist communities, witness the brilliant reconciliation of state and geometrical reason by Hobbes or state and rational history by Hegel. In this reading, the historicity of states is frequently ignored altogether, an ignorance that is further encouraged by the construction of a mythic antitradition of theories of international relations to complement the mythic tradition of theory about statist community.

Third, though consistent with the principle of sovereign equality or with understandings of the state as an embodiment of an abstract general will, national interest or national insecurity, the story detracts from the great historical, geographical and sociological variety of state forms. Certainly the dry codifications of so much legal history provide a significant contrast with attempts to develop an historical sociology or political economy of the state, although they readily confirm currently popular analogies with utilitarian accounts of rational action by possessive individuals in a capitalist market.

Fourth, the precise timetable of the emergence of state sovereignty is contested in the literature.[5] Some writers focus on the late fifteenth century and the emergence of a recognisably coherent system of states. Here the Franco-Spanish struggle over Italy in 1494 or Columbus' meeting with the Americas in 1492 becomes symbolic. Others focus on the formalisations of legal theory symbolised by the Peace of Augsburg (1515), the Treaty of Westphalia (1648), and the writings of Vattel. Others, like F. H. Hinsley, stress later dates on the grounds that only in the eighteenth or nineteenth centuries are there clearly cohesive nation-states in the modern sense, or a clearly cohesive states-system, such as was defined by the Congress of Vienna of 1815; or that only in the twentieth century does the principle of sovereign statehood become universalised with the ending of formal colonialism.

Finally, the state appears in the conventional story as a formal and almost lifeless category, when in fact states are constantly maintained, defended, attacked, reproduced, undermined, and relegitimised on a daily basis. The conventional story combines with a legalistic reading of the state to mystify the minute rituals through which states are constantly made and remade. Again, appeals to state sovereignty serve to maintain the high ground of timelessness (epistème, eternity) against the flux (doxa) of time, and to confirm the existence of the state as something 'out there' separate from the ordinary experience of people's lives.

Taken together, such objections suggest that the principle of state sovereignty is rather more interesting than it has been made to appear, whether through attempts to provide a clear definition, to resolve fundamental contradictions between power and authority, or to reproduce conventional accounts of the history of state sovereignty. It is more interesting, not least, because the conventional story of state sovereignty can be given slightly different readings in relation to the historically situated discursive spaces that are themselves defined by the principle of state sovereignty. As an historical achievement, the principle of state sovereignty affirms a particular reading of history. As a demarcation of political space/time, state sovereignty prescribes three distinct places, each with their own account of temporal possibility, in which to think about political space/time. Attempts to construct a history of sovereignty have varied according to whether it is examined from the perspective of life within states, or of relations between states, or in terms of some broader enterprise in which the distinction between inside and outside is subsumed as one – highly problematic – aspect of the dynamics of some more inclusive form of world politics and human identity.

Both the presence and the possibility of something that might usefully be called world politics or human identity flatly contradict the understanding of political identity affirmed by claims to state sovereignty. Yet, paradoxically, it is precisely the possibility, and in some respects the presence of some kind of world politics and common human identity that has continued to produce an account of the world as a spatially demarcated array of political identities fated to clash in perpetual contingency or to converge somewhere over the distant horizon at a time that is always deferred. This paradox continues to be the primary condition governing our ability, or inability, to think about struggles for political identity in a world in which it has become exceptionally unclear who this 'we' is.

Sovereignty from the inside

Once state sovereignty is defined as a centring of power/authority within a given territory, the way is open for emphasis on other things, like justice and law, freedom and social progress. In this context, concern with sovereignty occurs in three primary forms: as a given, as the outer limit of a society, a limit occurring as geographical frontier and maintained by procedures of defence and diplomacy; as a technical legal problem, especially in the construction of constitutional and institutional politics; and as a concept always in uneasy motion between power and authority, and thus between state and civil society or state and nation. This latter form has been of primary interest to political theorists. For, although the concept of sovereignty provides a constitutional account of the state as somehow (abstractly) synonymous with society, there remains the difficulty of determining exactly how the relationship between power and authority is to be specified or achieved in practice, a difficulty that has provided one of the core themes of European political thought since the age of social contract theory. Thus attention shifts to other dilemmas, notably those concerning the cultural or national content of the space contained within state boundaries and the precise democratic procedures that might permit some convergence between sovereign state and sovereign people. The claims of state sovereignty itself recede into the background, into the silence of received wisdom and legal convention. All that is needed are the appropriate constitutional and institutional arrangements to ensure a practical continuity over time and the clear affirmation of a spatial limit beyond which democracy and nation cannot trespass: matters that can be left safely in the hands of lawyers and soldiers as the twin guardians of sovereign enclosure. Though the weapons may be pointed out, the effects are clearly felt within.

Viewed in this internal context, the problematic character of the principle of state sovereignty takes two primary forms. The first involves continuing tensions between power and authority and between sovereign state and sovereign people, tensions that have come to be resolved either through binary distinctions between state and civil society or through unitary claims to national identity. While these resolutions continue to be of crucial importance as pressing aspirations in many places, they also continue to be put in doubt by the continuing recourse to various forms of authoritarian state and the demands of an increasingly global capitalist economy. From this direction, claims about state sovereignty have come to be identified both with the increasing strength of the state measured in terms of the state's capacity to coerce civil society, but also with an increasing weakness of the state in relation to the global structures in which it has become embedded. Though socialism has come to be seen as the most vulnerable of modern political doctrines, it is far from clear that the classic aspirations of liberalism or nationalism are any better founded in this respect.

The second, and closely related, form concerns the extent to which the concept of political community embodied in the principle of state sovereignty is compatible with the economic, social, cultural and political processes in which people now participate. Two subthemes can be loosely distinguished here. On the one hand, there are renewed assertions of various cosmopolitan claims. Some of these attempt to reassert the priority of the claims of people as people over the claims of people as citizens; hence, for example, the popularity of ideas derived from traditions of natural law and Enlightenment universalism in contemporary discussions about universal human rights. Others suggest that as a matter of empirical fact, people have become not only the subjects of sovereign states but subject to forces that are beyond the control of state authority, whether in terms of territorial reach or instrumental capacity. The threat of universal annihilation in nuclear war or ecological collapse is symbolic here. Many of the most crucial issues of our time seem to be beyond the scope of our understanding of democracy if democracy is understood in terms of the claims of sovereign states. On the other hand, there are also assertions of claims to some kind of local community. The limited diversity of a system of nation states, for example, seems increasingly inadequate to contain the contemporary profusion of ethnic and cultural identities. Similarly, neither unitary nor federal institutional arrangements seem able to maintain the single-minded allegiance either of particular locales or of some social movements.

Whether in relation to fears of authoritarianism and a crisis of legitimation or to claims about the increasing salience of both global and local processes, the established routines of democratic theory and nationalist aspiration must become increasingly tenuous once the guarantees of state sovereignty lose their credibility. Rather a lot hangs on whether the assumptions and silences of received wisdom and legal convention can remain relatively undisturbed, and on whether we can remain convinced that there is a here here as well as a there there.

Sovereignty from the outside

Relations between states are conventionally understood as the negation of the community presumed to be possible within the sovereign state. Whether characterised as politics without centralised authority, as an international anarchy, or as a more or less mechanical (automatic rather than political) system, international relations is defined both by the presence of sovereign states as primary actors and by the absence of a sovereign power/authority governing the system itself. Consequently, there is always a double elaboration of the argument that international relations is necessarily a matter of potentially – in the last instance – unlimited power and conflict. This double move is visible, for example, when different analytical traditions explain international relations primarily in terms of the behaviour of states or in relation to the structure of the international system. On the one hand, states are presumed to act autonomously, according to their own self-interest, as in the (neo-Weberian) tradition which identifies the pursuit of some mystical national interest as an assertion of power or will, and thus as a decisionism about national values. On the other hand, the international system is claimed to have no overarching authority through which conflicts of interest can be resolved. Hence there is the possibility of explaining international relations according to the operation of certain systemic or structural principles (balance of power theory), as well as of justifying the tragic legitimacy of war as a mechanism of system change.

In this world of sovereignty/lack of sovereignty, of supposedly autonomous states in an unregulated contest of wills, sovereignty is both constitutive of the system and a problem to be overcome. The problematic nature of the concept of sovereignty has thus remained on the active agenda of those concerned with international relations in a way that remains rather alien to those concerned with justice, freedom, community and progress within states, where sovereignty has become normalised or at least reduced to the conventional modern routines of state building or national liberation.

This double move also gives rise to the most basic theoretical problems associated with the principle of state sovereignty in this context, for it is unclear just how the principle of sovereign autonomy is compatible with the requirements of participation in a states-system. At one extreme, one can argue that the states-system is apolitical, that it is simply an automatic arrangement in which structural mechanisms respond to the assertions of autonomous states, as with attempts to apply mechanistic or utilitarian metaphors to international relations and with positivistic conceptions of international law. At the other extreme, one can suggest that the states-system constitutes a kind of society to which states are somehow obligated, so that the principle of sovereignty is understood to be compatible with emerging norms of international law. In this case an understanding of sovereignty as the locus of autonomous decisions requires considerable qualification, and an insistence that participation is in fact a condition of the possibility of autonomy rather than a threat to it. It is reaffirmed, however, in the Kantian aspiration for a perpetual peace, for a more positive resolution of the demands of particularistic autonomy with those of universal reason that earlier writers had assumed could only result in the possibility of domestic peace and the inevitability of external war.

In view of the abstract quality of Kant's proposed resolution, the tension between international anarchy and international society frames a wide field of practical dilemmas in which claims about state sovereignty have come to seem especially problematic. These can be grouped under at least five headings, all of which are now quite familiar to students of international relations:

i. Continuing general debates concerning:
    the constitutive principles of international law and the extent to which the law is binding in the absence of decisive centralised authority;
    the relationship between international law and *droit interne* (monism and dualism), particularly in view of claims about how international law effectively reduces the decision-making power of the modern state;
    the relationship between the principle of sovereignty and a variety of cosmopolitan claims about, for example, natural law, universal human rights, species identity, and so on.

ii. More specific problems arising from interpretations of sovereignty as implying a rigorous autonomy, especially in the context of processes of formal decolonisation:
    those concerning the principles of domestic jurisdiction and nonintervention;
    those concerning specific disputes over particular territories;
    those concerning the criteria for statehood and recognition for small states, divided states, and so on.

iii. Problems arising from the relationship between the principle of sovereignty and the claims of a society of states:
    those resulting from the de facto hegemony of great powers (vertical and in relation to omnipotence);
    those resulting from established norms of international law, regimes, or interdependence (horizontal and in relation to independence).

iv. Problems arising from the increasing significance of territorialities beyond existing claims of sovereignty:
    those involving the law of the sea;
    those involving space law;
    those involving speculative claims about a global commons or planetary habitat.

v. Problems arising from the institutionalisation of structures that somehow transcend state sovereignty:

formal constitutional arrangements, as with the European Community or United Nations;

de facto arrangements, as with multinational corporations and the complex relationships referred to under the term dependency.

Where much if not most of the conventional literature on state sovereignty in the context of international relations has placed greatest stress on (i) and (ii), more recent concerns stress (iii), (iv) and (v). And, as we engage with these more recent concerns, it seems more and more difficult to believe that here is indeed here and there is still there. Like the routines of modern political theory, accounts of international relations can still assume that inside and outside can be easily distinguished, but this is an assumption that is now very difficult to take for granted.

Sovereignty deferred

These two ways of reading state sovereignty, from the inside and the outside, are both readily familiar and seemingly exhaustive. Indeed, they seem to express the decisive demarcation between inside and outside, between self and other, identity and difference, community and anarchy that is constitutive of our modern understanding of political space. They affirm a clear sense of here and there. Here we are safe to work out the characteristic puzzles of modernity, about freedoms and determinations, the subjectivities and objectivities of a realm in which we might aspire to realise our peace and potential, our autonomy, our enlightenment, our progress and our virtù(e). There, we must beware. The outside is alien and strange, mysterious or threatening, a realm in which to be brave against adversity or patient enough to tame those whose life is not only elsewhere but also back then. Knowing the other outside, it is possible to affirm identities inside. Knowing identities inside, it is possible to imagine the absences outside. These routines, too, are familiar. They affirm the codes of nationalism and patriotism, the play of sanctimony and projection, the implausibility of strangers in a world of friend and foe and the impossibility of any real choice between tradition and modernity.

Yet, as I have sketched the puzzles generated by claims about state sovereignty both inside and outside, it is possible to get a sense of the significance of temporality, of the extent to which these puzzles of geopolitical space have changed or become more pressing over time. Here we run into a further familiar problematic in which claims about modernity as a culture of spatial chasms – between *res extensa* and *res cogitans*, words and things, subjects and objects – clash with claims about modernity as a process of historical acceleration, of modernisation and development, of all things solid melting into air. Many have argued that such processes of temporal development imply the eventual erasure of old spatial demarcations.

Nevertheless, many of these demarcations seem rather persistent. Contemporary accounts of political life – perhaps unlike contemporary accounts of social and economic life – remain impressed by the resilience of boundaries, by the sheer difficulty of imagining a politics beyond the horizons of a sovereign space. For where would one look? What could it mean to transcend the horizons of the sovereign state? To claim sovereignty is already to know what lies beyond, for there can be nothing beyond the horizon of that absence. The absence itself might become even darker, the horrors of war might become even more barbaric, but the important horizon is the one between it and home, between the terrors of international violence and our peace, order and good government. The obvious alternative is to bring the outside in, to speak of a global space, to act in the name of a planet or a humanity, to engage in the characteristic erasure of difference through an affirmation of the same. The domestic analogy, it can be said, must no longer be refused.

And, in any case, when could a breach of these horizons be achieved? Again, it might be possible to envisage a straight-line trajectory to some global community understood as a state writ large, but the trajectory is more likely to drop sharply into patterns of contingency once the lines of domestic jurisdiction are crossed. The domestic analogy, always so tempting, always so natural, reappears as a grim warning about confusing the universalising aspirations of one state with the distinctly undomesticated character of life on one planet.

Thus the principle of state sovereignty not only suggests how it is necessary to defend the borders but also how it is necessary to think about borders, about the delineation of political possibility in both space and time. It not only distinguishes between two spatial realms, each with their own characteristic mode of temporality, but also projects those temporalities into non-spaces, into imaginary realms where contradictions might be resolved in principle but which can never be reached. Or, at least, they can be reached only if all difference is erased, if the homogenising spaces of modernity are extended in all directions. Yes, we are all neo-utilitarian rational actors, say some. Yes, we must all become Kantian moralists, say others. But, the sceptic is likely to murmur, while observing new patterns of violence and exclusion on a global scale, even heaven on earth will require its own dark counterpoint in hell.

Sovereignty, identity, difference

Simply put, then, the principle of state sovereignty expresses an historically specific articulation of the relationship between universality and particularity in space and time. As such, it both affirms a specific resolution of philosophical and political options that must be acknowledged everywhere and sets clear limits to our capacity to envisage any other possibility. As both resolution and limit, it enters into the practices of states, the categories of those who analyse states and even the aspirations of those who would like to dispense with states. As a practice of states, it is easily mistaken for their essence. As a category of analysis, it is easily treated as the silent condition guaranteeing all other categories. As source of inspiration, it affirms that the only alternative to it is a return to the same, albeit on a larger – global – scale.

As an articulation of the relationship between universality and particularity in space and time, however, it is far from simple. The resolution of all philosophical and political options is not only elegant, but also densely textured. Three moments of this resolution are crucial and continually re-enforce each other.

With the collapse of feudal hierarchies and the delineation of the flat Euclidean spaces of modernity, political life was confronted with its own variation of the puzzles that had perplexed late mediaeval theologians, notably those concerning the proper relationship between the finite and the infinite, and consequently those concerning the relationship between the claims of men in general to those of the citizens of particular places. Despite all the one-sided references to the tragic demands of international anarchy, the modern states-system offers precisely a way of responding to both claims simultaneously: one system, many states; one Europe, or Christianity, or modernity and many (European, Christian or modern) peoples, cultures, nations and jurisdictions. Like all the grand dualisms of modern thought, of course, this one is rife with incipient monisms: the priority of national interests or the priority of international society; explanations of state behaviour or explanations of international structure; the possibility of international order or the inevitability of international conflict. As with all those other great dualisms, also, familiarity may have bred contempt but has not made it any easier to escape their tenacious grasp.

This primary resolution is replayed in twin discourses about life inside and outside the state. Within any particular constituent of the states-system, within the secure confines of particular states, it becomes possible to aspire to the universal. Indeed, as with most of the classic texts of modern political thought, it is possible to almost forget about the particularity of the community that is shown to be capable of reason and justice, democracy and liberty. Those marginal references to external troubles that manage to find a small place in the canonical texts of political theory have to be taken up by others, by theorists of international relations, who in turn easily lose sight of the extent to which their depictions of international disorder are coloured by the positive aspirations that are deemed to be legitimate within states. The effectiveness with which the principle of state sovereignty marks a distinction between political life inside and mere relations outside the modern state is still felt in the double reification of the two canons of political thought, the canon of presence and the canon of absence, the serious theory of established political community and the depressing theory of guns, bombs, lies and the occasional butter.

This double resolution of universal and particular inside and outside is initially made possible by a sharp distinction in space. But this distinction in space also permits a distinction in time. Inside, the spatial consciousness that informed early-modern contract theory gradually gave way to theories of history. The architectonics of *Leviathan* gave way to the dialectics of *Geist*. But if progress could be articulated within, it has remained notoriously scarce without. International relations remains a discourse about contingency, about barbarism and violence and war. The future can only be deferred. The present is destined to return. The political theorists may have their hidden hand and their optimistic teleologies, but theorists of international relations always remember Augustine, and shape their doctrines of realism as a peon to a temporality without hope of redemption.

One system and many states; the possibility of universality inside and the violent play of particularities outside; a spatial order in which history can unravel as it should and a spatial disorder in which contingent forces can only clash as they must. As a response to the puzzles of unity and diversity, presence and absence, and space and time, the principle of state sovereignty says all that is to be said, indeed all that can be said about the character and location of modern political life. All contradictions are resolved, and they are resolved with great elegance and style, with an apparent simplicity that masks the density of metaphysical achievement.

But it expresses a particular conception of elegance and a specific

177

sense of style, and its metaphysical achievements have become both more visible and less convincing. Its grand motif of straight lines retains a certain charm, and an enormously powerful grip on the contemporary political imagination, but we are no longer so easily fooled by the objectivity of the ruler, by the Euclidean theorems and Cartesian coordinates that have allowed us to situate and naturalise a comfortable home for power and authority. The difficulty of thinking about contemporary political identities comes not only from the profusion of struggles and uncertainties that has become even more obvious with the thawing of Cold War structures, but from an increasingly widespread sense that the metaphysical achievements of the principle of state sovereignty have less and less political relevance. Lines drawn in the desert sand bespeak the nostalgia of those reduced to force, to the self-righteous virtue of those who violently inscribe a here here and a there there. They say little about the *virtù* required to comprehend the wiles of approaching fortune, let alone the uncertainties of a new world order that will not lie still.

Neither nostalgia nor self-righteousness have ever been sufficient to prevent metaphysical collapse, and their capacity for political mobilisation is sometimes sweet but always short. Despite the immediate appeal to a common sense that will insist that there is indeed a here here and a there there, it is unlikely that any analysis of contemporary world politics – of the world economy, of nuclear strategy, of communications technologies, of cultural inclusions or social exclusions, of refugees or tourists, of investments, ecologies, markets or literatures – will now avoid some mention of how this once uncommon sense is not quite right. The clean lines of state sovereignty, it will be said, are less impressive than the startling velocity of contemporary accelerations. Temporality can no longer be contained within spatial coordinates. Given the history of thinking about concepts of space and time since Isaac Newton stopped underwriting the guarantees for modernity, this should not be surprising. But given the extent to which modern political thought has depended on the claim that temporality can and must be tamed and shaped by the spatial certainties of sovereign states, it is undoubtedly quite perplexing, even threatening.

To understand the elegance of the resolution of all philosophical and political options by the principle of state sovereignty, at least to the satisfaction of the modern imagination, is to understand how we do find it possible to think about the struggles for political identity that seem so pressing all around us. The usual categories and valorisations express all the usual answers to questions about who this 'we' is. This 'we' shifts rapidly back and forth between an invocation of humanity in general and an admission of the parochial ground from which the claimant to humanity speaks. We may aspire to be a good citizen and an exemplary expression of the species. Alternatively, we may resist claims about the species that are issued as the conceits of hegemonic powers by privileging the particular struggles of national citizenship or liberation. And as nationalist or globalist, we can know who we are through knowing where we are. Dislodged from the Great Chain of Being and pitched into the empty spaces of modernity, we claim autonomy and identity as particulars – individuals and nations – ever in search of reconciliation with the universal, or ever resigned to the unhappy condition in which reconciliation is known to be impossible. Though many complaints have been issued about the impossibility of *this* rendition of the available alternatives, the silent reifications of the principle of state sovereignty testify to *its* hegemony both over what it means to aspire to some other identity and to resist the identities constructed by hegemonic powers.

Rearticulations of political space/time

Once upon a time, the world was not as it is. The patterns of inclusion and exclusion we now take for granted are historical innovations. The principle of state sovereignty is the classic expression of those patterns, an expression that encourages us to believe that either those patterns are permanent or that they must be erased in favour of some kind of global cosmopolis. It is possible to understand how this claim to resolve all contradictions works. It, most of all, is not simply there. Its fixing of unity and diversity, or inside and outside, or space and time is not natural. Nor is it inevitable. It is a crucial part of the practices of all modern states, but they are not natural or inevitable either.

And yet, states have become (second) nature, and come to seem inevitable. We have inherited not Machiavelli's sense of the sheer difficulty and contingency of state formation, but Hobbes' sense that there can be no solution to the difficulties and contingencies of modern life without the eternal presence of the sovereign state. Of course, it might be argued that this is because the world is indeed made up of clean-cut parcels of territorial jurisdiction, because the claims of state sovereignty accurately reflect an empirical reality which we have only to recognise and acknowledge. Though some may be convinced that this must be the essence of a realistic politics, others are more likely to be persuaded about the purely formal and even utopian quality of state sovereignty given the messy picture that can appear through other constructions of the empirical evidence. Even – or perhaps especially – large states are liable to experience sovereignty as a tremendous problem rather than as a simple given. Even the most self-satisfied states exert enormous energies sustaining a sense of national identity and integrity. At best, theories of international relations predicated upon the claim to state sovereignty involve an extraordinary degree of oversimplification and wishful thinking. In this sense, they offer an explicitly normative account of how the world must be, a way of constructing empirical evidence on the basis of prior assumptions about how lines are to be drawn through messy appearances and contested subjectivities. The practices through which these lines are drawn, and by which profound metaphysics is rooted in an implicit geometry, I have argued, are much more interesting than the substantive claims that these practices have made so familiar.

Through these practices, it has become possible to present once highly controversial claims as unproblematic assertions. The ontological density of the principle of state sovereignty can be turned into vacuous claims about an international anarchy. Weber's struggles with the rationality/irrationality of modernity, with the problematic status of autonomy in a world torn between Kant and Nietzsche, can be turned into the six banalities of Morgenthau's discipline-defining text. The achievement of a horizontal space in which modern individuals can realise their sovereign identities within the sovereign state can be turned into a mere typology of pseudo-hierarchical levels, into a hierarchy that can neither reach to a transcendent eternity nor admit the possibility of a temporality that might erase its privileged spaces.

Through these practices, too, it has been possible to stop thinking about other claims to political identity. For a discipline preoccupied with the diversity of peoples, for example, there has been very little concern with processes usually grasped under the category of culture. On the one hand, the diversity of cultures has been reduced to questions about 'values' which can be either opposed to the eternal truths of 'power', or equated with the hegemony of rational action under modernity.[6] It is here that the similarities between theories of international relations and the crudest forms of reductionist Marxism have been particularly striking. For all its ambition to explain the world, the modern theory of international relations remains intensely parochial, and not just because it has been developed primarily in relation to the interests of hegemonic states. If culture is read through the principle of state sovereignty, it can only refer to the diversity of national cultures. If culture is read through a geometry of territorial exclusions, through a metaphysics of identity here and a non-identity there, it can only refer to an absence of community, a relativity of values and a clash of different ways of life; unless, of course, some convergence theory can chart a way through to an eternal peace and a kitsch Kantianism can solve the riddles of culture once and for all.

Similar problems beset attempts to understand international relations theory as an explicitly gendered practice and to suggest how an alternative feminist theory of international relations might be constructed. There is no doubt at all that a feminist critique of international relations theory is required, and required urgently. But, after pointing to the obviously gendered character of this discipline, it is far from clear what a feminist theory of international relations must involve. Leaving aside the considerable variation and controversy inherent in any contemporary claim about feminism or gender, a feminist critique of international relations theory must necessarily come to terms with the crucial gendering of political identities – the universal man – that informs the privileged principles of modern political life, and not least the principle of state sovereignty.

There is obviously little point in attempting to add gender to a discipline while simply taking for granted the gendered concepts through which that discipline has been constructed. A feminist critique of international relations theory must also be a critique of modern politics, of the fixing of possible identities as a binary choice between a citizenship and a humanity. At least to the extent that feminism itself is understood as a politics of identity, rather than as an apolitical essentialism or an extrapolation of classical liberalism, it can hardly afford to take this choice as the condition under which other ways of being human can be explored. As a politics of identity, the critique of modern theories of international relations must give way to an ambition to understand the gendered character of contemporary world politics. This ambition *must* involve a suspicion of the ethnocentricism and modernist hubris of theories of international relations for these are precisely conditions under which it has been possible to read women – among others – right out of the script.[7]

The pattern is familiar but not always easy to see. Through the separation of theories of international relations from those of an international political economy, it has become possible to ignore categories of class in favour of those of state and nation; so national chauvinism always triumphs over class solidarity, and national interests always heal the wounds of class division. Through the grand antinomy of political realism and utopianism, between the hardheaded and the normative, the righteously cynical and the righteously naive, it has been possible to consign all critique of international relations theory to the ghettos of 'peace research' or 'world order studies'.[8] Through the rituals of 'national security', it has become possible to link all forms of human insecurity to the military defence of the state, despite the fact that states have become increasingly important sources of contemporary insecurity and increasingly unable to provide security from environmental collapse and economic maldevelopment.[9] But again, while the problematic character of contemporary accounts of human security, or the rituals of realism and utopianism, or assumptions about a simple rift between politics and economics has attracted considerable critical commentary, the implications of the critique are perhaps more profound than even most of the critics are prepared to admit.

If an alternative account of human security is needed, for example, it will have to arise from some understanding of who it is that is to be made secure. If alternative accounts of peace and world order are to emerge from the debris of Cold War stereotypes, they will have to refuse the discursive and ontological options through which critique has been so easily trivialised. And if it is important to understand class divisions in order to explain contemporary patterns of violence and inequality, then it will have to be an analysis that is usurped neither by categories of state and nation nor by some abstract account of a humanity beyond power.

Whether in relation to culture, class or gender, to the demands of security or the possibilities of equity, a critique of modern theories of international relations, and thus of the principle of state sovereignty that has set the conditions under which those theories could be articulated, must lead to very difficult questions about principles and aspirations that presuppose a nice tidy world of Cartesian coordinates, at least as a regulative ambition. How is it possible to articulate a plausible account of identity, democracy, community, responsibility or security without assuming the presence of a territorial space, a sharp line between here and there, the celebratory teleologies of modern political life within the great universalising particular, the modern state? How is it possible to engage with aspirations for emancipation knowing that so many of those aspirations have merely affirmed a parochial particularity masquerading as universal? How is it possible to engage with others without relapsing into the rituals of identity and non-identity, affirmation and denial, the great battle between the righteous and the barbarian that is so deeply inscribed in the constitutive discourses of modern politics?

The principle of state sovereignty affirms the specifically modern conditions under which such questions can be answered. Many continue to affirm that modernity offers the *only* conditions under which these questions can be answered. But while states are still with us, their borders offer no theoretical or practical guarantees. Given contemporary rearticulations of political space/time, it is unlikely that contemporary struggles for political identity can afford to be so apolitical, or that attempts to make some sense of emerging forms of world politics can continue blithely to affirm categories that explicitly deny the possibility of a world politics. The politics of becoming otherwise will have to be a politics that challenges the modern framing of other as Other, the framing expressed, reproduced and legitimised by the very distinction between international relations and political theory. There is certainly no possibility of becoming otherwise if that account is assumed to provide an accurate portrayal of where we are now. As the discursive strategies through which we have come to believe in the natural necessity of that historical claim become more and more transparent, however, at least we may be spared the interminable self-righteousness of those who know what we cannot be because they are so sure of where we are. I would count this as a considerable achievement.

NOTES

1 International relations as political theory

1 Karl Marx, *The Communist Manifesto*, 1848.
2 The relevant literature here is enormous, encompassing, say, the link between geometry and Platonist accounts of truth, beauty and goodness, the categorical schemes of Kantian philosophy, and the spatiotemporal modalities of capitalist economies. My own reading of this theme is especially influenced by the literature on the relationship between spatial extension and the articulation of autonomous subjectivities in late-medieval theology and early-modern science and philosophy. In this context, see especially such classic texts as Ernst Cassirer, *Individual and Cosmos in Renaissance Philosophy* (1927) trans. M. Domandi (New York: Harper and Row, 1963); Pierre Duhem, *Medieval Cosmology: Theories of Infinity, Place, Time, Void, and the Plurality of Worlds* (abridged edition of *Le Système du monde*, 10 vols., 1913–1959), trans. and ed. Roger Ariew (Chicago: University of Chicago Press, 1985); Edmund Husserl, *The Crisis of European Sciences and Transcendental Phenomenology: An Introduction to Phenomenological Philosophy* (1954) trans. David Carr (Evanston: Northwestern University Press, 1970); and Michel Foucault, *The Order of Things* (London: Tavistock, 1970).
3 The most sustained exploration of this theme in the context of contemporary world politics is the work of James Der Derian; see his 'The (S)pace of International Relations: Simulation, Surveillance and Speed', *International Studies Quarterly*, 34:3, September 1990, 295–310; and *Anti-Diplomacy: Speed, Spies and Terror in International Relations* (Oxford: Basil Blackwell, 1992). It has become especially apparent in some of the most thoughtful interpretations of the Gulf War and its aftermath; see especially Stephen Gill, 'Reflections on Global Order and Sociohistorical Time', *Alternatives*, 16:3, Summer 1991, 275–314; and Timothy W. Luke, 'The Discipline of Security Studies and the Codes of Containment; Learning from Kuwait', *Alternatives*, 16:3, Summer 1991, 315–44. Among the many recent general texts that affirm both the significance of and the difficulty of responding to this theme in the specific context of international relations theory, see especially James N. Roseneau, *Turbulence in World Politics: A Theory of Change and Continuity* (Princeton: Princeton University Press, 1990); and Ernst-Otto Czempiel and J. N. Rosenau, eds., *Global Change and Theoretical Challenges* (Lexington: Lexington Books, 1989).

As I suggest later in this chapter, much of the pertinent general literature expresses an ambivalence as to whether modernity and its contemporary expressions are best characterised as a privileging of space or of time, an ambivalence that I interpret as a crucial effect of the modern resolution of all philosophical options through a claim to an autonomous subject capable of preserving its self-identity in time and space (see note 2 above). For especially provocative discussions, see Paul Virilio, *Speed and Politics* (New York: Semiotext(e), 1987); Virilio, *War and Cinema: The Logistics of Perception* (New York: Verso, 1989); and Gilles Deleuze, *Bergsonism*, trans. Hugh Tomlinson and Barbara Habberjam (New York: Zone Books, 1988). See also Donald M. Lowe, *History of Bourgeois Perception* (Chicago: University of Chicago Press, 1982); Timothy W. Luke, *Screens of Power: Ideology, Domination and Resistance in Informational Society* (Urbana and Chicago: University of Illinois Press, 1989); Harold A. Innis, *The Bias of Communication* (Toronto: University of Toronto Press, 1951); Marshall McLuhan, *The Gutenberg Galaxy* (Toronto: University of Toronto Press, 1962); Steven Connor, *Postmodernist Culture: An Introduction to Theories of the Contemporary* (Oxford: Basil Blackwell, 1989); Fredric Jameson, *Postmodernism, or The Cultural Logic of Late Capitalism* (Durham, NC: Duke University Press, 1991); Douglas Kellner, ed., *Postmodernism/Jameson/Critique* (Washington, DC: Maisonneuve Press, 1989); David Harvey, *The Condition of Postmodernity* (Oxford: Basil Blackwell, 1989); Edward Soja, *Postmodern Geographies: The Reassertion of Space in Critical Social Theory* (London: Verso, 1989); and Anthony Giddens, *The Consequences of Modernity* (Cambridge: Polity Press, 1990).

The problem of temporality, of course, has long been treated as a key theme of Western political thought. For my present purposes, it is especially important to remember the degree to which early-modern political thought involved a struggle to take the temporal realm seriously in relation to the claims of Heaven. In the shadow of Augustine's grand schism, of the devaluation of a life on earth in relation to the transcendental guarantees of eternity, a Machiavelli or a Hobbes can be read – as I tend to read them in this book – as moments in a broader attempt to constitute a positive vision of human existence in time. On this general theme, see, for example, John Gunnell, *Political Philosophy and Time*, 2nd edn, (Chicago: Chicago University Press, 1987); and Sheldon Wolin, *Politics and Vision* (Boston: Little Brown, 1960). See also John Bender and David E. Wellberg, eds., *Chronotypes: The Construction of Time* (Stanford: Stanford University Press, 1991).

4 In this book, I refer to international relations as a specific Anglo-American academic discipline that developed as a semi-autonomous enterprise from the 1920s onwards, and especially since 1945; to theories of international relations as an analytical and prescriptive literature produced by that discipline; to relations between states or the states system as the primary substantive concern of those theories; and to world politics as a broader array of processes – also often the focus of those theories – that extend beyond the territoriality and competence of particular states.

All these terms are highly problematic. Loose usages of the term international relations, for example, tend to reify a specific convergence between state and nation; references to the states system encourage a conflation of accounts of the state as territorial space and as governmental apparatus; ambivalent references to international relations and international politics signify some uncertainty about exactly what it is that goes on between states; most significantly, world politics appears both as a synonym for relations between states and as a way of referring to processes that largely escape prevailing analytical categories. The significance of the manner in which such terms slip from being innocuous synonyms to indicators of profound theoretical controversy should become clearer as the analysis proceeds.

The development of international relations as a discipline is explored in Kenneth W. Thompson, 'The Study of International Relations: Trends and Developments', *Review of Politics*, XIV, October 1952, 433–67; Hedley Bull, 'The Theory of International Politics, 1919–1969', in Brian Porter, ed., *International Politics 1919–1969: The Aberystwyth Papers* (Oxford: Oxford University Press, 1972), 30–55; Stanley Hoffman, 'An American Social Science: International Relations', *Daedalus*, 106, Summer 1977, 41–59; and William Olson and Nicholas Onuf, 'The Growth of a Discipline: Reviewed' in Steve Smith, ed., *International Relations: British and American Perspectives* (Oxford: Basil Blackwell, 1985), 1–28.

Recent attempts to assess the general achievements and present status of the discipline include Smith, ed., *International Relations*; K.J. Holsti, *The Dividing Discipline: Hegemony and Diversity in International Theory* (Boston: Allen and Unwin, 1985); Hayward R. Alker Jr, and Thomas J. Biersteker, 'The Dialectics of World Order: Notes for a Future Archeologist of International Savoir faire', *International Studies Quarterly*, 28:2, June 1984, 121–42; Yale Ferguson and Richard W. Mansbach, *The Elusive Quest: Theory and International Politics* (Columbia: University of South Carolina Press, 1988); Richard Higgott, ed., *New Directions in International Relations? Australian Perspectives*, Canberra Studies in World Affairs, No. 23, (Canberra: Australian National University Department of International Relations, 1988); Richard Higgott and J. L. Richardson, eds., *International Relations: Global and Australian Perspectives on an Evolving Discipline* (Canberra: Department of International Relations, Australian National University, 1991); and Hugh Dyer and Leon Mangasarian, eds., *The Study of International Relations: The State of the Art* (London: Macmillan, 1989).

For more focused controversies about the significance of converging claims about empirical social science, rational choice theory and 'neorealism', on the one hand, and about emerging forms of 'critical theory', on the other, see especially Robert O. Keohane, ed. *Neorealism and Its Critics* (New York: Columbia University Press, 1986); Hayward Alker and Richard K. Ashley, eds., *After Neo-Realism: The Institutions of Anarchy in World Politics* (in preparation); and Richard K. Ashley and R. B. J. Walker, eds., 'Speaking the Language of Exile: Dissidence in International Studies', special issue of *International Studies Quarterly*, 34:3, September 1990. These controversies provide the most immediate context in which the present analysis has been framed.

5 For helpful introductions to this theme see, for example, Marshall Bermam,

All That is Solid Melts into Air: The Experience of Modernity (New York: Simon and Schuster, 1982); David Frisby, *Fragments of Modernity: Theories of Modernity in the Work of Simmel, Kracauer and Benjamin* (Cambridge, MA: The MIT Press, 1986); and Stephen Kern, *The Culture of Time and Space, 1880–1918* (Cambridge, MA: Harvard University Press, 1983).

6 Because I am primarily concerned with the analysis of controversies that have developed within the theory of international relations, I pay relatively little attention to important literatures that have challenged the manner in which theories of international relations have been developed on the basis of a systematic amnesia about the international and global organisation of economic life. And because I am concerned to problematise the principle of state sovereignty, I also largely ignore literatures that challenge the absence of much analysis of the state as a complex historical phenomenon, an absence that has permitted so much empty speculation about the behaviour of black boxes, national interests, rational actors and the like. I share much of the critique that emerges from such literatures while remaining concerned about the extent to which it often remains caught within modernist assumptions about the character and location of political practice or informed by reductionist assumptions about the relative autonomies of economy, polity, society and culture. Many of the most helpful commentaries on literatures which I marginalise here have been informed by the counter-reductionist account of hegemony associated with Antonio Gramsci. See especially Robert W. Cox, *Production, Power, and World Order: Social Forces in the Making of History* (New York: Columbia University Press, 1987); Stephen Gill and David Law, *The Global Political Economy* (Baltimore: Johns Hopkins University Press, 1988); Gill, *American Hegemony and the Trilateral Commission* (Cambridge: Cambridge University Press, 1990); Craig Murphy and Roger Tooze, eds., *The New International Political Economy* (Boulder: Lynne Rienner, 1991); and Enrico Augelli and Craig Murphy, *America's Quest for Supremacy and the Third World: A Gramscian Analysis* (London: Francis Pinter, 1988).

The key connection between this literature and the present analysis is a shared concern with practices of reification, although I focus more explicitly on some aspects of the discursive economy of the modern state. Consequently, I also adopt a broader interpretation of the meaning of economy than is usual among economists, though it is one that has become increasingly familiar in the analysis of political discourse. See, for example, Jean-Joseph Gouz, *Symbolic Economies: After Marx and Freud*, trans. Jennifer Curtis Gage (Ithaca, NY: Cornell University Press, 1990); Friedrich A. Kittler, *Discourse Networks, 1800/1900* trans. Michael Metteer (Stanford: Stanford University Press, 1990); Michael Shapiro, 'Sovereignty and Exchange in the Orders of Modernity', *Alternatives*, 16:4, Fall 1991, 447–77; and Shapiro, *Reading the Postmodern Polity: Political Theory as Textual Practice* (Minneapolis: University of Minnesota Press, 1992).

7 Geoffrey Hawthorn, *Enlightenment and Despair: A History of Social Theory*, 2nd edn (Cambridge: Cambridge University Press, 1987). See also Zygmunt Bauman, *Modernity and the Holocaust* (Cambridge: Polity Press, 1989).

8 In keeping with current conventions, I treat postmodernity as a broad term

encompassing a complex historical/cultural condition, and poststructuralism as a reference to a more specific response to philosophical dilemmas that have become especially pressing under postmodern conditions. However, even this distinction encourages a premature attribution of coherence to both terms. I prefer to use these terms very loosely to refer to complex and contradictory forms of contemporary cultural practice and to literatures that seek to rethink the possibilities of being/acting/knowing in response to fundamental – Nietzschean, Heideggerian – critiques of modern accounts of universality/diversity and space/time relations. Accounts – and critiques – of postmodernity which simply stress a new celebration of diversity and the supposed liberation from foundationalist epistemologies especially seem to me to miss the significance of poststructuralist suspicions of the prior framing of relations of identity/difference and space/time which permit such accounts and critiques to be turned into a trivial replay of Romantic subjectivisim.

For a helpful brief discussion of the multiple meanings expressed by these terms see Wayne Hudson, 'Postmodernity and Contemporary Social Thought' in Peter Lassman, ed., *Politics and Social Theory* (London: Routledge, 1989): 138–60. Of the myriad contemporary attempts to make sense of modernity as a critical category of analysis, I have drawn especially on the diverse perspectives canvassed in Matei Calinescu, *Five Faces of Modernity* (Durham, NC: Duke University Press, 1987); William E. Connolly, *Political Theory and Modernity* (Oxford: Basil Blackwell, 1988); David Kolb, *The Critique of Pure Modernity: Hegel, Heidegger, and After* (Chicago: University of Chicago Press, 1986); Barry Smart, *Modern Conditions, Postmodern Controversies* (London: Routledge, 1992); and Zygmunt Bauman, *Intimations of Postmodernity* (London: Routledge, 1992).

9 See especially the work collected in James Der Derian and Michael J. Shapiro, eds., *International/Intertextual Relations: Postmodern Readings of World Politics* (Lexington: Lexington Books, 1989); and Ashley and Walker, eds., 'Speaking the Language of Exile'.

10 See Richard K. Ashley and R. B. J. Walker, 'Reading Dissidence/Writing the Discipline: Crisis and the Question of Sovereignty in International Studies', in Ashley and Walker, eds., Speaking the Language of Exile, 367–416.

11 It is, moreover, an insight that has been developed in quite diverse directions by Michel Foucault, Jacques Derrida, and the now extensive litany of names associated with postmodernist critique. This litany ought to be enough to forestall any expectations of a single poststructuralist approach to international relations/world politics. As with the more general literature, the differences among poststructuralist approaches in this context are often more striking than the convergences. Compare, for example, Richard K. Ashley, *Statecraft as Mancraft* (in preparation); William Connolly, *Identity\ Difference: Democratic Negotiation of Political Paradox* (Ithaca: Cornell University Press, 1991); Michael Shapiro, *The Politics of Representation* (Madison: University of Wisconsin Press, 1988); David Campbell, *Writing Security: United States Foreign Policy and the Politics of Identity* (Manchester: Manchester University Press, 1992); and D. M. Dillon, *Security and Modernity* (in preparation). On the heterogeneity of sources at work in such literature, see

Jim George and David Campbell, 'Patterns of Dissent and the Celebration of Difference: Critical Social Theory and International Relations', in Ashley and Walker, eds., Speaking the Language of Exile, 269-93.

Attempts to depict some central insight of postmodern and poststructural thought are notoriously fraught with contradictions, as with Lyotard's well-known sweeping narrative about the end of 'master narratives'; see Jean-François Lyotard, The Postmodern Condition: A Report on Knowledge, trans. Geoff Bennington and Brian Massumi, (Minneapolis: University of Minnesota Press, 1984). In a related manner, Jameson argues that it is 'safest to grasp the concept of the postmodern as an attempt to think the present historically in an age that has forgotten how to think historically in the first place'; Jameson, Postmodernism, ix. In each case, totalising claims pose severe difficulties, although I take it that the contradictory character of such diagnoses express a serious philosophical, cultural and political problematic rather than a simple minded failure of logic. In the case of Lyotard, it is a problematic that can be linked to the dissolution of modern conceptions of the transparency of language, while in the case of Jameson it can be linked to the difficulty of analysing late capitalism. Though both avenues of inquiry are undoubtedly crucial for analyses of contemporary world politics, they are beyond the scope of the present inquiry.

Contrary to such totalising strategies, I prefer to treat the postmodern turn and the literature of poststructuralism as opening up a range of critical possibilities, many of them at odds with each other, rather than as names for yet another grand solution to all philosophical and political puzzles. For helpful discussions of the difficulties of precise navigation in these waters, see Spivak, The Post-Colonial Critic; William Connolly, Politics and Ambiguity (Madison: University of Wisconsin Press, 1987); and Zygmunt Bauman, Modernity and Ambivalence (Cambridge: Polity Press, 1991).

12 See, for example, John Dunn, Western Political Theory in the Face of the Future (Cambridge: Cambridge University Press, 1979); Dunn, Rethinking Modern Political Theory (Cambridge: Cambridge University Press, 1985); Dunn, Interpreting Political Responsibility (Cambridge: Polity, 1990); Connolly, Political Theory and Modernity; David Held, Political Theory and the Modern State (Cambridge: Polity, 1989); Held, ed., Political Theory Today (Cambridge: Cambridge University Press, 1991); Jean Elshtain, Public Man, Private Woman (Princeton: Princeton University Press, 1981); and Wendy Brown, Manhood and Politics: A Feminist Reading in Political Theory (Totowa, NJ: Rowman and Littlefield, 1988).

13 One of the more perplexing characteristics of critical responses to forms of inquiry that depart from postmodern and poststructural premises has been an indiscriminate indulgence in the charge of relativism, an indulgence predicated on the assumption that those making the charge are standing on the firmest of epistemological terrain. In fact, of course, this terrain is notoriously swampy, to borrow a metaphor from Karl Popper, and the piles that have been driven into it, whether in the name of science, empiricism, rationalism, Kant or Hegel are decidedly flimsy. This much, at least, seems especially clear from the intense controversies that undermined the more pretentious claims of empiricist and positivistic philosophies of physical

science in the 1960s and 1970s. Even the curious combinations of conventionalism and sociology of knowledge shared by, say Popper, T. S. Kuhn and Imre Lakatos, are a long way removed from the presumed certainties that are still so often claimed in the name of scientific method.

Such charges of relativism tend to wish away two rather large problems that have dominated contemporary discussions of the possibility of objective knowledge but which are of concern for the present analysis. One, especially characteristic of debates about scientific epistemology, has involved the difficulty of holding apart the claims of objectivity from those of subjectivity given an acknowledgement of the constitutive role of the knowing subject in constructing the object to be known. The enormous sociological and cultural weight of naive empiricism has not entirely erased the memory of Hume and Kant in this respect, although the prevalence of simple-minded appeals to commonsense and brute reality among students of international relations is certainly disconcerting. The other, involving serious problems even for neo-Kantian critiques of naive empiricism, has involved the critique of the ontological conditions under which epistemology came to be construed as a dualistic encounter between subject and object in the first place.

This latter critique, especially, has been one of the crucial themes explored by postmodern and especially by poststructuralist thinkers. From this point of view, much of the concern about relativism merely confirms the limits of the historically specific ontologies that have produced relativism as a characteristically modern stance. While it may remain quite unclear how the dualistic ontologies that have informed our understanding of knowledge since the era of Galileo and Descartes might now be reconstructed, the dubious character of those ontologies has been sufficiently affirmed by almost all the influential philosophical movements of this century. Consequently, I judge the readiness with which so much modern social science is willing to proclaim standards of empirical method and rational action despite the widely acknowledged fragility of claims about rationalism and empiricism to be far more worrying than postmodern and poststructuralist celebrations of uncertainty.

Contrary to those who insist that critical scholarship, ethical conduct or progressive political practice require a prior commitment to universal reason (or to the breezier aspirations of a Jürgen Habermas, or at least to the American way of life), I work from the assumption that a certain scepticism about the idols of modern epistemology is a necessary condition for critical scholarship, ethical conduct and progressive political practice. In this respect, Foucault's attempt to articulate a moment of critique through a genealogical interrogation captures an attitude that has partly informed the conception of critical possibility assumed here:

I do not know whether we will ever reach mature adulthood. Many things in our experience convince us that the historical events of the Enlightenment did not make us mature adults, and we have not reached that stage yet. However, it seems to me that a meaning can be attributed to that critical interrogation on [sic] the present and on [sic] ourselves which Kant formulated by reflecting on the enlightenment. It seems to me that Kant's reflection is even a way of philosophizing that has not been without its importance or effectiveness during the last two centuries. The critical ontology of ourselves has to be considered not, certainly, as a theory, a doctrine, nor even as a permanent body of knowledge that is accumulating; it has to be conceived as an attitude, an ethos, a philosophical life in which the critique of what we are is at one and the same time the historical analysis of the limits that are imposed on us and an experiment with the possibility of going beyond them. Michel Foucault, 'What is Enlightenment?', in Paul Rabinow, ed., *The Foucault Reader* (New York: Pantheon, 1984), 32–50.

14 For a concise statement synthesising an enormous literature, see Joseph A. Camilleri, 'Rethinking Sovereignty in a Shrinking, Fragmented World', in R. B. J. Walker and Saul H. Mendlovitz, eds., *Contending Sovereignties: Rethinking Political Community* (Boulder: Lynne Rienner, 1990), 13–44.

15 Hoffmann, 'An American Social Science'; Robert W. Cox, 'Social Forces, States and World Orders: Beyond International Relations Theory', *Millennium: Journal of International Studies*, 10:2, 1981, 126–55; Roy Jones, 'The English School of International Relations: A Case for Closure', *Review of International Studies*, 7:1, 1981, 1–13; Smith, ed., *International Relations: British and American Perspectives*; and Dyer and Mangasarian, eds., *The Study of International Relations*.

16 Most notably concerning the positivist distinction between empirical and normative inquiry, the ethnocentric character of comparative and developmental analysis, and the need for a more historically sensitive approach to the relation between statist and interstate politics. See, for example, David Ricci, *The Tragedy of Political Science: Politics, Scholarship and Democracy* (New Haven: Yale University Press, 1984); John Gunnell, *Between Philosophy and Politics* (Amherst, MA: University of Massachusetts Press, 1986); Theda Scocpol, *States and Social Revolutions* (Cambridge: Cambridge University Press, 1979); Michael Mann, *The Sources of Social Power*, 3 vols. (Cambridge: Cambridge University Press, 1986–); and Gabriel Almond, 'Review Article: The International–National Connection', *British Journal of Political Science*, 19:2, April 1989, 237–59.

17 It is curious how few of the already scarce studies of the emergence of theorising about the modern states system pay much attention to the profound implications of this transition from medieval hierarchies to modern autonomies. For many analysts, of course, the very fact of statist fragmentation is enough, just as the fact of a new conception of individual subjectivity has often been enough to justify the construction of universalising accounts of, say, 'rational man' within liberal political theory. The historical diversity of state forms, like the historically constituted character of claims about individuality, is then easily erased in favour of ahistorical abstractions.

Some of the best-known expositions of the supposed classics of international relations theory simply ignore this transition, preferring instead to enlist everyone into analytical schemas (or ideological conceits) about 'man, the state and the international system' or grand metaphysical battles between realists and idealists, or optimists and pessimists. See, for example, E. H. Carr, *The Twenty-Years Crisis, 1919–1939*, 2nd edn (London: Macmillan, 1946); John Herz, *Political Realism and Political Idealism* (Chicago: University of Chicago Press, 1951); Michael Howard, *War and the Liberal Conscience* (Oxford: Oxford University Press, 1978); Hans J. Morgenthau, *Politics Among Nations* (New York: Knopf, 1948); Kenneth N. Waltz, *Man, the State and War* (New York: Columbia University Press, 1959); Charles R. Beitz, *Political Theory and International Relations* (Princeton: Princeton University Press, 1979); and Ian Clark, *The Hierarchy of States: Reform and Resistence in the International Order* (Cambridge: Cambridge University Press, 1989). Others, while generally much more helpful, are more concerned with the emergence of claims about an international society from the eighteenth century onwards. See, for example, F. H. Hinsley, *Power and the Pursuit of Peace* (Cambridge: Cambridge University Press, 1967); and W. B. Gallie, *Philosophers of Peace and War* (Cambridge: Cambridge University Press, 1978). Important detailed studies have also been made, for example, of continuities and discontinuities in the natural law tradition or the emergence of modern diplomacy, but their influence has been quite limited, especially in the United States. See, for example, E. B. F. Midgley, *The Natural Law Tradition and the Theory of International Relations* (London: Elek Books, 1975); Garrett Mattingly, *Renaissance Diplomacy* (London: Jonathan Cape, 1955); and Martin Wight, *Systems of States*, edited by Hedley Bull (Leicester: Leicester University Press, 1977). Much of the literature on ethics and international relations alludes to the implications of this transition but is usually more concerned with establishing a plausible account of a universalist ethics given the achievement of modern autonomies – and statist fragmentations – or simply establishing the importance of historical, normative or critical scholarship in the face of positivist and realist dogmas. These are all themes that will be taken up in subsequent chapters.

Against this background, two recent studies stand out as important and innovative explorations. In one, Andrew Linklater has focused explicitly on the early-modern tension between claims to a universalist conception of humanity and claims to citizenship within particular states. Linklater seeks to resolve this tension through an appeal to a universalising conception of history that draws much of its inspiration from Kant, Hegel and Marx, a conception of history that I prefer to hold under considerable suspicion even though it is perhaps difficult to avoid entirely. See Linklater, *Men and Citizens in the Theory of International Relations* (London: Macmillan, 1982); *Beyond Realism and Marxism: Critical Theory and International Relations* (London: Macmillan, 1989); and especially 'The Problem of Community in International Relations', *Alternatives*, 15:2, Spring 1990, 135–53. In the other, James Der Derian develops a genealogical reading of diplomatic practices as the mediation of estrangement. See Der Derian, *On Diplomacy: A Genealogy of Western Estrangement* (Oxford: Basil Blackwell, 1987). While my formulation of the problem to be addressed is often close to that of Linklater, my overall argument is more sympathetic to Der Derian's emphasis on the extent to which modern theories of international relations both express and rely on a reification of others as Other, and thus to his conception of the problematic character of universalist aspirations framed within particularistic communities. For a collection of recent essays that explore distinctive dimensions of the intervening terrain, see Walker and Mendlovitz, eds., *Contending Sovereignties*.

18 Despite the influence of positivistically inclined conceptions of research method in international relations, there have been relatively few sustained discussions – as opposed to brief invocations – of scientific inquiry in this discipline. For notable exceptions, all of which advance warnings about positivist caricatures, see Charles Reynolds, *Theory and Explanation in International Politics* (London: Martin Robertson, 1973); Martin Hollis and Steve Smith, *Explaining and Understanding International Relations* (Oxford: Clarendon Press, 1990); and Friedrich Kratochwil, 'Regimes, Interpretation and the "Science" of Politics: A Reappraisal', *Millennium: Journal of International Studies*, 17:2, Summer 1988, 263–84. For a broad survey of the implications of recent controversies about science and epistemology for theories of international relations, see George and Campbell, 'Patterns of Dissent and the Celebration of Difference: Critical Social Theory and International Relations'.

19 See especially Michael Doyle, 'Kant, Liberal Legacies and Foreign Affairs', Parts 1 and 2, *Philosophy and Public Affairs*, 12:3, Summer 1983, 205–35 and 12:4, Fall 1983, 323–53.

20 Linklater, *Beyond Realism and Marxism*; Cox, 'Social Forces, States and World Orders'; Mark Hoffman, 'Critical Theory and the Inter-Paradigm Debate', in Dyer and Mangasarian, eds., *The Study of International Relations*, 60–86; John Maclean, 'Political Theory, International Theory and Problems of Ideology', *Millennium: Journal of International Studies*, 10:2, Summer 1981, 102–25; and Maclean, 'Marxism and International Relations: A Strange Case of Mutual Neglect', *Journal of International Studies*, 17:2, Summer 1988, 295–319.

Earlier attempts to develop an explicitly critical theory of international relations have largely disappeared without trace. See, for example, the phenomenological perspective canvassed in Herbert G. Reid and Ernest J. Yanarella, 'Towards a Critical Theory of Peace Research in the United States: the Search for an "Intelligible Core"', *Journal of Peace Research*, 13:4, 1976, 315–41.

21 Jurgen Habermas, *The Philosophical Discourse of Modernity*, trans. Frederick Lawrence (Cambridge, MA: MIT Press, 1987).

22 Hans Blumenberg, *The Legitimacy of the Modern Age* (Cambridge, MA: MIT Press, 1983).

23 Charles Taylor, *Sources of the Self: The Making of the Modern Identity* (Cambridge, MA: Harvard University Press, 1989).

24 In this respect, much of my account of modern theories of international relations has been informed by an attempt to make sense of the contemporary strategies of social movements in relation to globally organised practices of power; see Walker, *One World, Many Worlds* (Boulder: Lynne Rienner, 1988); and Warren Magnusson and R. B. J. Walker, 'Decentring the State: Political Theory and Canadian Political Economy', *Studies in Political Economy*, 27, Summer 1988, 37–71.

25 See the important critical survey by Hidemi Suganami, *The Domestic Analogy and World Order Proposals* (Cambridge: Cambridge University Press, 1989).

26 John Dunn, *Western Political Theory in the Face of the Future*, 78–9.

27 Indeed, I would stress that such a pairing is likely to lead to a very narrow reading of the implications of Foucault's work, though one that is especially useful for my much more limited purposes here. For a helpful general discussion of Weber and Foucault see Colin Gordon, 'The Soul of the Citizen: Max Weber and Michel Foucault on Rationality and Government', in Sam Whimster and Scott Lash, eds., *Max Weber, Rationality and Modernity* (London: Allen and Unwin, 1987), 293–316.

2 *The Prince* and 'the pauper'

1 K. J. Holsti, *The Dividing Discipline: Hegemony and Diversity in International Theory* (Boston: Allen & Unwin, 1985): 1.

2 Meditations on this theme constitute the staple fare of discussions about the character and method of the history of ideas, especially the history of political and philosophical thought. They extend into complex metatheoretical problems involving the politics and epistemology of interpretation as well as into ontological controversies about history and time. This chapter skates over the surface of these more complex themes. My intention is simply to insist on the highly problematic nature of any reference to a tradition in the context of one specific academic discipline, one that is constantly relegitimised by what ought to be embarrassing claims about the origin, continuity and transformation of a tradition of theory about international relations or politics.

The underlying problems involved have been sharply articulated both by those associated with 'hermeneutics', such as R. G. Collingwood and Hans-Georg Gadamer, and those associated with 'poststructuralism', such as Michel Foucault and Jacques Derrida. Any extended discussion of these problems must necessarily engage in a complex conversation in which the names of Hegel, Nietzsche and Heidegger would find a prominent place. Relatively accessible general discussions, which speak more directly to the argument I want to develop here, include: John Gunnell, 'The Myth of the Tradition', *American Political Science Review*, 72:1, March 1978, 122–34; Gunnell, *Between Philosophy and Politics*; John S. Nelson, ed., *Tradition, Interpretation and Science: Political Theory in the American Academy* (Albany: State University of New York Press, 1986); Richard Ashcraft, 'Political Theory and the Problem of Ideology', *Journal of Politics*, 42:3, August 1980; James Tully, ed., *Meaning and Context: Quentin Skinner and his Critics* (Princeton: Princeton University Press, 1988); Richard Rorty, J. B. Schneedwind and Quentin Skinner, eds., *Philosophy and History* (Cambridge: Cambridge University Press, 1984); Jonathan Rée *et al.*, *Philosophy and its Past* (Brighton: Harvester, 1978); Edward Said, *Beginnings* (New York: Basic Books, 1975): 29–78; Dominique La Capra, *Rethinking Intellectual History: Texts, Contexts, and Language* (Ithaca, NY: Cornell University Press, 1983); David Carr, *Time, Narrative and History* (Bloomington and Indianapolis: Indiana University Press, 1986); Paul Veyne, *Did the Greeks Believe in their Myths?* (Chicago: University of Chicago Press, 1988); Michel de Certeau, *The Writing of History*, trans. Tom Conley, (New York: Columbia University Press, 1988); and Paul Ricoeur, *History and Truth*, trans. C. A. Kelbey, (Evanston, Illinois: Northwestern University Press, 1965).

It is worth noting that much of the discussion of this theme in American political science has involved challenges to the specific version of a tradition associated with Leo Strauss, not least for the role 'Machiavelli' plays in Strauss's story as the point of collapse in the 'great tradition' that Strauss counterposes the modernity. This specific version of a tradition is arguably of overriding importance of the way the 'American science of international relations' has been constituted since 1945. The differing responses by Strauss and Hans J. Morgenthau to Max Weber's rendition of modernity, and their role in the institutionalisation of the academic disciplines of political theory and international relations in the USA, are particularly interesting in this respect.

3 See, e.g., Eric Wolf, *Europe and the People without History* (Berkeley: University of California Press, 1982); George E. Marcus and Michael M. J. Fischer, *Anthropology as Cultural Critique* (Chicago: University of Chicago Press, 1986); Edward Said, *Orientalism* (New York: Random House, 1979); Johannes Fabian, *Time and the Other: How Anthropology Makes its Object* (New York: Columbia University Press, 1983); Tzvetan Todorov, *The Conquest of America* (New York: Harper and Row, 1982); Robert Young, *White Mythologies: Writing History and the West* (London: Routledge, 1990); Ashis Nandy, *Traditions, Tyranny and Utopias: Essays in the Politics of Awareness* (Delhi: Oxford University Press, 1987); Nandy, *The Intimate Enemy: Loss and Recovery of Self Under Colonialism* (Delhi: Oxford University Press, 1983); Ashis Nandy, *The Tao of Cricket: On Games of Destiny and the Destiny of Games* (New Delhi: Penguin, 1989); Gayatri Chakravorty Spivak, *In Other Worlds: Essays in Cultural Politics* (London: Methuen, 1987); and Partha Chatterjee, *Nationalist Thought and the Colonial World: A Derivative Discourse* (London: Zed/UNU, 1986).

4 A challenge initiated by Richard K. Ashley, 'The Poverty of Neo-Realism', *International Organization*, 38:2, Spring 1984, 225–86.

5 See, for example, Michael Donelan's argument that insofar as it is useful to speak of a tradition, it is better understood as a conversation among five distinctive positions: Historicism, Natural Law, Realism, Fideism and Rationalism. See his *Elements of International Political Theory* (Oxford: Clarendon Press, 1990).

6 E. H. Carr, *The Twenty-Years Crisis*; Ian Clark, *The Hierarchy of States*.

7 Hedley Bull, *The Anarchical Society* (London: Macmillan, 1977); Martin Wight, 'An Anatomy of International Thought' (1960), *Review of International Studies*, 13:3, July 1987, 221–27.

8 Stanley Hoffmann, *The State of War: Essays in the Theory and Practice of International Politics* (New York: Praeger, 1965); Hans J. Morgenthau, *Scientific Man vs. Power Politics* (Chicago: Chicago University Press, 1946).

9 R. N. Berki, *On Political Realism* (London: J. M. Dent, 1981) and Friedrich Meinecke, *Machiavellianism: The Doctrine of Raison D'Etat and Its Place in Modern History* (London: Routledge and Kegan Paul, 1957).

10 Martin Wight, 'Why is There No International Theory?' in H. Butterfield and M. Wight, eds., *Diplomatic Investigations* (London: George Allen & Unwin, 1966): 17–34. For commentary, see Hedley Bull, 'Martin Wight and the Theory of International Relations: The Second Martin Wight Memorial Lecture', *British Journal of International Studies*, 2: 1976, 101–16; and Robert H.

Jackson, 'Martin Wight, International Theory and the Good Life', *Millennium: Journal of International Studies*, 19:2, Summer 1990, 261–72.

11 Martin Wight, *Systems of States*, edited by Hedley Bull (Leicester: Leicester University Press, 1977).

12 See, for example, Felix Raab, *The English Face of Machiavelli: A Changing Interpretation* (London: Routledge and Kegan Paul, 1964); and Isaiah Berlin, 'The Originality of Machiavelli', in Berlin, *Against the Current* (Oxford: Oxford University Press, 1979): 25–79.

13 See, for example, J. G. A. Pocock, *The Machiavellian Moment: Florentine Political Thought and the Atlantic Republican Tradition* (Princeton: Princeton University Press, 1975); Pocock, 'Machiavelli and Guicciardini: Ancients and Moderns', *Canadian Journal of Political and Social Theory*, 2:3, Fall 1978, 93–107; Quentin Skinner, *The Foundations of Modern Political Thought*, 2 vols. (Cambridge: Cambridge University Press, 1978); Skinner, *Machiavelli* (Oxford: Oxford University Press, 1981); Felix Gilbert, *Machiavelli and Guicciardini* (Princeton: Princeton University Press, 1965); Hans Baron, *The Crisis of the Early Italian Renaissance*, 2nd edn (Princeton: Princeton University Press, 1966); and J. H. Hexter, *The Vision of Politics on the Eve of the Reformation* (New York: Basic Books, 1973).

14 Wolin, *Politics and Vision*, 195–238.

15 Niccolò Machiavelli, *The Prince*, edited by Quentin Skinner and Russell Price (Cambridge: Cambridge University Press, 1988): 75–6.

16 For helpful discussions of this familiar theme see Hanna Fenichel Pitkin, *Fortune is a Woman: Gender and Politics in the Thought of Niccolo Machiavelli* (Berkeley and Los Angeles: University of California Press, 1984); Mark Hulliung, *Citizen Machiavelli* (Princeton: Princeton University Press, 1983); and Maurice Merleau-Ponty, 'A Note on Machiavelli' in his *Signs*, trans. Richard C. McCleary, (Evanston, Ill: Northwestern University Press, 1964): 211–23.

17 Machiavelli, *The Prince*, chapter 25.

18 On this general theme see Gunnell, *Political Philosophy and Time*. In the specific case of Machiavelli, see Robert Orr, 'The Time Motif in Machiavelli' in M. Fleisher, ed., *Machiavelli and the Nature of Political Thought* (New York: Atheneum, 1972): 185–208; and Thomas M. Greene, 'The End of Discourse in Machiavelli's "Prince"', *Yale French Studies*, 67, 1984, 57–71.

19 Although greatness in time was not necessarily incompatible with the achievement of ultimate grace through the achievement of God's desire; see Sebastian de Grazia, *Machiavelli in Hell* (Princeton: Princeton University Press, 1989).

20 Thomas Hobbes, *Leviathan*, edited by C. B. Macpherson, (London: Penguin Books, 1968), chapter 21.

21 Hence the contrast between the reification of the distinction between 'inside' and 'outside' in the categories adopted by Martin Wight and the exploration of the practices of negation and displacement that has been central to recent attempts to develop a more critical understanding of contemporary world politics. See especially Richard K. Ashley, 'Untying the Sovereign State: A Double Reading of the Anarchy Problematique', *Millennium: Journal of International Studies*, 17:2, Summer 1988, 227–62;

Ashley, 'Living on Border Lines: Man, Post-structuralism and War' in Der Derian and Shapiro, eds., *International/Intertextual Relations*, 259–321; and Der Derian, *On Diplomacy*.

22 Machiavelli, *The Prince*, chapter 25.

23 See Pitkin, *Fortune is a Woman*; and Brown, *Manhood and Politics*. Machiavelli's chauvinism, of course, which implies an eventual submission to *fortuna*, is perhaps more positively ambiguous than the erasure of all questions about gender through rationalist claims about universal man. Nevertheless, it remains one of the crucial constitutive moves in the construction of an explicitly gendered account of the boundaries of inclusion and exclusion in modern political life, a theme that has recently become a focus for feminist critiques of international relations theory. See, for example, Anne Sisson Runyon and V. Spike Peterson, 'The Radical Future of Realism: Feminist Subversions of International Relations Theory', *Alternatives*, 16:1, Winter 1991, 67–106. I return to this theme in the final chapter.

24 See Eric Havelock, *Preface to Plato* (Cambridge, MA: Harvard University Press, 1963); and Hans-Georg Gadamer, 'Plato and the Poets', in *Dialogue and Dialectic: Eight Hermeneutical Studies in Plato*, trans. Christopher Smith (New Haven: Yale University Press, 1980): 39–72.

25 See, for example, Robert Harriman, 'Composing Modernity in Machiavelli's *Prince*', *Journal of the History of Ideas*, 1989, 3–29; and Eugene Garver, *Machiavelli and the History of Prudence* (Madison: University of Wisconsin Press, 1987).

26 For recent examples of this aspiration see, for example, W. B. Gallie, *Philosophers of Peace and War* (Cambridge: Cambridge University Press, 1978); Michael C. Williams, 'Rousseau, Realism and *Realpolitik*', *Millennium: Journal of International Studies* 18:2, Summer 1989, 163–87; Williams, 'Reason and Realpolitik: Kant's "Critique of International Politics"', *Canadian Journal of Political Science*, 25:1, March 1992, 99–119; N. J. Rengger, 'An Arrow in the Heart of the Present: Kant and International Theory' in Howard Williams, ed., *Kant's Political Theory* (forthcoming); and Cornelia Navari, 'Hobbes and the Hobbesian Tradition in International Thought', *Millennium: Journal of International Studies*, 11:3, 1982, 202–22.

3 Ethics, modernity, community

1 Stanley Hoffmann, *The Political Ethics of International Relations* (New York: Carnegie Council on Ethics and International Affairs, 1988). See also Hoffmann, *Duties Beyond Borders: On the Limits and Possibilities of Ethical International Relations* (Syracuse, NY: Syracuse University Press, 1981). For a brief introduction and bibliographical guide to the literature that is conventionally included under the heading of ethics and international relations see Mark J. Hoffman, 'Normative Approaches', in Margot Light and A. J. R. Groom, eds., *International Relations: A Handbook of Current Theory* (London: Francis Pinter, 1985, 27–45). For a helpful discussion of the positivist context in which questions about ethics and international relations have been marginalised see Mervyn Frost, *Towards a Normative Theory of International Relations* (Cambridge: Cambridge University Press, 1988).

2 While I am not specifically concerned with the current state of debate about ethics within contemporary social and political theory and philosophy, it is worth noting, first, that much of this debate is explicitly focused on the constraints imposed by a continuing opposition between universalist and communitarian standards, and second, that very few champions of the communitarian position seem perturbed by the problematic character of community in contemporary world politics. Working within explicitly modern accounts of individual agency and tacitly modern accounts of community within a single sovereign state, much of the contemporary literature on ethics continues to simply take for granted that which theories of international relations simply presume to be absent.

3 On the connections between ethics, epistemology and modernity, and the extent to which these connections have become the focus of contemporary philosophical debate, I have found the following discussions to be especially helpful: Bernard Williams, *Ethics and the Limits of Philosophy* (Cambridge, MA: Harvard University Press, 1985); Stuart Hampshire, *Innocence and Experience* (Cambridge, MA: Harvard University Press, 1987); Alasdair MacIntyre, *After Virtue* (Notre Dame: University of Notre Dame Press, 1981); Richard Rorty, *Philosophy and the Mirror of Nature* (Princeton: Princeton University Press, 1980); David Hiley, *Philosophy in Question: Essays on a Pyrrhonian Theme* (Chicago: University of Chicago Press, 1988); David Kolb, *The Critique of Pure Modernity: Hegel, Heidegger and After* (Chicago: University of Chicago Press, 1986); and William E. Connolly, *Political Theory and Modernity* (Oxford: Basil Blackwell, 1988).

4 Hence part of what is at stake in recent distinctions between ahistorical or structuralist forms of neo-realism and the historicist sensitivities informing the classic texts of writers like E. H. Carr and Hans J. Morgenthau. These distinctions are explored from a variety of directions in Keohane, ed., *Neorealism and Its Critics*; and Alker and Ashley, eds., *After Neorealism*. See also chapter 5 below.

5 See, for example, Raymond Aron, 'Max Weber and Power Politics', in Otto Stammer, ed., *Max Weber and Sociology Today*, trans. K. Morris (Oxford: Basil Blackwell, 1979), 83–100; and Hans J. Morgenthau, 'Fragment of an Intellectual Autobiography: 1904–1932', in K. W. Thompson, et al., eds., *Truth and Tragedy: A Tribute to Hans J. Morgenthau* (Washington, DC: New Republic Book Co., 1977). For commentary on the connection between Weber and political realism in international relations, see Michael Joseph Smith, *Realist Thought from Weber to Kissinger* (Baton Rouge: Louisiana State University Press, 1986); and, more helpfully, Stephen Turner and Regis A. Factor, *Max Weber and the Dispute Over Reason and Value* (London: Routledge and Kegan Paul, 1984). I return to this theme in chapter 8.

6 See especially F. H. Tenbruck, 'The Problem of Thematic Unity in the Work of Max Weber', *British Journal of Sociology* 31, 1980, 316–51; Wilhelm Hennis, *Max Weber: Essays in Reconstruction*, trans. Keith Tribe (London: Allen and Unwin, 1988); Wolfgang J. Mommsen, *Max Weber and German Politics, 1880–1920*, trans. Michael S. Steinberg (Chicago: University of Chicago Press, 1984); and Mommsen, *The Political and Social Theory of Max Weber* (Chicago: University of Chicago Press, 1989). See also David Beetham, *Max Weber*

and the Theory of Modern Politics, 2nd edn (Cambridge: Polity Press, 1985); Wolfgang J. Mommsen and Jurgen Osterhammel, eds., *Max Weber and his Contemporaries* (London: Allen and Unwin, 1987); and Harry Liebersohn, *Fate and Utopia in German Sociology, 1870–1923* (Cambridge, MA: MIT Press, 1988).

7 Whether mediated through Weber or not, the link between Augustinian and Lutheran theologies on twentieth-century claims to political realism has been both profound and relatively unexplored. For an account of this link that is especially sensitive to the diversity of positions that resort to such claims see Roger Epp, 'Power Politics and the *Civitas Terrena*: The Augustinian Sources of Anglo-American Theory in International Relations' (unpublished doctoral dissertation, Queen's University, Kingston, Ontario, 1989). More generally, see William E. Connolly, 'A Letter to St Augustine', in his *Identity\Difference*.

8 Carl Schmitt, *Political Theology: Four Chapters on the Concept of Sovereignty* (1922), trans. George Schwab (Cambridge, MA: MIT Press, 1985); and Alfons Söllner, 'German Conservatism in America: Morgenthau's Political Realism', *Telos*, 72, Summer 1987, 161–72.

9 Smith, *Realist Thought from Weber to Kissinger*, 15.

10 Hoffmann, *The Political Ethics of International Relations*, 12.

11 Albert J. Hirshmann, *The Passions and the Interests* (Princeton: Princeton University Press, 1979). This brilliant essay offers an especially insightful perspective from which to read the literature on what Robert Keohane calls 'neoliberal institutionalism'. See Robert O. Keohane, *International Institutions and State Power: Essays in International Relations Theory* (Boulder: Westview Press, 1989).

12 Charles Beitz, *Political Theory and International Relations* (Princeton: Princeton University Press, 1979); and 'Sovereignty and Morality in International Affairs', in Held, ed., *Political Theory Today*, 236–54.

13 Onora O'Neill, 'Transnational Justice', in Held, ed., *Political Theory Today*, 276–304; and *Faces of Hunger: An Essay on Poverty, Development and Justice* (London: Allen and Unwin, 1986).

14 Linklater, *Men and Citizens in the Theory of International Relations*.

15 W. B. Gallie, 'Kant's View of Reason in Politics', *Philosophy*, 54, 1979, 19–33; 'Wanted: A Philosophy of International Relations', *Political Studies* 37:3, September 1979, 484–92; and *Philosophers of Peace and War*. See also Roger J. Sullivan, *Immanuel Kant's Moral Theory* (Cambridge: Cambridge University Press, 1989).

16 Hedley Bull and Adam Watson, eds., *The Expansion of International Society* (Oxford: Clarendon Press, 1984).

17 Saul H. Mendlovitz, ed., *On the Creation of a Just World Order* (New York: Free Press, 1975); Richard A. Falk, *A Study of Future Worlds* (New York: Free Press, 1975); Richard A. Falk, Samuel Kim and Saul H. Mendlovitz, eds., *Towards a Just World Order* (Boulder: Westview Press, 1982); Falk, *The Promise of World Order* (Philadelphia: Temple University Press, 1987); Falk, *Explorations at the Edge of Time: The Prospects for World Order* (Philadelphia: Temple University Press, 1992) and R. Falk, Samuel S. Kim, and Robert C. Johansen, eds., *The Constitutional Foundations of World Peace* (Albany: State University of New York Press, 1993).

18 Joseph Nye and Robert O. Keohane, *Power and Interdependence* (Boston: Little Brown, 1977).

19 Wight, 'Why is there no International Theory?'

20 François Hartog, *The Mirror of Herodotus: The Representation of the Other in the Writing of History*, trans. Janet Lloyd (Berkeley and Los Angeles: University of California Press, 1988). For a helpful discussion of the dangers of anachronism in this general context, see Peter T. Mancias, 'War, Stasis and Greek Political Theory', *Comparative Studies in Society and History*, 24:4, October 1982, 673–88.

21 Bull, *The Anarchical Society*.

22 R. J. Vincent, 'Hedley Bull and Order in International Politics', *Millennium: Journal of International Studies* 17:2, Summer 1988, 195–213.

23 Terry Nardin, *Law, Morality and the Relations of States* (Princeton: Princeton University Press, 1983).

24 Friedrich Kratochwil, *Rules, Norms and Decisions: On the Conditions of Practical and Legal Reasoning in International Relations and Domestic Affairs* (Cambridge: Cambridge University Press, 1989).

25 Nicholas Greenwood Onuf, *World of Our Making: Rule and Rule in Social Theory and International Relations* (Columbia: University of South Carolina Press, 1989).

26 Ashley, 'The Poverty of Neorealism'; 'The Geopolitics of Geopolitical Space', *Alternatives*, 12, October 1987, 403–34; 'Untying the Sovereign State'; and 'Living on Border Lines'.

27 Der Derian, *On Diplomacy*.

28 Bull and Roberts, eds., *The Expansion of International Society*.

29 For this argument see, for example, Michael Doyle, 'Kant, Liberal Legacies and Foreign Affairs'.

30 Important expressions include Beitz, *Political Theory and International Relations*; Beitz, 'Cosmopolitan Ideals and National Sentiment', *Journal of Philosophy* 80, No. 10, October 1983, 591–600; and Marshall Cohen, 'Moral Skepticism and International Relations', in Beitz, et al., eds., *International Ethics* (Princeton: Princeton University Press, 1985), 3–50.

31 Beitz, et al., eds., *International Ethics*; Michael Walzer, *Just and Unjust Wars* (New York: Basic Books, 1977); James Turner Johnson, *Just War Tradition and the Restraint of War* (Princeton: Princeton University Press, 1981); Johnson, *The Quest for Peace: Three Moral Traditions in Western Cultural History* (Princeton: Princeton University Press, 1987); Robert L. Holmes, *On War and Morality* (Princeton: Princeton University Press, 1989); Barrie Paskins and Michael Dockrill, *The Ethics of War* (Minneapolis: University of Minnesota Press, 1979); Jean Bethke Elshtain, *Women and War* (New York: Basic Books, 1987).

32 Hedley Bull, ed., *Intervention in World Politics* (Oxford: Clarendon Press, 1984); R. J. Vincent, *Nonintervention and International Order* (Princeton: Princeton University Press, 1974); Vincent, *Human Rights and International Relations* (Cambridge: Cambridge University Press, 1986); and Richard A. Falk, *Human Rights and State Sovereignty* (New York: Holmes and Meier, 1981).

33 Walker and Mendlovitz, eds., *Contending Sovereignties*.

34 Foucault, 'What is Enlightenment?'.

4 History, structure, reification

1 See George and Campbell, 'Patterns of Dissent and the Celebration of Difference'. Characteristically diverse accounts of what it now means to speak of a philosophy of science can be found in, for example, Peter Achinstein and Stephen F. Barker, eds., *The Legacy of Logical Positivism* (Baltimore: Johns Hopkins, 1969); Harold I. Brown, *Perception, Theory and Commitment: The New Philosophy of Science* (Chicago: University of Chicago Press, 1977); Len Doyal and Roger Harris, *Empiricism, Explanation and Rationality: An Introduction to the Philosophy of the Social Sciences* (London: Routledge and Kegan Paul, 1986); Peter Manicas, *A History and Philosophy of the Social Sciences* (Oxford: Basil Blackwell, 1987); Sandra Harding, *The Science Question in Feminism* (Ithaca: Cornell University Press, 1986); Helen E. Longino, *Science as Social Knowledge: Values and Objectivity in Scientific Enquiry* (Princeton: Princeton University Press, 1990); and Joseph Rouse, *Knowledge and Power: Toward a Political Philosophy of Science* (Ithaca: Cornell University Press, 1987).

It is worth recalling the extent to which contemporary debates about explanation and understanding have long been caught up in contending claims about modernity. Rudolph Carnap's verifiability theory of meaning or attempts by Karl Popper and Imre Lakatos to prescribe a criterion for distinguishing science from non-science, now fading landmarks of post-war positivism, were themselves part of a concerted reaction to historicist and counter-empiricist philosophies that had become influential earlier in this century. Indeed, useful perspective on contemporary debates is still provided by texts like Ernst Cassirer, *The Philosophy of the Enlightenment*, trans. F. C. A. Koelln and J. P. Pettegrove (Princeton: Princeton University Press, 1951), and Leszek Kolakowski, *The Alienation of Reason*, trans. Norbert Guterman (Garden City, NY: Doubleday Anchor, 1972), which examine even earlier trends.

2 Robert Keohane, 'International Institutions: Two Approaches', chapter 7 of his *International Institutions and State Power*, 158–79. I am not concerned here with the multiple controversies within contemporary social and political thought generated by claims about rationality. Keohane's own understanding of the relation between rationalism and his own explicitly liberal commitments is sketched in the earlier chapters of *International Institutions and State Power*. For more nuanced discussions, see, for example, Brian Wilson, ed., *Rationality* (Oxford: Basil Blackwell, 1970); Martin Hollis and Steven Lukes, eds., *Rationality and Relativism* (Oxford: Basil Blackwell, 1982); Martin Hollis, *The Cunning of Reason* (Cambridge: Cambridge University Press, 1997); Barry Hindess, *Choice, Rationality and Social Theory* (London: Unwin Hyman, 1988); and Hollis and Smith, *Explaining and Understanding International Relations*.

3 Kenneth Waltz, *Theory of International Politics* (Reading, MA: Addison-Wesley, 1979); Kenneth Oye, ed., *Cooperation Under Anarchy* (Princeton: Princeton University Press, 1986).

4 See, for example, Michael Shapiro, *The Politics of Representation*; Paul Rabinow and William Sullivan, eds., *Interpretive Social Science: A Second Look*

(Berkeley and Los Angeles: University of California Press, 1987); Michael T. Gibbons, ed., *Interpreting Politics* (Oxford: Basil Blackwell, 1987); Paul Ricoeur, *Hermeneutics and the Human Sciences* trans. and edited by John B. Thompson (Cambridge: Cambridge University Press, 1981); Hans-Georg Gadamer, *Philosophical Hermeneutics*, trans. and ed. David E. Linge (Berkeley and Los Angeles: University of California Press, 1976); Richard Harvey Brown, *Society as Text: Essays on Rhetoric, Reason and Reality* (Chicago: University of Chicago Press, 1987); David Carroll, *Paraaesthetics: Foucault, Lyotard, Derrida* (London: Methuen, 1987); Toril Moi, *Sexual/Textual Politics* (London: Methuen, 1985); Brian Fay, *Critical Social Science* (Cambridge: Polity, 1987); Georg Henryk von Wright, *Explanation and Understanding* (Ithaca: Cornell University Press, 1971); and Quentin Skinner, ed., *The Return of Grand Theory in the Human Sciences* (Cambridge: Cambridge University Press, 1985).

5 The main papers from this debate were collected in Klaus Knorr and James N. Rosenau, eds., *Contending Approaches to International Politics* (Princeton: Princeton University Press, 1969).

6 See, for example, the relatively accessible discussions in R. J. Holton, *The Transition from Feudalism to Capitalism* (London: Macmillan, 1985) and Michael Mann, *The Sources of Social Power*, Volume 1.

7 Compare, for example, Wight, *Systems of States*, and Hinsley, *Power and the Pursuit of Peace*.

8 See, for example, the qualification that Hobbes adds to a passage that is frequently cited in the context of claims about an international anarchy: 'Yet in all times, Kings, and Persons of Soveraigne authority, because of their Independency, are in continuall jealousies, and in the state and posture of Gladiators; having their weapons pointing, and their eyes fixed on one another ... But because they uphold thereby, the Industry of their Subjects; there does not follow from it, that misery, which accompanies the Liberty of particular men.' Thomas Hobbes, *Leviathan* (1651), chapter 13, C. B. Macpherson, ed. (London: Penguin, 1968), 188.

9 Robert Gilpin, *The Political Economy of International Relations* (Princeton: Princeton University Press, 1987); Immanuel Wallerstein, 'The Rise and Future Demise of the World Capitalist System: Concepts for Comparative Analysis', *Comparative Studies in Society and History*, 16, 1974, 387–415; Robert W. Cox, *Production, Power and World Order*; and Gill and Law, *The Global Political Economy*.

10 See John O'Neill, ed., *Modes of Individualism and Collectivism* (London: Heinemann, 1973); Steven Lukes, *Individualism* (Oxford: Blackwell, 1973); Marx Wartofsky, *Conceptual Foundations of Scientific Thought* (New York: Macmillan, 1968), 344–402.

11 See, for example, Vincent Descombes, *Modern French Philosophy*, trans. L. Scott-Fox and J. M. Harding (Cambridge: Cambridge University Press, 1980); and Eve Taylor Bannet, *Structuralism and the Logic of Dissent: Barthes, Derrida, Foucault, Lacan* (Urbana: University of Illinois Press, 1989).

12 Helpful secondary literature in this context includes Jonathan Culler, *On Deconstruction* (Routledge and Kegan Paul, 1983); and Rudolphe Gasché, *The Tain of the Mirror: Derrida and the Philosophy of Reflection* (Cambridge, MA: Harvard University Press, 1986).

13 See the important analysis in Friedrich Kratochwil and John Gerald Ruggie, 'International Organizations: A State of the Art on an Art of the State', *International Organization*, 40:4, Autumn 1986, 753–76. See also Kratochwil, *Rules, Norms and Decisions*; and Susan Strange, '*Cave! hic dragones*: a critique of regimes analysis', in Stephen D. Krasner, ed., *International Regimes* (Ithaca: Cornell University Press, 1983).

14 In international relations the adequacy of these images has become especially important in the literature on systems analysis. For a helpful discussion see Richard Little, 'Three Approaches to the International System: Some Ontological and Epistemological Considerations', *British Journal of International Studies* 3, 1977, 269–85.

15 See Roger Hurwitz, 'Strategic and Social Fictions in the Prisoner's Dilemma', in Der Derian and Shapiro, eds., *International/Intertextual Relations*, 113–34.

16 See, for example, Paul Chilton, ed., *Language and the Nuclear Arms Debate: Nukespeak Today* (London: Francis Pinter, 1985); Simon Dalby, *Creating the Second Cold War: The Discourse of Politics* (London: Francis Pinter, 1990); and R. B. J. Walker, 'Culture, Discourse, Insecurity', in Saul Mendlovitz and R. B. J. Walker, eds., *Towards a Just World Peace: Perspectives From Social Movements* (London: Butterworths, 1987), 171–90. More generally, see Der Derian and Shapiro, eds., *International/Intertextual Relations*.

17 The most explicit attempts to treat this as a serious problem for theories of international relations are Alex Wendt, 'The Agent-Structure Problem in International Relations Theory', *International Organization* 41, 1987, 335–70; and David Dessler, 'What's at Stake in the Agent-Structure Debate?' *International Organization* 43:3, Summer 1989, 441–73. Cf. Anthony Giddens, *Central Problems in Social Theory* (London: Macmillan, 1979), 9–95; and Roy Bhaskar, *Scientific Realism and Human Emancipation* (London: Verso, 1988). Like the treatment of questions about freedom and necessity in the literature on political realism, much of the literature on 'agency and structure' can be read as a series of variations on a theme by St Augustine.

18 See the classic text by Michel Foucault, 'What is an Author?' in Rabinow, ed., *The Foucault Reader*, 101–20.

19 Keohane, 'International Institutions: Two Approaches', 162.

5 Realism and change

1 Ashley, 'The Poverty of Neo-Realism'. Cf. Karl Marx, 'The Eighteenth Brumaire of Louis Bonapart', in Marx, *Surveys From Exile*, edited by David Fernbach (New York: Random House, 1973), 143–249.

2 This theme has received surprisingly little attention in the critical response to Ashley's critique. Of the three immediate responses to Ashley, Bruce Andrews and Friedrich Kratochwil do raise some of the issues to be addressed here; see Andrews, 'The Domestic Content of International Desire', *International Organization*, 38:2, 1984, 321–37; and Kratochwil, 'Errors Have Their Advantages', *International Organization*, 38:2, 1984, 305–20. Andrews focuses his attention primarily (and quite correctly) on the frailty of the conceptualisation of the state in international political theory, but skips rather lightly over the theoretical and ideological origins

of the problems he identifies. Kratochwil confirms once again the limited epistemological resources of the would-be positivists, but does not pursue the debate much beyond the bounds of epistemology. As I suggest below, the most interesting aspect of Robert Gilpin's response ('The Richness of the Tradition of Political Realism', *International Organization*, 38:2, 1984, 287–304) is its silence on precisely those metatheoretical assumptions that are so problematic in his own empirical work.

3 John G. Ruggie, 'Continuity and Transformation in the World Polity: Toward a Neorealist Synthesis', *World Politics*, 35:2, 1983, 261–85.

4 Especially Robert Gilpin, *War and Change in World Politics* (Cambridge: Cambridge University Press, 1981).

5 Robert Cox, 'Social Forces, States and World Orders: Beyond International Relations Theory', *Millennium: Journal of International Studies*, 10:2, 1981, 126–55.

6 Berki, *On Political Realism*.

7 Barry Buzan and R. Barry Jones, eds., *Change and the Study of International Relations* (London: Francis Pinter, 1981); Ole Holsti et al. eds., *Change in the International System* (Boulder: Westview Press, 1981); Czempiel and Rosenau, eds., *Global Changes and Theoretical Challenges*.

8 R. J. Vincent, 'Change and International Relations', *Review of International Studies*, 9:1, 1983, 63–70.

9 Berki, *On Political Realism*, 69.

10 For critical commentaries on the appropriation of Thucydides in the theory of international relation, see Daniel Garst, 'Thucydides and Neorealism', *International Studies Quarterly*, 33:1, March 1989, 3–27; and Richard D. Sears, 'Thucydides and the Scientific Approach to International Relations', *Australian Journal of Politics and History*, 23:1, April 1977, 28–40.

11 Hedley Bull, 'Hobbes and the International Anarchy', *Social Research*, 48:4, 1981, 717–38.

12 See D. W. Hanson, 'Thomas Hobbes' "Highway to Peace"', *International Organization*, 38:2, 1984, 329–54; Murray Forsyth, 'Thomas Hobbes and the External Relations of States', *British Journal of International Studies*, 5:3, 1979, 196–209; and especially Cornelia Navari, 'Hobbes and the "Hobbesian Tradition" in International Thought'.

13 For especially helpful discussions, see Alfred Schmidt, *History and Structure: An Essay on Hegelian-Marxist and Structuralist Theories of History*, trans. Jeffrey Herf (Cambridge, MA: MIT Press, 1981); T. K. Seung, *Structuralism and Hermeneutics* (New York: Columbia University Press, 1982); and Vincent Descombes, *Modern French Philosophy*.

14 See, especially, Jacques Derrida, *Writing and Difference*, trans. Alan Bass (Chicago: University of Chicago Press, 1978); Derrida, *Margins of Philosophy* trans. Alan Bass (Chicago: University of Chicago Press, 1982); Derrida, *Of Grammatology*, trans. Gayatri Chakravorty Spivak (Baltimore: Johns Hopkins University Press, 1976); and Derrida, *Positions*, trans. Alan Bass (Chicago: University: University of Chicago Press, 1981).

15 This was the crucial issue posed by T. S. Kuhn in *The Structure of Scientific Revolutions* (Chicago: University of Chicago Press, 1962), but which was largely diverted in subsequent controversies into subsidiary problems

NOTES TO PAGES 118–128

about the sociology of knowledge. For more sustained treatments see Gaston Bachelard, *La formation de l'esprit scientifique* (Paris: Vrin, 1938); and Micheal Foucault, *The Order of Things*.

16 Karl Marx, *Grundrisse*, trans. Martin Nicolaus (London: Penguin, 1973), 83.

17 Gilpin, 'The Richness of the Tradition of Political Realism'.

18 E. H. Carr's *The Twenty Years Crisis* is paradigmatic in this respect.

19 R. N. Berki, *Insight and Vision: The Problem of Communism in Marx's Thought* (London, J. M. Dent, 1983).

20 Berki, *Insight and Vision*, 172.

21 Berki, *Insight and Vision*, 173.

6 The territorial state and the theme of Gulliver

1 Some idea of the complexity of contemporary theorisations of the state can be gleaned from, say, David Held, *Political Theory and the Modern State: Essays on State, Power and Democracy* (Cambridge: Polity Press, 1989); Kenneth Dyson, *The State Tradition in Western Europe* (Oxford: Martin Robertson, 1980); Martin Carnoy, *The State and Political Theory* (Princeton: Princeton University Press, 1984); Andrew Vincent, *Theories of the State* (Oxford: Basil Blackwell, 1987); Anthony Giddens, *The Nation State and Violence* (Cambridge: Polity Press, 1985); and James A. Caporaso, ed., *The Elusive State: International and Comparative Perspectives* (London: Sage, 1989).

2 Max Weber, 'Politics as a Vocation', 78.

3 Stanley Hoffman, 'Obstinate or Obsolete? The Fate of the Nation-State and the Case of Western Europe', *Daedalus*, 95, (Summer 1966) 862–915.

4 John Herz, *International Politics in the Atomic Age* (New York: Columbia University Press, 1959); and *The Nation State and the Crisis of World Politics* (New York: David McKay, 1976).

5 Maurice Merleau-Ponty, *Phenomenology of Perception*, trans. Colin Smith (London: Routledge and Kegan Paul, 1962); and Donald M. Lowe, *History of Bourgeois Perception*. See also Ernst Cassirer, *The Philosophy of Symbolic Forms*, 3 vols. (1923–1927) trans. Ralph Mannheim (New Haven: Yale University Press, 1955–1957); and Cassirer, 'Mythic, Aesthetic and Theoretical Space', *Man and World*, 2:1, 1969, 3–17.

6 Gaston Bachelard, *The Poetics of Space*, trans. Maria Jolas (Boston: Beacon Press, 1969).

7 Derek Gregory and John Urry, eds., *Social Relations and Spatial Structures* (London: Macmillan, 1985); Yi-Fu Tuan, *Space and Place* (Minneapolis: University of Minnesota Press 1977); Robert David Sack, *Conceptions of Space in Social Thought* (London: Macmillan 1980); Neil Smith, *Uneven Development: Nature, Capital and the Production of Space* (Oxford: Basil Blackwell, 1985); David Harvey, *The Condition of Postmodernity*; E. P. Thompson, 'Time, Work-Discipline and Industrial Capitalism', *Past and Present*, 38:1, December 1967, 56–97; and David Gross, 'Temporality and the Modern State', *Theory and Society*, 14:2, 1985, 53–82.

8 Henri Lefebvre, 'Reflections on the Politics of Space', trans. Michael J. Enders, *Antipode*, 8 May 1976, 31. See also Lefebvre, *The Production of Space* (1974) translated by Donald Nicholson-Smith (Oxford: Blackwell, 1991).

9 Max Jammer, *Concepts of Space: The History of Theories of Space in Physics* 2nd edn, (Cambridge, MA: Harvard University Press 1969).

10 Cassirer, *Individual and Cosmos in Renaissance Philosophy*.

11 Edmund Husserl, *The Crisis of European Sciences and Transcendental Phenomenology*, (previously cited ch. 1 note 2) trans. David Carr (Evanston: University of Illinois Press, 1970).

12 Milič Čapek, *The Philosophical Impact of Contemporary Physics* (New York: Van Nostrand 1961), 28. See also Alexander Koyré, *From the Closed World to the Infinite Universe* (Baltimore: Johns Hopkins Press 1957).

13 On the broad historical and cultural impact of this new understanding of space, see, for example, Morris Kline, *Mathematics in Western Culture* (New York: Oxford University Press 1953); and Dan Pedoe, *Geometry and the Liberal Arts* (Harmondsworth: Penguin 1976).

14 John Locke, chapter 5 of *Two Treatises of Government*, ed. Peter Laslett (Cambridge: Cambridge University Press, 1988).

15 Edward W. Soja, *The Political Organization of Space*, Commission on College Geography, Resource Paper No. 8 (Washington DC: Association of American Geographers 1971), 9.

16 Ernest Gellner, *Nations and Nationalism* (Oxford: Basil Blackwell 1983), 139–40.

17 Kenneth Waltz, *Man, the State and War* (New York: Columbia University Press 1954). See also J. David Singer, 'The level of analysis problem in international relations', in Klaus Knorr and Sidney Verba, eds., *The International System: Theoretical Essays* (Princeton: Princeton University Press 1961), 77–92. More recently, Robert C. North has attempted to extend the number of levels to four by insisting on the importance of global as well as interstate systems; see North, *War, Peace and Survival: Global Politics and Conceptual Synthesis* (Boulder: Westview, 1990). While I share his judgment about the importance of global processes, the spatial imagery of levels necessarily provides an inappropriate guide to what these processes involve.

18 Inis Claude, Jr., *Power and International Relations* (New York: Random House, 1962).

19 Ernst Haas, 'The Study of Regional Integration: Reflections on the Joy and Anguish of Pretheorizing', *International Organization*, 24:4, Autumn 1970, 361.

20 Pierre-Maxime Schuhl, 'Le Thème du Gulliver et le postulat de Laplace', *Journal de psychologie normal et pathologique*, 40:211, avril–juin 1947, 169–84; and Milič Čapek, 'The "theme of Gulliver" and the relativity of magnitude', in Čapek, *The Philosophical Impact of Contemporary Physics*, 21–6. Cf. Jonathan Swift, *Gulliver's Travels*, 1726.

21 For a recent succinct statement, see Waltz, 'Realist Thought and Neorealist Theory', *Journal of International Studies*, 44:1, Spring/Summer 1990, 20–37. Waltz's desire both to keep and swallow his cake, both to affirm and deny the boundary between inside and outside encourages two crucial moves in his substantive theory: i. the charge of reductionism against those who do not abstract the logic of supposedly anarchical relations from the actions of states, and ii. the resort to conceptions of a system informed by assumptions about a market economy rather than by the rather long and contentious discussions about reductionisms, hierarchies and levels from which contemporary systems theories have emerged.

Some sense of the ontological controversies that Waltz manages to elide with respect to systems theory can be found in, for example, Walter Buckley, ed., *Modern Systems Research for the Behavioral Scientist: A Sourcebook* (Chicago: Aldine, 1968); and Buckley, *Sociology and Modern Systems Theory* (Englewood Cliffs, NJ: Prentice Hall, 1967). For a sharp discussion of the controversies that Waltz has generated, though one which continues to take the levels of hierarchy for granted, see Hollis and Smith, *Explaining and Understanding International Relations*, 104–18. For a sustained, incisive and, in my view, decisive critique of Waltz's commitment to a modernist account of sovereign subjectivity, see Ashley, 'Living on Border Lines'.

22 Herz, 'The Rise and Demise of the Territorial State', *World Politics*, 9:4, 1957, 473–93, reprinted in Herz, *The Nation-State and the Crisis of World Politics*, 99–123. The quotations here are from the Introduction to this collection of essays, 15–16.

23 Herz, 'The Territorial State Revisited: Reflections on the Future of the Nation-State', *Polity*, 1:1, Fall 1968, 11–34, reprinted in Herz, *The Nation-State and the Crisis of World Politics*, 226–253.

24 Herz, *The Nation-State and the Crisis of World Politics*, 19.

25 The connection is especially stressed in Hans Saner, *Kant's Political Thought*, trans. E. B. Ashton (Chicago: University of Chicago Press, 1973).

26 Barry Buzan, *People, States and Fear: The National Security Problem in International Relations* (Brighton: Wheatsheaf, 1983, 2nd edn 1991). One of the positive achievements of Buzan's analysis here is the seriousness with which it treats economic aspects of national security policy, an achievement that is nevertheless compromised by restricting conceptions of economic life to an opposition between 'liberal' and 'mercantilist' accounts of the world economy. See also Buzan, 'Economic Structure and International Security: the Limits of the Liberal Case', *International Organization*, 38:4, Autumn 1984, 597–624.

27 R. B. J. Walker, 'Contemporary Militarism and the Discourse of Dissent', in Walker, ed., *Culture, Ideology and World Order*, 302–22; and Walker, 'Culture, Discourse, Insecurity'.

28 This opposition was invoked in a later revision of Buzan's analysis. Both peace and power are said to provide partial and complementary insights which can be synthesised into something more suitably comprehensive, a claim which depends on the dubious assumption that the two ends of the spectrum provide an adequate terrain on which to delineate a middle. See Buzan, 'Peace, Power and Security: Contending Concepts in the Study of International Relations', *Journal of Peace Research*, 21:2, 1984, 109–25.

29 See, for example, Buzan, 'Systems, Structures and Units: Reconstructing Waltz's Theory of International Politics', paper delivered at the British International Studies Association/International Studies Association Annual Conference, London, February 1989.

30 See, for example, Michael T. Klare and Daniel Thomas, eds., *World Security: Trends and Challenges at Century's End* (New York: St Martins, 1991); Simon Dalby, 'Security, Modernity, Ecology: The Dilemmas of Post-Cold War Security Discourse', *Alternatives*, 17:1, Winter 1992, 95–133; and Walker, *One World, Many Worlds*.

7 On the spatio-temporal conditions of democratic practice

1 John Dunn, *Western Political Theory in the Face of the Future* (Cambridge: Cambridge University Press, 1979), 2.

2 For a brief discussion of the problematic relationship between democracy and foreign policy, for example, see Steve Smith, 'Reasons of State', in David Held and Christopher Pollitt, eds., *New Forms of Democracy* (London: Sage, 1986), 192–217.

3 Lawrence Whitehead, 'International Aspects of Democratization', in Guillermo O'Donnell, Philippe Schmitter and Lawrence Whitehead, eds., *Transitions from Authoritarian Rule: Prospects for Democracy* (Baltimore: Johns Hopkins University Press, 1986).

4 Dunn, *Western Political Theory*, 64.

5 See, for example, C. B. Macpherson, *Democratic Theory: Essays in Retrieval* (Oxford: Clarendon Press, 1973).

6 John Keane, *Democracy and Civil Society* (London: Verso, 1988); Keane, ed., *Civil Society and the State* (London: Verso, 1988); Keane, *Public Life and Late Capitalism* (Cambridge: Cambridge University Press, 1984); David Held, *Political Theory and the Modern State* (Cambridge: Polity Press, 1989); and Held, *Models of Democracy* (Cambridge: Polity, 1987).

7 Norberto Bobbio, *Democracy and Dictatorship*, trans. P. Kennealy (Minneapolis: University of Minnesota Press, 1989).

8 Ernesto Laclau and Chantal Mouffe, *Hegemony and Socialist Strategy: Towards a Radical Democratic Politics* (London: Verso, 1985).

9 See, for example, the comments on the relationship between democracy and socialist ideals of the self-governing community by Barry Hindess, 'Imaginary Presuppositions of Democracy', *Economy and Society*, 20:2, May 1991, 173–95.

10 David Campbell, 'Global Inscription: How Foreign Policy Constitutes the United States', *Alternatives*, 15:3, Summer 1990, 263–86; G. M. Dillon, *Security and Modernity*; Bradley Klein 'How the West was One: The Representational Politics of NATO', in Ashley and Walker, eds., 'Speaking the Language of Exile', 311–25; Peter T. Manicas, *War and Democracy* (Oxford: Basil Blackwell, 1989).

11 Marc Managaro, ed., *Modernist Anthropology: From Fieldwork to Text* (Princeton: Princeton University Press, 1990); James Clifford, *The Predicament of Culture: Twentieth-Century Ethnography, and Art* (Cambridge, MA: Harvard University Press, 1988); James Clifford and George Marcus, eds., *Writing Culture: The Poetics and Politics of Ethnography* (Berkeley: University of California Press, 1986); George E. Marcus and Michael M. J. Fischer, eds., *Anthropology as Cultural Critique: An Experimental Moment in the Human Sciences* (Chicago: University of Chicago Press, 1986).

12 Warren Magnusson, 'The Reification of Political Community', in Walker and Mendlovitz, eds., *Contending Sovereignties*, 45–60; and Magnusson, 'Bourgeois Theories of Local Government', *Political Studies*, 34:1, 1986, 1–18.

13 Which is certainly not to say that such sustenance and revitalisation is unimportant. For a helpful attempt to think through the implications of such a project in the context of contemporary global processes see David

Held, 'Democracy, the Nation-State and the Global System', in Held, ed., *Political Theory Today* (Cambridge: Polity, 1990), 214–42.

14 This is, of course, a widely recognised problem: See, for example, John Dunn, 'Reconceiving the Content and Character of Modern Political Community', chapter 12 of his *Interpreting Political Responsibility* (Cambridge: Polity, 1990); and Andrew Linklater, 'The Problem of Community in International Relations', *Alternatives*, 15:2, Spring 1990, 135–54.

15 Dunn, *Western Political Theory*, 78.

16 See, for example, Scott Lash and John Urry, *The End of Organized Capitalism* (Cambridge: Polity, 1987); and Luke, *Screens of Power*.

17 Among a vast literature, see, for example, Anne Norton, *Reflections on Political Identity* (Baltimore: Johns Hopkins University Press, 1988); Partha Chatterjee, *Nationalist Thought and the Colonial World* (London: Zed, 1986); Gayatri Spivak, *In Other Worlds: Essays in Cultural Politics* (London: Methuen, 1987); Spivak, *The Post-Colonial Critic*; Homi Bhabha, *Nation and Narration* (London and New York: Routledge, 1990); Mike Featherstone, ed., *Global Culture: Nationalism, Globalism and Modernity* (London: Sage, 1990); David Cairns and Shaun Richards, *Writing Ireland: Colonialism, Nationalism and Culture* (Manchester: Manchester University Press, 1988); Edward Said, *After the Last Sky: Palestinian Lives* (New York: Pantheon, 1986); and Michael M. J. Fisher and Mehd Abedi, *Debating Muslims: Cultural Dialogues in Postmodernity and Tradition* (Madison: University of Wisconsin Press, 1990).

18 Walker, *One World, Many Worlds*; Warren Magnusson and R. B. J. Walker, 'Decentring the State: Political Theory and Canadian Political Economy' *Studies in Political Economy*, 26, Summer 1988, 37–71; Saul H. Mendlovitz and R. B. J. Walker, eds., *Towards a Just World Peace: Perspectives From Social Movements* (London: Butterworths, 1987); Alberto Melucci, *Nomads of the Present: Social Movements and Individual Needs in Contemporary Societies*, ed. John Keene and Paul Meir (Philadelphia: Temple University Press, 1989); and The Lelio Basso Foundation, ed., *Theory and Practice of Liberation at the End of the XXth Century* (Brussels: Bruyland, 1988).

19 R. B. J. Walker, 'Security, Sovereignty and the Challenge of World Politics', *Alternatives*, 15:1, Winter 1991, 3–28; Klare and Thomas, eds., *World Security*; and Richard Falk, *Revolutionaries and Functionaries: The Dual Face of Terrorism* (New York: E. P. Dutton, 1988).

20 Rajni Kothari, *Rethinking Development: In Search of Humane Alternatives* (Delhi: Ajanta Books, 1989); Kothari, *State Against Democracy: In Search of Humane Governance* (Delhi: Ajanta Publications, 1989); Kothari, *Transformation and Survival: In Search of Humane World Order* (Delhi: Ajanta Publications, 1989); Björne Hettne, *Development Theory and the Three Worlds* (London: Longman, 1990); and Gerald J. Kruijer, *Development Through Liberation: Third World Problems and Solutions* (London: Macmillan, 1987).

21 Judith Butler, *Gender Trouble: Feminism and the Subversion of Identity* (New York and London: Routledge, 1990); Joan Cocks, *The Oppositional Imagination: Feminism, Critique and Political Theory* (London: Routledge, 1989); Linda J. Nicholson, ed., *Feminism/Postmodernism* (New York: Routledge, 1990); Irene Diamond and Lee Quimby, eds., *Feminism and Foucault: Reflections*

on Resistance (Boston: Northeastern University Press, 1988); Chris Weedon, *Feminist Practice and Poststructuralist Theory* (Oxford: Basil Blackwell, 1987); and Marianne Hirsch and Evelyn Fox Keller, eds., *Conflicts in Feminism* (New York and London: Routledge, 1990).

22 Michael Shapiro and Deanne Neaubauer, 'Spatiality and Policy Discourse: Reading the Global City', in Walker and Mendlovitz, eds., *Contending Sovereignties*, 97–124. See also Michel de Certeau, *The Practices of Everyday Life*, trans. Steven Rendall (Berkeley and Los Angeles: University of California Press, 1984); and Michel Foucault, *Politics, Philosophy, Culture: Interviews and Other Writings, 1977–1984*, ed. Lawrence D. Kritzman (New York and London: Routledge, 1988).

23 Zygmunt Bauman, *Freedom* (Minneapolis: University of Minnesota Press, 1988); Fred R. Dallmayr, *Twilight of Subjectivity: Contributions to a Post-Individualist Theory of Subjectivity* (Amherst: University of Massachusetts Press, 1981); Eduardo Cadava, Peter Connor and Jean-Luc Nancy, eds., *Who Comes After the Subject?* (London: Routledge, 1991).

24 Ashis Nandy, 'The Politics of Secularism and the Recovery of Religious Tolerance', in Walker and Mendlovitz, eds., *Contending Sovereignties*, 125–44; and Kirstie M. McClure, 'Difference, Diversity, and the Limits of Toleration', *Political Theory*, 18:3, August 1990, 361–91.

25 Though it is more usually a resonance of aspiration. For a broad range of perspectives, see, for example, Laclau and Mouffe, *Hegemony and Socialist Strategy*; Linda Hutcheon, *The Politics of Postmodernism* (London: Routledge, 1989); Claude Lefort, *Democracy and Political Theory* (Cambridge: Polity Press, 1988); Connolly, *Politics and Ambiguity*; Connolly, *Political Theory and Modernity*; Connolly, *Identity\Difference: Democratic Negotiations of Political Paradox*; Gary Wickham, 'The Political Possibilities of Postmodernism', *Economy and Society*, 19:1, Feb. 1990, 121–49; Michael Ryan, *Marxism and Deconstruction: A Critical Deconstruction* (Baltimore: The Johns Hopkins University Press, 1982); Andrew Ross, ed., *Universal Abandon: The Politics of Postmodernism* (Minneapolis: University of Minnesota Press, 1988); Roy Boyne and Ali Rattansi, eds., *Postmodernism and Society* (London: Macmillan, 1990); and Fred Dallmayr, *Margins of Political Discourse* (Albany: State University of New York Press, 1989).

8 Sovereign identities and the politics of forgetting

1 See, among many others, Ashley, 'Untying the Sovereign State'; Ashley and Walker, 'Reading Dissidence/Writing the Discipline'; Walker and Mendlovitz, eds., *Contending Sovereignties*; David Campbell, 'Global Inscription: How Foreign Policy Constitutes the United States', *Alternatives*, 15:3, Summer 1990, 263–86; Janice E. Thomson, 'Sovereignty in Historical Perspective: The Evolution of State Control Over Extraterritorial Violence', in James A. Caporoso, ed., *The Elusive State: International and Comparative Perspectives* (Newbury Park, CA: Sage, 1989), 227–54; Janice Thomson, *Defining Sovereignty: State Practices and the Organisation of Violence*; in preparation. Janice Thomson and Stephen D. Krasner, 'Global Transactions and the Consolidation of Sovereignty', in Czempiel and Rosenau, eds., *Global*

Changes and Theoretical Challenges, 195–220; Cynthia Weber, *Writing the State: Political Intervention and the Historical Constitution of State Sovereignty*, in preparation; Robert H. Jackson, *Quasi-States: Sovereignty, International Relations and the Third World* (Cambridge: Cambridge University Press, 1990); and Michael Shapiro, 'Sovereignty and Exchange in the Orders of Modernity', *Alternatives*, 16:4, Fall 1991, 447–77.

2 For a more extensive exploration of the rituals of eternal presence and imminent absence that have been such an important part of attempts to analyse change in international relations, see my 'Sovereignty, Identity, Community: Reflections on the Horizons of Contemporary Political Practice', in Walker and Mendlovitz, eds., *Contending Sovereignties*, 159–85.

3 These last two names, an intentional transgression of the conventional canon, are intended to serve as a reminder of the extent to which codifications of state sovereignty in international law often have been cleansed of references to the statist power politics with which they are nevertheless indelibly associated. See, especially, Carl Schmitt, *Political Theology: Four Chapters on the Concept of Sovereignty*; and Max Weber, 'Politics as a Vocation', in *From Max Weber: Essays in Sociology* trans. and ed. H. H. Gerth and C. Wright Mills (New York: Oxford University Press, 1946), 77–128. Cf. W. J. Stankiewitz, ed., *In Defence of Sovereignty* (New York: Oxford University Press, 1969); and F. H. Hinsley, *Sovereignty* 2nd edn (Cambridge: Cambridge University Press, 1986).

4 For a helpful discussion of the relevant historiography, see Nicholas Onuf, 'Sovereignty: Outline of a Conceptual History', *Alternatives*, 16:4, Fall 1991, 425–46. The classic text by Otto Gierke, *Political Theories of the Middle Age* trans. F. W. Maitland (Cambridge: Cambridge University Press, 1900) remains an important guide in this context.

5 Compare, for example, Martin Wight, *Systems of States* (Leicester: Leicester University Press, 1977); Perry Anderson, *Lineages of the Absolutist State* (London: New Left Books, 1974); Immanuel Wallerstein, *The Modern World System I: Capitalist Agriculture and the Origins of the European World Economy in the Sixteenth Century* (New York: Academic Press, 1974); Joseph Strayer, *On the Medieval Origins of the Modern State* (Princeton: Princeton University Press, 1970); Charles Tilly, ed., *The Formation of National States in Western Europe* (Princeton: Princeton University Press, 1975); Hinsley, *Sovereignty*; Alan James, *Sovereign Statehood* (London: George, Allen and Unwin, 1986); and Kenneth Dyson, *The State Tradition in Western Europe* (Oxford: Martin Robertson, 1980).

6 For a more extended discussion of the absence of cultural analysis in the theory of international relations, see my 'The Concept of Culture in the Theory of International Relations', in John Chay, ed., *Culture and International Relations* (New York: Praeger, 1990), 3–17.

7 For an elaboration of this argument, see my 'Gender and Critique in the Theory of International Relations', in V. Spike Peterson, ed., *Gendered States* (Boulder: Lynne Rienner, 1992), 179–202. This volume offers a good introduction to and an extensive bibliography of recent work in this area. See also, for example, Anne Sisson Runyan and V. Spike Peterson, 'The Radical Future of Realism: Feminist Subversions of IR Theory', *Alternatives* 16:1, Winter

1991, 67–106; Cynthia Enloe, *Bananas, Beaches and Bases: Making Feminist Sense of International Relations* (Berkeley: University of California Press, 1989); Rebecca Grant and Kathleen Newland, eds., *Gender and International Relations* (Milton Keynes: Open University Press, 1991); and Ann Tickner, *Gender and International Relations* (New York: Columbia University Press, 1992).

8 For an argument to this effect, see my 'World Order and the Reconstitution of Political Life', in R. Falk, R. Johansen and S. Kim, eds., *The Constitutional Foundations of World Order* (cited earlier in ch. 3, note 17.

9 For further discussion, see my 'Sovereignty, Security and the Challenge of World Politics'.

BIBLIOGRAPHY

Abedi, Mehd, and Michael M. J. Fisher. *Debating Muslims: Cultural Dialogues in Postmodernity and Tradition*. Madison: University of Wisconsin Press, 1990.

Achinstein, Peter, and Stephen F. Barker, eds. *The Legacy of Logical Positivism*. Baltimore: Johns Hopkins, 1969.

Alker, Jr., Hayward R., and Richard K. Ashley, eds. *After Neo-Realism: The Institutions of Anarchy in World Politics*. In preparation.

Alker, Jr., Hayward R., and Thomas J. Biersteker. 'The Dialectics of World Order: notes for a future archeologist of international savoir faire', *International Studies Quarterly*, 28:2, June 1984, 121–42.

Almond, Gabriel. 'Review Article: The International–National Connection', *British Journal of Political Science*, 19:2, April 1989, 237–59.

Anderson, Perry. *Lineages of the Absolutist State*. London: New Left Books, 1974.

Andrews, Bruce. 'The Domestic Content of International Desire', *International Organization*, 38:2, 1984, 321–7.

Aron, Raymond 'Max Weber and Power Politics', in Otto Stammer, ed., *Max Weber and Sociology Today*, trans. K. Morris. Oxford: Basil Blackwell, 1979, 83–100.

Ashcraft, Richard. 'Political Theory and the Problem of Ideology', *Journal of Politics*, 42:3, August 1980.

Ashley, Richard K. 'The Geopolitics of Geopolitical Space', *Alternatives*, 12, October 1987, 403–34.

'Living on Border Lines: Man, Post-structuralism and War', in James Der Derian and Michael Shapiro, eds., *International/Intertextual Relations*. Lexington: Lexington Books, 1989, 259–321.

'The Poverty of Neo-Realism', *International Organization*, 38:2, Spring 1984, 225–86.

Statecraft as Mancraft. In preparation.

'Untying the Sovereign State: A Double Reading of the Anarchy Problematique', *Millennium: Journal of International Studies*, 17:2, Summer 1988, 227–62.

Ashley, Richard K., and R. B. J. Walker. 'Speaking the Language of Exile: Dissidence in International Studies', Special Issue of *International Studies Quarterly*, 34:3, September 1990.

'Reading Dissidence/Writing the Discipline: Crisis and the Question of Sovereignty in International Studies', *International Studies Quarterly*, 34:3, September 1990, 367–416.

Augelli, Enrico, and Craig Murphy. *America's Quest For Supremacy and the Third World: A Gramscian Analysis*. London: Francis Pinter, 1988.

Bachelard, Gaston. *La Formation de l'esprit scientifique*. Paris: Vrin, 1938.
  The Poetics of Space, trans. Maria Jolas. Boston: Beacon Press, 1969.
Bannet, Eve Taylor. *Structuralism and the Logic of Dissent: Barthes, Derrida, Foucault, Lacan*. Urbana: University of Illinois Press, 1989.
Baron, Hans. *The Crisis of the Early Italian Renaissance*, 2nd edn. Princeton: Princeton University Press, 1966.
Bauman, Zygmunt. *Freedom*. Minneapolis: University of Minnesota Press, 1988.
  Modernity and the Holocaust. Cambridge: Polity Press, 1989.
  Modernity and Ambivalence. Cambridge: Cambridge University Press, 1991.
  Intimations of Postmodernity. London: Routledge, 1992.
Beetham, David. *Max Weber and the Theory of Modern Politics*, 2nd edn Cambridge: Polity Press, 1985.
Beitz, Charles. 'Cosmopolitan Ideals and National Sentiment', *Journal of Philosophy*, 80:10, October 1983, 591–600.
  Political Theory and International Relations. Princeton: Princeton University Press, 1979.
Bender, John, and David Wellbery, eds. *Chronotypes: The Construction of Time*. Stanford: Stanford University Press, 1991.
Berki, R. N. *Insight and Vision: The Problem of Communism in Marx's Thought*. London: J. M. Dent, 1983.
  On Political Realism. London: J. M. Dent, 1981.
Berlin, Isaiah. 'The Originality of Machiavelli', in Berlin, *Against the Current*. Oxford: Oxford University Press, 1979, 29–79.
Berman, Marshall. *All That is Solid Melts Into Air: The Experience of Modernity*. New York: Simon and Schuster, 1982.
Bhabha, Homi. *Nation and Narration*. London and New York: Routledge, 1990.
Bhaskar, Roy. *Scientific Realism and Human Emancipation*. London: Verso, 1988.
Blumenberg, Hans. *The Legitimacy of the Modern Age*. Cambridge, MA: MIT Press, 1983.
Bobbio, Norberto. *Democracy and Dictatorship*, trans. P. Kennealy. Minneapolis: University of Minnesota Press, 1989.
Boyne, Roy, and Ali Rattansi, eds. *Postmodernism and Society*. London: Macmillan, 1990.
Brown, Harold I. *Perception, Theory and Commitment: The New Philosophy of Science*. Chicago: University of Chicago Press, 1977.
Brown, Richard Harvey. *Society as Text: Essays on Rhetoric, Reason and Reality*. Chicago: University of Chicago Press, 1987.
Brown, Wendy. *Manhood and Politics: A Feminist Reading of Political Theory*. Totowa, NJ: Rowman and Littlefield, 1988.
Buckley, Walter, ed. *Modern Systems Research for the Behavioral Scientist: A Sourcebook*. Chicago: Aldine, 1968.
  Sociology and Modern Systems Theory. Englewood Cliffs, NJ: Prentice Hall, 1967.
Bull, Hedley. *The Anarchical Society*. London: Macmillan, 1977.
  'Hobbes and the International Anarchy', *Social Research*, 48:4, 1981, 717–38.
  'Martin Wight and the Theory of International Relations: The Second Martin Wight Memorial Lecture', *British Journal of International Studies*, 2: 1976, 101–16.

'The Theory of International Politics, 1919–1969', in Brian Porter, ed., *International Politics 1919–1969: The Aberystwyth Papers*, Oxford: Oxford University Press, 1972, 30–55.

Bull, Hedley, ed. *Intervention in World Politics*. Oxford: Clarendon Press, 1984.

Bull, Hedley and Adam Watson, eds. *The Expansion of International Society*. Oxford: Clarendon Press, 1984.

Butler, Judith. *Gender Trouble: Feminism and the Subversion of Identity*. New York and London: Routledge, 1990.

Buzan, Barry. 'Economic Structure and International Security: the Limits of the Liberal Case', *International Organization*, 38:4, Autumn 1984.

'Peace, Power and Security: Contending Concepts in the Study of International Relations', *Journal of Peace Research*, 21:2, 1984, 109–25.

People, States and Fear: The National Security Problem in International Relations. Brighton: Wheatsheaf, 1983, 2nd edn 1991.

'Systems, Structures and Units: Reconstructing Waltz's Theory of International Politics'. Paper delivered at the British International Studies Association/International Studies Association Annual Conference, London, February, 1989.

Buzan, Barry and R. Barry Jones, eds. *Change and the Study of International Relations*. London: Francis Pinter, 1981.

Cadava, Eduardo, Peter Connor and Jean-Luc Nancy, eds., *Who Comes After the Subject?* London: Routledge, 1991.

Cairns, David, and Shaun Richards, *Writing Ireland: Colonialism, Nationalism and Culture*. Manchester: Manchester University Press, 1988.

Calinescu, Matei. *Five Faces of Modernity*. Durham, NC: Duke University Press, 1987.

Camilleri, Joseph A. 'Rethinking Sovereignty in a Shrinking, Fragmented World', in R. B. J. Walker and Saul H. Mendlovitz, eds., *Contending Sovereignties: Rethinking Political Community*. Boulder: Lynne Rienner, 1990, 13–44.

Campbell, David. 'Global Inscription: How Foreign Policy Constitutes the United States', *Alternatives*, 15:3, Summer 1990, 263–86.

Writing Security: United States Foreign Policy and the Politics of Identity. Manchester: Manchester University Press, 1992.

Čapek, Milič. *The Philosophical Impact of Contemporary Physics*. New York: Van Nostrand, 1961.

Caporaso, James A., ed. *The Elusive State: International and Comparative Perspective's*. London: Sage, 1989.

Carnoy, Martin. *The State and Political Theory*. Princeton: Princeton University Press, 1984.

Carr, David. *Time, Narrative and History*. Bloomington and Indianapolis: Indiana University Press, 1986.

Carr, E. H. *The Twenty-Years Crisis, 1919–1939*, 2nd edn London: Macmillan, 1946.

Carroll, David. *Paraesthetics: Foucault, Lyotard, Derrida*. London: Methuen, 1987.

Chatterjee, Partha. *Nationalist Thought and the Colonial World: A Derivative Discourse*. London: Zed/UNU, 1986.

Chilton, Paul, ed. *Language and the Nuclear Arms Debate: Nukespeak Today*. London: Francis Pinter, 1985.

Clark, Ian. *The Hierarchy of States: Reform and Resistance in the International Order*. Cambridge: Cambridge University Press, 1989.

Claude, Jr., Inis. *Power and International Relations*. New York: Random House, 1962.

Clifford, James. *The Predicament of Culture: Twentieth-Century Ethnography, and Art*. Cambridge, MA: Harvard University Press, 1988.

Clifford, James and George Marcus, eds. *Writing Culture: The Poetics and Politics of Ethnography*. Berkeley: University of California Press, 1986.

Cocks, Joan. *The Oppositional Imagination: Feminism, Critique and Political Theory*. London: Routledge, 1989.

Cohen, Marshall. 'Moral Skepticism and International Relations', in Beitz, et al., eds., *International Ethics*. Princeton: Princeton University Press, 1985.

Connolly, William E. *Identity\Difference: Democratic Negotiation of Political Paradox*. Ithaca: Cornell University Press, 1991.

Political Theory and Modernity. Oxford: Basil Blackwell, 1988.

Politics and Ambiguity. Madison: University of Wisconsin Press, 1987.

Connor, Steven. *Postmodernist Culture: An Introduction to Theories of the Contemporary*. Oxford: Basil Blackwell, 1989.

Cox, Robert W. *Production, Power, and World Order: Social Forces in the Making of History*. New York: Columbia University Press, 1987.

'Social Forces, States and World Orders: Beyond International Relations Theory', *Millennium: Journal of International Studies*, 10:2, 1981, 126–55.

Culler, Jonathan. *On Deconstruction*. London: Routledge and Kegan Paul, 1983.

Czempiel, Ernst-Otto, and J. N. Rosenau, eds. *Global Change and Theoretical Challenges*. Lexington: Lexington Books, 1989.

Dalby, Simon. *Creating the Second Cold War: The Discourse of Politics*. London: Francis Pinter, 1990.

'Security, Modernity, Ecology: The Dilemmas of Post-Cold War Security Discourse', *Alternatives*, 17:1, Winter 1992, 95–133.

Dallmayr, Fred R. *Margins of Political Discourse*. Albany: State University of New York Press, 1989.

Twilight of Subjectivity: Contributions to a Post-Individualist Theory of Subjectivity. Amherst: University of Massachusetts Press, 1981.

de Certeau, Michel. *The Practices of Everyday Life*, trans. Steven Rendall. Berkeley and Los Angeles: University of California Press, 1984.

The Writing of History, trans., Tom Conley. New York: Columbia University Press, 1988.

de Grazia, Sebastian. *Machiavelli in Hell*. Princeton: Princeton University Press, 1989.

Deluze, Gilles. *Bergsonism*, trans. Hugh Tomlinson and Barbara Habberjam. New York: Zone Books, 1988.

Der Derian, James. *Anti-Diplomacy: Speed, Spies and Terror in International Relations*. Oxford: Basil Blackwell, 1992.

On Diplomacy: A Genealogy of Western Estrangement. Oxford: Basil Blackwell, 1987.

'The (S)pace of International Relations: Simulation, Surveillance and Speed', *International Studies Quarterly*, 34:3, September 1990, 295–310.

Der Derian, James, and Michael J. Shapiro, eds. *International/Intertextual Relations: Postmodern Readings of World Politics*. Lexington: Lexington Books, 1989.

Derrida, Jacques. *Margins of Philosophy*, trans. Alan Bass. Chicago: University of Chicago Press, 1982.

　Of Grammatology, trans. Gayatri Chakravorty Spivak. Baltimore: Johns Hopkins University Press, 1976.

　Positions, trans. Alan Bass. Chicago: University of Chicago Press, 1981.

　Writing and Difference, trans. Alan Bass. Chicago: University of Chicago Press, 1978.

Descombes, Vincent. *Modern French Philosophy*, trans. L. Scott-Fox and J. M. Harding. Cambridge: Cambridge University Press, 1980.

Dessler, David. 'What's at Stake in the Agent-Structure Debate?', *International Organization*, 43:3, Summer 1989, 441–73

Diamond, Irene, and Lee Quimby, eds. *Feminism and Foucault: Reflections on Resistance*. Boston: Northeastern University Press, 1988.

Dillon, G. M. *Security and Modernity*. In preparation.

Dockrill, Michael, and Barrie Paskins. *The Ethics of War*. Minneapolis: University of Minnesota Press, 1979.

Donelan, Michael. *Elements of International Political Theory*. Oxford: Clarendon Press, 1990.

Doyal, Len, and Roger Harris. *Empiricism, Explanation and Rationality: An Introduction to the Philosophy of the Social Sciences*. London: Routledge and Kegan Paul, 1986.

Doyle, Michael. 'Kant, Liberal Legacies and Foreign Affairs', Parts 1 and 2, 205–35, and 12:4, Fall 1983, 323–53.

Duhem, Pierre. *Medieval Cosmology: Theories of Infinity, Place, Time, Void, and the Plurality of Worlds*, abridged edition of *Le Système du monde*, 10 vols., 1913–59, trans. and ed., Roger Ariew. Chicago: University of Chicago Press, 1985.

Dunn, John. *Interpreting Political Responsibility*. Cambridge: Polity, 1990.

　Rethinking Modern Political Theory. Cambridge: Cambridge University Press, 1985.

　Western Political Theory in the Face of the Future. Cambridge: Cambridge University Press, 1979.

Dyer, Hugh, and Leon Mangasarian, eds. *The Study of International Relations: The State of the Art*. London: Macmillan, 1989.

Dyson, Kenneth. *The State Tradition in Western Europe*. Oxford: Martin Robertson, 1980.

Elshtain, Jean. *Public Man, Private Woman*. Princeton: Princeton University Press, 1981.

　Woman and War. New York: Basic Books, 1987.

Enloe, Cynthia. *Bananas, Beaches and Bases: Making Feminist Sense of International Relations*. Berkeley: University of California Press, 1989.

Epp, Roger. 'Power Politics and the *Civitas Terrena*: The Augustinian Sources of Anglo-American Theory in International Relations', Unpublished dissertation, Queen's University, Kingston, Ontario, 1989.

Fabian, Johannes. *Time and the Other: How Anthropology Makes its Object*. New York: Columbia University Press, 1983.

217

Falk, Richard A. *Human Rights and State Sovereignty*. New York: Holmes and Meier, 1981.

The Promise of World Order. Philadelphia: Temple University Press, 1987.

Revolutionaries and Functionaries: The Dual Face of Terrorism. New York: E. P. Dutton, 1988.

A Study of Future Worlds. New York: Free Press, 1975.

Explorations at the Edge of Time: The Prospects for World Order. Philadelphia: Temple University Press, 1992.

Falk, Richard, Samuel S. Kim, and Robert C. Johansen, eds. *The Constitutional Foundations of World Peace*. Albany: State University of New York Press, 1993.

Falk, Richard, Samuel S. Kim, and Saul H. Mendlovitz, eds. *Towards a Just World Order*. Boulder: Westview Press, 1982.

Fay, Brian. *Critical Social Science*. Cambridge: Polity, 1987.

Featherstone, Mike, ed. *Global Culture: Nationalism, Globalism and Modernity*. London: Sage, 1990.

Ferguson, Yale, and Richard W. Mansbach. *The Elusive Quest: Theory and International Politics*. Columbia: University of South Carolina Press, 1988.

Fischer, Michael M. J., and George E. Marcus, eds. *Anthropology as Cultural Critique: An Experimental Moment in the Human Sciences*. Chicago: University of Chicago Press, 1986.

Forsyth, Murray. 'Thomas Hobbes and the External Relations of States', *British Journal of International Studies*, 5:3, 1979, 196–209.

Foucault, Michel. *The Order of Things*. London: Tavistock, 1970.

Politics, Philosophy, Culture: Interviews and Other Writings, 1977–1984, ed. Lawrence D. Kritzman. New York and London: Routledge, 1988.

'What is an Author?', in Paul Rabinow, ed., *The Foucault Reader*. New York: Pantheon Books, 1984.

'What is Enlightenment?', in Paul Rabinow, ed., *The Foucault Reader*. New York: Pantheon Books, 1984.

Frisby, David. *Fragments of Modernity: Theories of Modernity in the Work of Simmel, Kracauer and Benjamin*. Cambridge, MA: The MIT Press, 1986.

Frost, Mervyn. *Towards a Normative Theory of International Relations*. Cambridge: Cambridge University Press, 1988.

Gadamer, Hans-Georg. *Philosophical Hermeneutics*, trans. and ed., David E. Linge. Berkeley and Los Angeles: University of California Press, 1976.

'Plato and the Poets', in *Dialogue and Dialectic: Eight Hermeneutical Studies in Plato*, trans. Christopher Smith. New Haven: Yale University Press, 1980, 39–72.

Gallie, W. B. 'Kant's View of Reason in Politics', *Philosophy*, 54, 1979, 19–33.

Philosophers of Peace and War. Cambridge: Cambridge University Press, 1978.

'Wanted: A Philosophy of International Relations', *Political Studies*, 27:3, September 1979, 484–92.

Garst, Daniel. 'Thucydides and Neorealism', *International Studies Quarterly*, 33:1, March 1989, 3–27.

Garver, Eugene. *Machiavelli and the History of Prudence*. Madison: University of Wisconsin Press, 1987.

Gasché, Rudolphe. *The Tain of the Mirror: Derrida and the Philosophy of Reflection.* Cambridge, MA: Harvard University Press, 1986.

Gellner, Ernest. *Nations and Nationalism.* Oxford: Basil Blackwell, 1983.

George, Jim and David Campbell. 'Patterns of Dissent and the Celebration of Difference: Critical Social Theory and International Relations', *International Studies Quarterly*, 34:3, September 1990, 269–93.

Gibbons, Michael T., ed. *Interpreting Politics.* Oxford: Basil Blackwell, 1987.

Giddens, Anthony. *Central Problems in Social Theory.* London: Macmillan, 1979.

The Consequences of Modernity. Cambridge: Polity Press, 1990.

The Nation State and Violence. Cambridge: Polity Press, 1985.

Gierke, Otto. *Political Theories of the Middle Age*, trans. F. W. Maitland. Cambridge: Cambridge University Press, 1900.

Gilbert, Felix. *Machiavelli and Guicciardini.* Princeton: Princeton University Press, 1965.

Gill, Stephen. *American Hegemony and the Trilateral Commission.* Cambridge: Cambridge University Press, 1990.

'Reflections on Global Order and Sociohistorical Time', *Alternatives*, 16:3, Summer 1991, 275–314.

ed. *Gramsci and International Relations.* Cambridge: Cambridge University Press, forthcoming.

Gill, Stephen and David Law. *The Global Political Economy.* Baltimore: Johns Hopkins University Press, 1988.

Gilpin, Robert. *The Political Economy of International Relations.* Princeton: Princeton University Press, 1987.

'The Richness of the Tradition of Political Realism', *International Organization*, 38:2, 1984, 287–304.

War and Change in World Politics. Cambridge: Cambridge University Press, 1981.

Gordon, Colin. 'The Soul of the Citizen: Max Weber and Michel Foucault on Rationality and Government', in Sam Whimster and Scott Lash, eds., *Max Weber, Rationality and Modernity.* London: Allen and Unwin, 1987, 293–316.

Goux, Jean-Joseph. *Symbolic Economies: After Marx and Freud*, trans. Jennifer Curtiss Cage. Ithaca, NY: Cornell University Press, 1990.

Grant, Rebecca, and Kathleen Newland, eds. *Gender and International Relations.* Milton Keynes: Open University Press, 1991.

Greene, Thomas M. 'The End of Discourse in Machiavelli's "Prince"', *Yale French Studies*, 67, 1984, 57–71.

Gregory, Derek, and John Urry, eds. *Social Relations and Spatial Structures.* London: Macmillan, 1985.

Gross, David. 'Temporality and the Modern State', *Theory and Society*, 14:2, 1985, 53–82.

Gunnell, John. *Between Philosophy and Politics.* Amherst, MA: University of Massachusetts Press, 1986.

'The Myth of the Tradition', *American Political Science Review*, 72:1, March 1978, 122–34.

Political Philosophy and Time, 2nd edn Chicago: Chicago University Press, 1987.

Haas, Ernst. 'The Study of Regional Integration: Reflections on the Joy and Anguish of Pretheorizing', *International Organization*, 24:4, Autumn 1970, 361.

Habermas, Jürgen. *The Philosophical Discourse of Modernity*, trans. Frederick Lawrence. Cambridge, MA: MIT Press, 1987.

Hampshire, Stuart. *Innocence and Experience*. Cambridge, MA: Harvard University Press, 1987.

Hanson, D. W. 'Thomas Hobbes' "highway to peace"', *International Organization*, 38:2, 1984, 329–54.

Harding, Sandra. *The Science Question in Feminism*. Ithaca: Cornell University Press, 1986.

Harriman, Robert. 'Composing Modernity in Machiavelli's *Prince*', *Journal of the History of Ideas*, 1989, 3–29.

Hartog, François. *The Mirror of Herodotus: The Representation of the Other in the Writing of History*, trans. Janet Lloyd. Berkeley and Los Angeles: University of California Press, 1988.

Harvey, David. *The Condition of Postmodernity*. Oxford: Basil Blackwell, 1989.

Havelock, Eric. *Preface to Plato*. Cambridge, MA: Harvard University Press, 1963.

Hawthorn, Geoffrey. *Enlightenment and Despair: A History of Social Theory*, 2nd edn. Cambridge: Cambridge University Press, 1987.

Held, David. *Models of Democracy*. Cambridge: Polity, 1987.

Political Theory and the Modern State. Cambridge: Polity, 1989.

Held, David, ed. *Political Theory Today*. Cambridge: Cambridge University Press, 1991.

Hennis, Wilhelm. *Max Weber: Essays in Reconstruction*, trans. Keith Tribe. London: Allen and Unwin, 1988.

Herz, John. *Political Realism and Political Idealism*. Chicago: University of Chicago Press, 1951.

International Politics in the Atomic Age. New York: Columbia University Press, 1959.

The Nation State and the Crisis of World Politics. New York: David MacKay, 1976.

Hettne, Björne. *Development Theory and the Three Worlds*. London: Longman, 1990.

Hexter, J. H. *The Vision of Politics on the Eve of the Reformation*. New York: Basic Books, 1973.

Higgott, Richard, ed. *New Directions in International Relations? Australian Perspectives*, Canberra Studies in World Affairs, No. 23. Canberra: Australian National University Department of International Relations, 1988.

Higgott, Richard, and J. L. Richardson, eds. *International Relations: Global and Australian Perspectives on an Evolving Discipline*. Canberra: Department of International Relations, Australian National University, 1991.

Hiley, David. *Philosophy in Question: Essays on a Pyrrhonian Theme*. Chicago: University of Chicago Press, 1988.

Hindess, Barry. *Choice, Rationality and Social Theory*. London: Unwin Hyman, 1988.

'Imaginary Presuppositions of Democracy', *Economy and Society*, 20:2, May 1991, 173–95.

220

Hinsley, F. H. *Power and the Pursuit of Peace*. Cambridge: Cambridge University Press, 1967.

Sovereignty, 2nd edn. Cambridge: Cambridge University Press, 1986.

Hirsch, Marianne, and Evelyn Fox Keller, eds. *Conflicts in Feminism*. New York: Routledge, 1990.

Hobbes, Thomas. *Leviathan*, ed., C. B. Macpherson. London: Penguin Books, 1968.

Hoffman, Mark J. 'Normative Approaches', in Margot Light and A. J. R. Groom, eds., *International Relations: A Handbook of Current Theory*. London: Francis Pinter, 1985.

Hoffmann, Stanley. 'An American Social Science: International Relations', *Daedalus*, 106, Summer 1977, 41–59.

Duties Beyond Borders: On the Limits and Possibilities of Ethical International Relations. Syracuse, NY: Syracuse University Press, 1981.

'Obstinate or Obsolete? The Fate of the Nation-State and the Case of Western Europe', *Daedalus*, 95, Summer 1966, 862–915.

The Political Ethics of International Relations. New York: Carnegie Council on Ethics and International Affairs, 1988.

The State of War: Essays in the Theory and Practice of International Politics. New York: Praeger, 1965.

Hollis, Martin. *The Cunning of Reason*. Cambridge: Cambridge University Press, 1987.

Hollis, Martin and Steven Lukes, eds. *Rationality and Relativism*. Oxford: Basil Blackwell, 1982.

Hollis, Martin and Steve Smith. *Explaining and Understanding International Relations*. Oxford: Clarendon Press, 1990.

Holmes, Robert L. *On War and Morality*. Princeton: Princeton University Press, 1989.

Holsti, K. J. *The Dividing Discipline: Hegemony and Diversity in International Theory*. Boston: Allen & Unwin, 1985.

Holsti, Ole, et al., eds. *Change in the International Systems*. Boulder: Westview Press, 1981.

Holton, R. J. *The Transition from Feudalism to Capitalism*. London: Macmillan, 1985.

Howard, Michael *War and the Liberal Conscience*. Oxford: Oxford University Press, 1978.

Hudson, Wayne. 'Postmodernity and Contemporary Social Thought', in Peter Lassman, ed., *Politics and Social Theory*. London: Routledge, 1989, 138–60.

Hulliung, Mark. *Citizen Machiavelli*. Princeton: Princeton University Press, 1983.

Hurwitz, Roger. 'Strategic and Social Fictions in the Prisoner's Dilemma', in Der Derian and Shapiro eds. *International/Intertextual Relations*, Lexington: Lexington Books, 1989, 113–34.

Husserl, Edmund. *The Crisis of European Sciences and Transcendental Phenomenology*, trans. David Carr. Evanston: Northwestern University Press, 1970.

Hutcheon, Linda. *The Politics of Postmodernism*. London and New York: Routledge, 1989.

Innis, Harold. A. *The Bias of Communication*. Toronto: University of Toronto Press, 1951.

Jackson, Robert H. 'Martin Wight, International Theory and the Good Life', *Millennium: Journal of International Studies*, 19:2, Summer 1990, 261–72.
    Quasi-States: Sovereignty, International Relations and the Third World. Cambridge: Cambridge University Press, 1990.
Jameson, Fredric. *Postmodernism, or the Cultural Logic of Late Capitalism*. Durham, NC: Duke University Press, 1991.
Jammer, Max. *Concepts of Space: The History of Theories of Space in Physics*, 2nd edn. Cambridge, MA: Harvard University Press, 1969.
Johnson, James Turner. *Just War Tradition and the Restraint of War*. Princeton: Princeton University Press, 1981.
    The Quest for Peace: Three Moral Traditions in Western Cultural History. Princeton: Princeton University Press, 1989.
Jones, Roy. 'The English School of International Relations: A Case for Closure', *Review of International Studies*, 7:1, 1981, 1–13.
Keane, John, ed. *Civil Society and the State*. London: Verso, 1988.
    Democracy and Civil Society. London: Verso, 1988.
    Public Life and Late Capitalism. Cambridge: Cambridge University Press, 1984.
Kellner, Douglas, ed. *Postmodernism/Jameson/Critique*. Washington, DC: Maisonneuve Press, 1989.
Keohane, Robert O. *International Institutions and State Power: Essays in International Relations Theory*. Boulder: Westview Press, 1989.
Keohane, Robert O., ed. *Neorealism and Its Critics*. New York: Columbia University Press, 1986.
Keohane, Robert O. and Joseph Nye. *Power and Interdependence*. Boston: Little Brown, 1977.
Kern, Stephen. *The Culture of Time and Space, 1880–1918*. Cambridge, MA: Harvard University Press, 1983.
Kittler, Friedrich A. *Discourse Networks, 1800/1900*, trans. Michael Metteer. Stanford: Stanford University Press, 1990.
Klare, Michael T., and Daniel Thomas, eds. *World Security: Trends and Challenges at Century's End*. New York: St Martins, 1991.
Klein, Bradley. 'How the West was One: The Representational Politics of NATO', *International Studies Quarterly*, 34:3, September 1990, 311–25.
Kline, Morris. *Mathematics in Western Culture*. New York: Oxford University Press, 1953.
Knorr, Klaus, and James N. Rousenau, eds. *Contending Approaches to International Politics*. Princeton: Princeton University Press, 1969.
Kolakowski, Leszek. *The Alienation of Reason*, trans. Norbert Guterman. Garden City, NY: Doubleday Anchor, 1972.
Kolb, David. *The Critique of Pure Modernity: Hegel, Heidegger, and After*. Chicago: University of Chicago Press, 1986.
Kothari, Rajni. *Rethinking Development: In Search of Humane Alternatives*. Delhi: Ajanta Publications, 1989.
    State Against Democracy: In Search of Humane Governance. Delhi: Ajanta Publications, 1989.
    Transformation and Survival: In Search of Humane World Order. Delhi: Ajanta Publications, 1989.
Krasner, Stephen D., and Janice Thomson. 'Global Transactions and the Con-

solidation of Sovereignty', in Ernst-Otto Czempiel and James N. Rosenau, eds., *Global Changes and Theoretical Challenges*. Lexington: Lexington Books, 1989, 195–220.

Kratochwil, Friedrich. 'Errors Have Their Advantages', *International Organization*, 38:2, 1984, 305–20.

'Regimes, Interpretation and the "Science" of Politics: A Reappraisal', *Millennium: Journal of International Studies*, 17:2, Summer 1988, 263–84.

Rules, Norms and Decisions: On the Conditions of Practical and Legal Reasoning in International Relations and Domestic Affairs. Cambridge: Cambridge University Press, 1989.

Kratochwil, Friedrich and John Gerald Ruggie. 'International Organizations: A State of the Art on an Art of the State', *International Organization*, 40:4, Autumn 1986, 753–76.

Kruijer, Gerald J. *Development Through Liberation: Third World Problems and Solutions*. London: Macmillan, 1987.

Kuhn, T. S. *The Structure of Scientific Revolutions*. Chicago: University of Chicago Press, 1962.

La Capra, Dominique. *Rethinking Intellectual History: Texts, Contexts, and Language*. Ithaca, NY: Cornell University Press, 1983.

Laclau, Ernesto, and Chantal Mouffe. *Hegemony and Socialist Strategy: Towards a Radical Democratic Politics*. London: Verso, 1985.

Lash, Scott, and John Urry. *The End of Organized Capitalism*. Cambridge: Polity, 1987.

Lefebre, Henri, *The Production of Space*. (1974) Oxford: Blackwell, 1991.

'Reflections on the Politics of Space', trans. Michael J. Enders, *Antipode*, 8, May 1976, 31.

Lefort, Claude. *Democracy and Political Theory*. Cambridge: Polity, 1988.

Lelio Basso Foundation, The, ed. *Theory and Practice of Liberation at the End of the XXth Century*. Brussels: Bruyland, 1988.

Liebersohn, Harry. *Fate and Utopia in German Sociology, 1870–1923*. Cambridge, MA: MIT Press, 1988.

Linklater, Andrew. *Beyond Realism and Marxism: Critical Theory and International Relations*. London: Macmillan, 1989.

Men and Citizens in the Theory of International Relations. London: Macmillan, 1982.

'The Problem of Community in International Relations', *Alternatives*, 15:2, Spring 1990, 135–53.

Little, Richard. 'Three approaches to the international system: some ontological and epistemological considerations', *British Journal of International Studies*, 3, 1977, 269–85.

Locke, John. *Two Treatises of Government*, ed. Peter Laslett. Cambridge: Cambridge University Press, 1988.

Longino, Helen E. *Science as Social Knowledge: Values and Objectivity in Scientific Inquiry*. Princeton: Princeton University Press, 1990.

Lowe, Donald M. *History of Bourgeois Perception*. Chicago: University of Chicago Press, 1982.

Luke, Timothy W. 'The Discipline of Security Studies and the Codes of Containment: Learning from Kuwait', *Alternatives*, 16:3, Summer 1991, 315–44.

Screens of Power: Ideology, Domination and Resistance in Informational Society.
Urbana and Chicago: University of Illinois Press, 1989.

Lukes, Steven. *Individualism.* Oxford: Basil Blackwell, 1973.

Lyotard, Jean-François. *The Postmodern Condition: A Report on Knowledge,* trans.
Geoff Bennington and Brian Massumi. Minneapolis: University of Minnesota Press, 1984.

Machiavelli, Niccolò. *The Prince,* eds. Quentin Skinner and Russell Price.
Cambridge: Cambridge University Press, 1988.

MacIntyre, Alasdair. *After Virtue.* Notre Dame; University of Notre Dame Press, 1987.

Maclean, John. 'Marxism and International Relations: A Strange Case of Mutual Neglect', *Journal of International Studies,* 17:2, Summer 1988, 295–319.

'Political Theory, International Theory and Problems of Ideology', *Millennium: Journal of International Studies,* 10:2, Summer 1981, 102–125.

Macpherson, C. B. *Democratic Theory: Essays in Retrieval.* Oxford: Clarendon Press, 1973.

Magnusson, Warren. 'Bourgeois Theories of Local Government', *Political Studies,* 34:1, 1986, 1–18.

'The Reification of Political Community', in R. B. J. Walker and Saul H. Mendlovitz, eds., *Contending Sovereignties.* Boulder and London: Lynne Rienner Publications, 1990, 45–60.

Magnusson, Warren and R. B. J. Walker, 'Decentring the State: Political Theory and Canadian Political Economy', *Studies in Political Economy,* 26, Summer 1988, 37–71.

Manganaro, Marc, ed. *Modernist Anthropology: From Fieldwork to Text.* Princeton: Princeton University Press, 1990.

Manicas, Peter. *A History and Philosophy of the Social Sciences.* Oxford: Basil Blackwell, 1987.

War and Democracy. Oxford: Basil Blackwell, 1989.

'War, Stasis and Greek Political Theory', *Comparative Studies in Society and History,* 24:4, October 1982, 673–88.

Mann, Michael. *The Sources of Social Power,* 3 vols. Cambridge: Cambridge University Press, 1986–.

Marx, Karl. *The Communist Manifesto.* 1848.

'The Eighteenth Brumaire of Louis Bonapart', in Marx, *Surveys From Exile,* ed., David Fernbach. New York: Random House, 1973.

Grundrisse, trans. Martin Nicolaus. London: Penguin, 1973.

Mattingly, Garrett. *Renaissance Diplomacy.* London: Jonathan Cape, 1955.

McLuhan, Marshall. *The Gutenberg Galaxy.* Toronto: University of Toronto Press, 1962.

Meinecke, Friedrich. *Machiavellianism: The Doctrine of Raison D'Etat and Its Place in Modern History.* London: Routledge and Kegan Paul, 1957.

Melucci, Alberto. *Nomads of the Present: Social Movements and Individual Needs in Contemporary Societies,* eds. John Keene and Paul Meir. Philadelphia: Temple University Press, 1989.

Mendlovitz, Saul H., ed. *On the Creation of a Just World Order.* New York: Free Press, 1975.

Mendlovitz, Saul H. and R. B. J. Walker, eds. *Towards a Just World Peace: Perspectives From Social Movements*. London: Butterworths, 1987.

Merleau-Ponty, Maurice. 'A Note on Machiavelli', in Merleau-Ponty, *Signs*, trans. Richard C. McCleary. Evanston: Northwestern University Press, 1964, 211–23.

Phenomenology of Perception, trans. Colin Smith. London: Routledge and Kegan Paul, 1962.

Midgley, E. B. F. *The Natural Law Tradition and the Theory of International Relations*. London: Elek Books, 1975.

Moi, Toril. *Sexual/Textual Politics*. London: Methuen, 1985.

Mommsen, Wolfgang J. *Max Weber and German Politics, 1920–1980*, trans. Michael S. Steinberg. Chicago: University of Chicago Press, 1984.

The Political and Social Theory of Max Weber. Chicago: University of Chicago Press, 1989.

Mommsen, Wolfgang J. and Jürgen Osterhammel, eds. *Max Weber and his Contemporaries*. London: Allen and Unwin, 1987.

Morgenthau, Hans J. 'Fragment of an Intellectual Autobiography: 1904–1932', in K. W. Thompson, et al., eds., *Truth and Tragedy: A Tribute to Hans J. Morgenthau*. Washington, D.C.: New Republic Book Co., 1977.

Scientific Man vs. Power Politics. Chicago: Chicago University Press, 1946.

Politics Among Nations. New York: Knopf, 1948.

Murphy, Craig, and Roger Tooze, eds. *The New International Political Economy*. Boulder: Lynne Rienner, 1991.

Nandy, Ashis. *The Intimate Enemy: Loss and Recovery of Self Under Colonialism*. Delhi: Oxford University Press, 1983.

'The Politics of Secularism and the Recovery of Religious Tolerance', in R. B. J. Walker and Saul H. Mendlovitz, eds., *Contending Sovereignties*. Boulder and London: Lynne Rienner Publishers, 1990, 125–44.

The Tao of Cricket: On Games of Destiny and the Destiny of Games. New Delhi: Penguin, 1989.

Traditions, Tyranny and Utopias: Essays in the Politics of Awareness. Delhi: Oxford University Press, 1987.

Nardin, Terry. *Law, Morality and the Relations of States*. Princeton: Princeton University Press, 1983.

Navari, Cornelia. 'Hobbes and the Hobbesian Tradition in International Thought', *Millennium: Journal of International Studies*, 11:3, 1982, 202–22.

Neaubauer, Deanne, and Michael Shapiro. 'Spatiality and Policy Discourse: Reading the Global City', in Saul H. Mendlovitz and R. B. J. Walker, eds., *Contending Sovereignties*. Boulder and London: Lynne Rienner Publishers, 1990, 97–124.

Nelson, John S., ed. *Tradition, Interpretation and Science: Political Theory in the American Academy*. Albany: State University of New York Press, 1986.

Nicholson, Linda J., ed. *Feminism/Postmodernism*. New York: Routledge, 1990.

North, Robert C. *War, Peace and Survival: Global Politics and Conceptual Synthesis*. Boulder: Westview, 1990.

Norton, Anne. *Reflections on Political Identity*. Baltimore: Johns Hopkins University Press, 1988.

Olson, William, and Nicholas Onuf. 'The Growth of a Discipline: Reviewed', in Steve Smith, ed., *International Relations: British and American Perspectives*. Oxford: Basil Blackwell, 1985, 1–28.

Onuf, Nicholas. 'Sovereignty: Outline of a Conceptual History', *Alternatives*, 16:4, Fall 1991, 425–46.

    World of Our Making: Rule and Rule in Social Theory and International Relations. Columbia: University of South Carolina Press, 1989.

O'Neill, John, ed. *Modes of Individualism and Collectivism*. London: Heinemann, 1973.

O'Neill, Onora. *Faces of Hunger: An Essay on Poverty, Development and Justice*. London: Allen and Unwin, 1986.

    'Transnational Justice', in David Held, ed., *Political Theory Today*. Cambridge: Cambridge University Press, 1991, 276–304.

Orr, Robert. 'The Time Motif in Machiavelli', in M. Fleisher, ed., *Machiavelli and the Nature of Political Thought*. New York: Atheneum, 1972, 185–208.

Oye, Kenneth, ed. *Cooperation Under Anarchy*. Princeton: Princeton University Press, 1986.

Pedoe, Dan. *Geometry and the Liberal Arts*. Harmondsworth: Penguin, 1976.

Peterson, V. Spike, ed. *Gendered States*. Boulder: Lynne Rienner, 1992.

    'The Radical Future of Realism: Feminist Subversions of International Relations Theory', *Alternatives*, 16:1, Winter 1991, 67–106.

Pitkin, Hanna Fenichel. *Fortune is a Woman: Gender and Politics in the Thought of Niccolo Machiavelli*. Berkeley and Los Angeles: University of California Press, 1984.

Pocock, J. G. A. 'Machiavelli and Guicciardini: Ancients and Moderns', Canadian Journal of Political and Social Theory, 2:3, Fall 1978, 93–107.

    The Machiavellian Moment: Florentine Political Thought and the Atlantic Republican Tradition. Princeton: Princeton University Press, 1975.

Raab, Felix. *The English Face of Machiavelli: A Changing Interpretation*. London: Routledge and Kegan Paul, 1964.

Rabinow, Paul, and William Sullivan, eds. *Interpretive Social Science: A second Look*. Berkeley and Los Angeles: University of California Press, 1987.

Rée, Jonathan, et al. *Philosophy and its Past*. Brighton: Harvester, 1978.

Reid, Herbert G., and Ernest J. Yanarella. 'Towards a Critical Theory of Peace Research in the United States: the Search for an "Intelligible Core"', *Journal of Peace Research*, 13:4, 1976, 315–41.

Rengger, N. J. 'An Arrow in the Heart of the Present: Kant and International Theory', in Howard Williams, ed., *Kant's Political Theory*. Forthcoming.

Reynolds, Charles. *Theory and Explanation in International Politics*. London: Martin Robertson, 1973.

Ricci, David. *The Tragedy of Political Science: Politics, Scholarship and Democracy*. New Haven: Yale University Press, 1984.

Ricoeur, Paul. *Hermeneutics and the Human Sciences*, trans. and ed., John B. Thompson. Cambridge: Cambridge University Press, 1984.

    History and Truth, trans. C. A. Kelbey. Evanston: Northwestern University Press, 1965.

Rorty, Richard. *Philosophy and the Mirror of Nature*. Princeton: Princeton University Press, 1980.

Rorty, Richard, J. B. Schneedwind and Quentin Skinner, eds. *Philosophy and History*. Cambridge: Cambridge University Press, 1984.

Rosenau, James N. *Turbulence in World Politics: A Theory of Change and Continuity*. Princeton: Princeton University Press, 1990.

Ross, Andrew, ed. *Universal Abandon: The Politics of Postmodernism*. Minneapolis: University of Minnesota Press, 1988.

Rouse, Joseph. *Knowledge and Power: Toward a Political Philosophy of Science*. Ithaca: Cornell University Press, 1987.

Ruggie, John G. 'Continuity and Transformation in the World Polity: Toward a Neorealist Synthesis', *World Politics*, 35:2, 1983, 261–85.

Ryan, Michael. *Marxism and Deconstruction: A Critical Articulation*. Baltimore: The Johns Hopkins University Press, 1982.

Sack, Robert David. *Conceptions of Space in Social Thought*. London: Macmillan, 1980.

Said, Edward. *After the Last Sky: Palestinian Lives*. New York: Pantheon, 1986.
Beginnings. New York: Basic Books, 1975.
Orientalism. New York: Random House, 1979.

Saner, Hans. *Kant's Political Thought*, trans. E. B. Ashton. Chicago: University of Chicago Press, 1973.

Schmidt, Alfred. *History and Structure: An Essay on Hegelian-Marxist and Structuralist Theories of History*, trans. Jeffrey Herf. Cambridge, MA: MIT Press, 1981.

Schmitt, Carl. *Political Theology: Four Chapters on the Concepts of Sovereignty*, trans. George Schwab. Cambridge, MA: MIT Press, 1985.

Schuhl, Pierre-Maxime. 'Le Thème du Gulliver et le postulat de Laplace,' *Journal de psychologie normal et pathologique*, 40:2, avril-juin 1947, 169–84.

Scocpol, Theda. *States and Social Revolutions*. Cambridge: Cambridge University Press, 1979.

Sears, Richard D. 'Thucydides and the Scientific Approach to International Relations,' *Australian Journal of Politics and History*, 23:1, April 1977, 28–40.

Seung, T. K. *Structuralism and Hermeneutics*. New York: Columbia University Press, 1982.

Shapiro, Michael. *The Politics of Representation*. Madison: University of Wisconsin Press, 1988.
Reading the Postmodern Polity: Political Theory as Textual Practice. Minneapolis: University of Minnesota Press, 1992.
'Sovereignty and Exchange in the Orders of Modernity', *Alternatives*, 16:4, Fall 1991, 447–77.

Singer, J. David. 'The Level of Analysis Problem in International Relations', in Klaus Knorr and Sidney Verba, eds., *The International System: Theoretical Essays*. Princeton: Princeton University Press, 1978.

Singer, Quentin, *Machiavelli*. Oxford: Oxford University Press, 1981.

Skinner, Quentin, ed. *The Return of Grand Theory in the Human Sciences*. Cambridge: Cambridge University Press, 1985.

Smart, Barry. *Modern Conditions, Postmodern Controversies*. London: Routledge, 1992.

Smith, Michael Joseph. *Realist Thought from Weber to Kissinger*. Baton Rouge: Louisiana State University Press, 1986.

Smith, Neil. *Uneven Development: Nature, Capital and the Production of Space.* Oxford: Basil Blackwell, 1985.

Soja, Edward W. *The Political Organization of Space.* Commission on College Geography, Resource paper no. 8. Washington, DC: Association of American Geographers, 1971.

Postmodern Geographies: The Reassertion of Space in Critical Social Theory. London: Verso, 1989.

Söllner, Alfons. 'German Conservatism in America: Morgenthau's Political Realism', *Telos*, 72, Summer 1987, 161–72.

Spivak, Gayatri Chakravorty. *In Other Worlds: Essays in Cultural Politics.* London: Methuen, 1987.

The Post-colonial Critic, ed., Sarah Harasym. New York and London: Routledge, 1990.

Stankiewitz, W. J., ed. *In Defence of Sovereignty.* New York: Oxford University Press, 1969.

Strange, Susan. '*Cave! hic dragones*: a Critique of Regimes Analysis', in Stephen D. Krasner, ed., *International Regimes.* Ithaca: Cornell University Press, 1983.

Strayer, Joseph. *On the Medieval Origins of the Modern State.* Princeton: Princeton University Press, 1970.

Suganami, Hidemi. *The Domestic Analogy and World Order Proposals.* Cambridge: Cambridge University Press, 1989.

Sullivan, Roger J. *Immanuel Kant's Moral Theory.* Cambridge: Cambridge University Press, 1989.

Taylor, Charles. *Sources of the Self: The Making of the Modern Identity.* Cambridge, MA: Harvard University Press, 1983.

Tenbruck, F. H. 'The Problem of Thematic Unity in the Work of Max Weber', *British Journal of Sociology*, 31, 1980, 316–51.

Thompson, E. P. 'Time, Work-Discipline and Industrial Capitalism', *Past and Present*, 38:1, December 1967, 56–97.

Thompson, Kenneth W. 'The Study of International Relations: Trends and Developments', *Review of Politics*, 14, October 1952, 433–67.

Thomson, Janice E. 'Sovereignty in Historical Perspective: The Evolution of State Control Over Extraterritorial Violence', in James A. Caporoso, ed., *The Elusive State: International and Comparative Perspectives.* Newbury Park, CA: Sage, 1989, 227–54.

Defining Sovereignty: State Practices and the Organization of Violence. In preparation.

Tickner, Ann. *Gender and International Relations.* New York: Columbia University Press, forthcoming.

Tilley, Charles, ed. *The Formation of National States in Western Europe.* Princeton: Princeton University Press, 1975.

Todorov, Tzvetan. *The Conquest of America.* New York: Harper and Row, 1982.

Tuan Yi-Fu. *Space and Place.* Minneapolis: University of Minnesota Press, 1977.

Tully, James, ed. *Meaning and Context: Quentin Skinner and his Critics.* Princeton: Princeton University Press, 1988.

Turner, Stephen P., and Regis A. Factor. *Max Weber and the Dispute over Reason and Value.* London: Routledge and Kegan Paul, 1984.

Veyne, Paul. *Did the Greeks Believe in their Myths?* Chicago: University of Chicago Press, 1988.

Vincent, Andrew. *Theories of the State*. Oxford: Basil Blackwell, 1987.

Vincent, R. J. 'Change and International Relations', *Review of International Studies*, 9:1, 1983, 63–70.

'Hedley Bull and Order in International Politics', *Millennium: Journal of International Studies*, 17:2, Summer 1988, 195–213.

Human Rights and International Relations. Cambridge: Cambridge University Press, 1986.

Nonintervention and International Order. Princeton: Princeton University Press, 1974.

Virilio, Paul. *Speed and Politics*. New York: Semiotext(e), 1987.

War and Cinema: The Logistics of Perception. New York: Verso, 1989.

von Wright, Georg Henryk. *Explanation and Understanding*. Ithaca: Cornell University Press, 1971.

Walker, R. B. J. 'The Concept of Culture in the Theory of International Relations', in John Chay, ed., *Culture and International Relations*. New York: Praeger, 1990, 3–17.

'Contemporary Militarism and the Discourse of Dissent', in R. B. J. Walker, ed., *Culture, Ideology and World Order*. Boulder and London: Westview Press, 1984, 302–22.

'Culture, Discourse, Insecurity', in Saul Mendlovitz and R. B. J. Walker, eds. *Towards a Just World Peace: Perspectives From Social Movements*. London: Butterworths, 1987, 171–90.

'Gender and Critique in the Theory of International Relations', in V. Spike Peterson, ed., *Gendered States*. Boulder: Lynne Rienner, 1992.

One World, Many Worlds. Boulder: Lynne Rienner, 1988.

'Security, Sovereignty and the Challenge of World Politics', *Alternatives*, 15:1, Winter 1991, 3–28.

'World Order and the Reconstitution of Political Life,' in R. Falk, R. Johansen and S. Kim, eds., *The Constitutional Foundations of World Order*. Albany: State University of New York Press, 1993.

Walker, R. B. J., and Saul H. Mendlovitz, eds. *Contending Sovereignties: Rethinking Political Community*. Boulder: Lynne Rienner, 1990.

Wallerstein, Immanuel. *The Modern World System I: Capitalist Agriculture and the Origins of the European World Economy in the Sixteenth Century*. New York: Academic Press, 1974.

'The Rise and Future Demise of the World Capitalist System: Concepts for Comparative Analysis', *Comparative Studies in Society and History*, 16, 1974, 387–415.

Waltz, Kenneth N. *Man, the State and War*. New York: Columbia University Press, 1959.

'Realist Thought and Neorealist Theory', *Journal of International Studies*, 44:1, Spring/Summer 1990, 20–37.

Theory of International Politics. Reading, MA: Addison-Wesley, 1979.

Walzer, Michael. *Just and Unjust Wars*. New York: Basic Books, 1977.

Wartofsky, Marx. *Conceptual Foundations of Scientific Thought*. New York: Macmillan, 1968.

Weber, Cynthia. 'Reconsidering Statehood: Examining the Sovereignty/ Intervention Boundary', *Review of International Studies*, 18:3, July 1992.

Writing the State: Political Intervention and the Historical Constitution of State Sovereignty. In preparation.

Weber, Max. 'Politics as a Vocation', in *From Max Weber: Essays in Sociology*, trans. and ed., H. H. Gerth and C. Wright Mills. New York: Oxford University Press, 1946, 77–128.

Weedon, Chris. *Feminist Practice and Poststructuralist Theory*. Oxford: Basil Blackwell, 1987.

Wendt, Alex. 'The Agent-Structure Problem in International Relations Theory', *International Organization*, 41:3, 1987, 335–70.

Whitehead, Lawrence. 'International Aspects of Democratization', in Guillermo O'Donnell, Phillippe Schmitter and Lawrence Whitehead, eds. *Transitions from Authoritarian Rule: Prospects for Democracy*. Baltimore; Johns Hopkins, 1986.

Wickham, Gary. 'The Political Possibilities of Postmodernism', *Economy and Society*, 19:1, February 1990, 121–49.

Wight, Martin. 'An Anatomy of International Thought', *Review of International Studies*, 13:3, July 1987, 221–27.

Systems of States, ed., Hedley Bull. Leicester: Leicester University Press, 1977.

'Why is There No International Theory?', in H. Butterfield and M. Wight, eds., *Diplomatic Investigations*. London: George Allen & Unwin, 1966, 17–34.

Williams, Bernard. *Ethics and the Limits of Philosophy*. Cambridge, MA: Harvard University Press, 1985.

Williams, Michael C. 'Reason and Realpolitik: Kant's "Critique of International Politics"', *Canadian Journal of Political Science*, 25:1, March 1992, 99–119.

'Rousseau, Realism and *Realpolitik*', *Millennium: Journal of International Studies*, 18:2, Summer 1989, 163–87.

Wilson, Brian, ed. *Rationality*. Oxford: Basil Blackwell, 1970.

Wolf, Eric. *Europe and the People Without History*. Berkeley: University of California Press, 1982.

Wolin, Sheldon. *Politics and Vision*. Boston: Little Brown, 1960.

Young, Robert. *White Mythologies: Writing History and the West*. London: Routledge, 1990.

INDEX

Printed in the United Kingdom
by Lightning Source UK Ltd.
9807900002B/176